INSIDERS TALK

Guide to Executive Branch

AGENCY RULEMAKING

INSIDERS TALK

Guide to Executive Branch

AGENCY RULEMAKING

Policy, Procedure, Participation, and Post-Promulgation Appeal

ROBERT L. GUYER
CHRIS MICHELI

LOBBY SCHOOL

Books by Robert L. Guyer

Guide to State Legislative Lobbying (2000-2007, 3 editions)

Insiders Talk Series of Best Practices Manuals:
Manual 1. *How to Get and Keep Your First Lobbying Job* (2020)
Manual 2. *Glossary of Legislative Concepts and Representative Terms* (2019)
Manual 3. *How to Successfully Lobby State Legislatures: Guide to State Legislative Lobbying, 4th edition*—Revised, Updated and Expanded (2020)
Manual 4. *Winning with Lobbyists*, Readers edition (2019)
Manual 5. *Winning with Lobbyists*, Professional edition (2019)
Manual 6. *Guide to Executive Branch Agency Rulemaking* (2021, with Chris Micheli)

INSIDERS TALK: GUIDE TO EXECUTIVE BRANCH AGENCY RULEMAKING

PRINT VERSION DATA
First Edition published 2021. Requests for permission to make copies of any part of this book should be sent to rlguyer@lobbyschool.com and:
Engineering THE LAW, Inc.
13714 N.W. 21 Lane
Gainesville, Florida 32606

Library of Congress Control Number: 2021904326
Print ISBN: 978-1-7323431-3-9
Ebook ISBN: 978-1-7323431-4-6

Book design by Sarah E. Holroyd (https://sleepingcatbooks.com)

To revise, not reflect, the status quo
to broaden, guide, and illuminate the practitioner's path
through legislating by the fourth branch of government.

Executive Branch Agency Rulemaking…

You don't have a law until the agency tells you that you have a law. And *you don't know what a law means* until they tell you what it means. Agencies do both via rulemaking.

Executive Branch Agency Rulemaking...

For every *one page* of broad legislature made law,
agencies make *ten pages* of highly detailed administrative law.

Executive Branch Agency Rulemaking...

What the legislature *giveth*, an executive agency can *taketh* away, and what the legislature wouldn't give you, an executive agency might.

Executive Branch Agency Rulemaking...

"The execution of laws is more important than
the making of them."
—Thomas Jefferson

TABLE OF CONTENTS

CHAPTER 2: THE AGENCY MODEL

CHAPTER 3: ADMINISTRATIVE PROCEDURE(S) ACT

CHAPTER 4: SETTING THE STAGE FOR EXECUTIVE AGENCY LOBBYING

CHAPTER 5: LOBBYING INTERNAL AND EXTERNAL INFLUENCERS ON THE RULEMAKING PROCEEDING

CHAPTER 6: RULE ADOPTION

CHAPTER 7: POST-RULEMAKING

CHAPTER 8: WHAT YOU SHOULD LEARN, ACCEPT AND CHALLENGE ON AGENCY REGULATORY ENFORCEMENT AND ADJUDICATIONS

FOREWORD

For those interested in the inner-workings of government, the word "advocacy" is typically associated with influencing elected policymakers in the *legislative process*. Often overlooked, however, is the advocacy that occurs to influence government officials—including gubernatorial appointees, elected officials, and state civil servants—during the *regulatory process*.

Indeed, major state laws often lack necessary detail to function as standalone measures. Federal and state rulemaking agencies are therefore tasked with putting the meat on the legal bones, which in some circumstances results in regulations that have a greater impact than the underlying laws themselves. For this reason, regulatory advocacy is an important component of any government affairs strategy; yet, the process and the tools needed to implement an effective regulatory advocacy strategy are not well-understood.

That is where this edition of *Insiders Talk: Guide to Executive Branch Agency Rulemaking* comes in. Whether you are a seasoned state regulatory advocate or just looking for a primer, Bob Guyer and Chris Micheli masterfully capture everything you need to know about the regulatory process and effective advocacy strategies, from the constitutional foundations of administrative law and preparing for a lobbying visit with regulatory officials and staff, all the way to the enforcement and adjudication of a final rule.

The book digs deep into a convoluted issue, but does so in a simple, easy-to-understand way. In the end, readers will understand how to become an effective regulatory advocate, and they will gain a true appreciation for the art of state regulatory advocacy. It is well worth the read in either case.

My experience as a policy advocate in California—a state with the most active regulatory agencies in the country—makes me appreciate this book even more. In my current role managing Arnold & Porter's California Government Affairs practice in Sacramento, and having previously been a Policy Advocate at the California Chamber of Commerce, I have had to navigate my way through dozens of regulatory agencies—ranging from the California Air Resources Board to the Department of Transportation—without the benefit of any valuable external resources.

I like to believe the "trial by fire" approach I took early in my advocacy career has made me an effective advocate, but the reality is that a resource like *Insiders Talk: Guide to Executive Branch Agency Rulemaking* will be an immense benefit to students studying administrative law and advocacy, as well as regulatory advocates at any time in their careers, including myself.

Anthony Samson
Managing Director
Arnold & Porter
Sacramento, California

WELCOME

Welcome from Bob Guyer
Author, *Insiders Talk* Series of Lobbying Practice Manuals

Just out of law school, my first job was lobbying and, as first jobs often do, it defined my career. My new employer gave me a title and an expense account and told me to change its regulatory world. However, I had little idea what to do. Neither practice manuals nor training seminars existed. I had to learn lobbying by experiencing it. In time, mistakes I made taught me lessons learned that increasingly led to successes. The *Insiders Talk* series passes on to readers those lessons learned while lobbying at the state, federal, and international levels.

Today's *Insiders Talk* sequence of six best practices lobbying manuals and the 15-video series *Campaign Method for More Effective State Government Affairs* will jump-start the careers of new lobbyists and improve veterans' skills. I wish I had had this training when I started out. It did not exist then, but it does now.

Even better, these publications share the experiences and advice of dozens of other experts with whom I have worked or who have attended *Lobby School* skills development workshops. These experts include Chris Micheli, co-author of this book. Chris is a prestigious Sacramento lobbyist, law school adjunct, and author of many articles on lobbying.

Guide to Executive Branch Agency Rulemaking completes the *Insiders Talk* series because it covers the final steps in *legislating* a regulatory environment, that is, *agency rulemaking*. My other books and videos teach advocates how to influence the first *ten percent of lawmaking*, that is, legislating *statutory law*. This closing book teaches them how to influence the remaining *90 percent*, that is, *legislating executive branch agency law.*

We hope this book helps you thrive in what for us have been successful, enjoyable, and meaningful careers. Let us know what you think.

Bob Guyer
rlguyer@lobbyschool.com
www.lobbyschool.com

Chris Micheli
cmicheli@apreamicheli.com
www.apreamicheli.com

PRELIMINARIES

All *Insiders Talk* manuals are *primers* based upon and reflecting commonalities of process, concepts, personalities, and application among U.S. states. However, individual states have their own peculiarities as to process, vocabulary, cultures, and specifics. The reader should review state-specific information in application of our manuals.

This book has an environmental regulation bias. Bob has worked as a pollution control inspector, environmental manager for a power company, and lobbied environmental matters at the international, federal, state, and local levels. He also served as a chairman and member of various corporate, state, and local government environmental advisory boards and his district's Human Rights Advocacy Committee serving clients of the Florida Department of Children and Families. His experience broadly applies *procedurally* and *temperamentally* to all agencies while recognizing that the particular fact patterns of his experiences do not.

For deeper understanding of this manual and application thereof, readers are advised to study the model rules found in the *State Administrative Procedure Act, Revised—Uniform Law Commission* (uniformlaws.org) which provisions and vocabulary are referred to repeatedly throughout this manual and are the focus of Chapter 3, *Administrative Procedure(s) Acts*. Ten states and the District of Columbia have enacted the model rules as their APAs and many more state APAs incorporate similar provisions.

LOBBYIST CAREER DEVELOPMENT PLAN

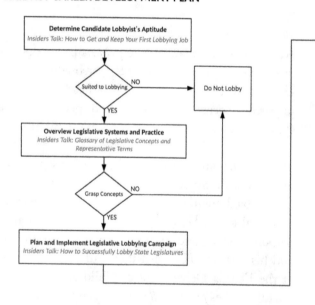

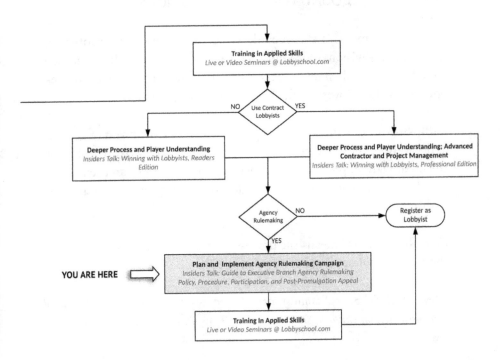

Training in Applied Skills
Live or Video Seminars @ Lobbyschool.com

NO / **Use Contract Lobbyists** \ YES

Deeper Process and Player Understanding
Insiders Talk: Winning with Lobbyists, Readers Edition

Deeper Process and Player Understanding; Advanced Contractor and Project Management
Insiders Talk: Winning with Lobbyists, Professional Edition

Agency Rulemaking NO → **Register as Lobbyist**

YES

Plan and Implement Agency Rulemaking Campaign
Insiders Talk: Guide to Executive Branch Agency Rulemaking Policy, Procedure, Participation, and Post-Promulgation Appeal

YOU ARE HERE

Training In Applied Skills
Live or Video Seminars @ Lobbyschool.com

Foundational Definitions

(3) "Agency" means a state board, authority, commission, institution, department, division, office, officer, or other state entity that is authorized by law of this state to make rules or to adjudicate. The term does not include the Governor, the [Legislature], or the Judiciary.

(30) "Rule" means the whole or a part of an agency statement of general applicability that implements, interprets, or prescribes law or policy or the organization, procedure, or practice requirements of an agency and has the force of law. The term includes the amendment or repeal of an existing rule.

(31) "Rulemaking" means the process for the adoption of a new rule or the amendment or repeal of an existing rule.

"Revised Model State Administrative Procedures Act," *National Conference of Commissioners on Uniform State Laws* (July 9–16, 2010) https://www.uniform-laws.org.

WHY A MANUAL ON EXECUTIVE BRANCH AGENCY RULEMAKING?

While some practical training exists about influencing lawmaking by the *legislative branch* of state government[1], very little, if any, practice guidance has been developed for successfully influencing lawmaking by the *executive branch* of state government. As you proceed through this primer, the highly technical side of the agency legislating process gradually will come together. But let us begin your training simply by answering the question, *Why a Manual on Executive Agency Rulemaking?*

Chris Micheli, as a contract lobbyist, and Robert Guyer, as in-house staff for government and business, have seen that too often managers, especially in the "C-suites[2]," do not grasp the significance of executive agency rulemaking. They presume that once the statute is enacted the heavy lifting is done. All that remains is for the executive agency to fill in details necessary to implement the legislature's direction. This view is woefully and dangerously mistaken. They are mistaken first because for every page of *broad legislative law* an agency may promulgate ten pages of *detailed administrative law*. In other words, 90 percent of the body of law regulating your principal(s) is written by executive branch agencies.

Further, agency experts have their own ideas about fixing a problem; they may object to legislative political deals watering down their technical solutions; and, they may intend to fix statutory shortfalls in the

1

rulemaking process. Agencies can effectively rewrite legislation in part because of the, albeit rebuttable, judicial presumption of agency correctness and because of judicial and legislative deference to the constitutionally coequal executive branch. The other part is both branches concede to the almost inarguable superior technical expertise residing within executive branch agencies.

Agencies make *administrative law* to implement *statutory law*, that is, law as enacted by the legislature. They do this in several ways. First, they make *unofficial law* which is law by custom, as for example how agencies enforce administrative laws. Bob as an agency inspector and later as a compliance manager for an electric utility found that a regulated party generally will do what an agency requests without formal agency enforcement. Similarly, agency-published guidance documents and policy, while not legally enforceable, in practice also become unofficial laws. This is because both regulator and regulated know, as we explain in Chapter 7, *Post-Rulemaking* that "the process is the punishment." Just the threat of being forced into an agency's bureaucratic process may be enough to elicit voluntary compliance.

Agencies also make entity-specific *private law* as when they issue a permit to operate a facility with provisos tailored to the permittee's operations or site conditions. They may impose for good cause additional requirements for a particular licensee to practice a profession. Private law also becomes administrative law when to settle litigation an agency agrees to promulgate rules. We touch upon this in Chapter 6, *Rule Adoption*, section, "Triggers to Motivating Agency Rulemaking," subsection, "Sue and Settle."

Agencies make *decreed law* when they issue a declaratory decree (called a *declaratory judgment* or *declaratory order*) interpreting how a law or application thereof impacts a party's set of facts. While a particular decree binds only the department and petitioner asking for it, the decree becomes precedent for future agency actions.

Agencies also make *adjudicatory law* when they administratively rule on a specific regulated party's case. Adjudication may be done internally by

2

staff, by an in-house hearing officer, or by an administrative law judge working for the state's division of administrative hearings.

Case law is binding law made by the judicial branch in settling agency litigation. And *attorney general advisory opinions*, while not binding, are persuasive authority for the courts and agencies.

And finally, agencies make *administrative legislative law*, that is, *regulations* or *rules*. Rather than ending a process, a statute initiates a constitutional process, that is, agency adoption of *administrative laws* to implement *legislative laws*. This type of lawmaking is the topic of this manual.

Some readers may find odd the idea that agencies like legislatures can *legislate*. But agencies do legislate using authority given to them by the legislature. This is called *delegated legislative authority*. Details are incrementally explained as we proceed.

EXECUTIVE BRANCH AGENCIES

Executive branch agencies in terms of money, staff numbers, and authority dwarf the rest of the executive, legislative, and judicial branches combined. While the legislative, executive, and judicial branches *pursuant to the federal and state constitutions* are coequal, in functional reality, the disproportionate size, power, wealth, and reach of the *administrative state* is so substantial that, since the 1930s, it has been called "the headless fourth branch of government."[3]

And, to support the administrative state, taxpayers invest billions of dollars per year to employ and equip millions of state government workers.[4] Each state has from dozens to hundreds of regulatory agencies, departments, boards, and commissions that implement public policy and adopt and enforce regulations using *legislatively delegated* authority. For example, as of this writing, California has 235 agencies employing 235,000 state workers that promulgate roughly 600 regulations each year. The single largest state agency of which we know employs 20,000 staff.

3

The reach of the administrative state is enormous. Former Illinois Governor Dan Walker observed, "Most of the people in the state of Illinois, and I think this is true across the country, are much more affected in their daily lives by operation of the administrative and executive part of government than they are by 90 percent of the bills [of] the General Assembly."[5]

Agencies are the face of the executive branch to the public, legislature, and courts. In many ways, agencies are the executive branch with the Governor as an actual or nominal head. As we proceed through the pages of this manual, you will see why the term *headless* and *fourth branch* aptly describes the administrative state.[6]

As in legislative lawmaking, so too in executive agency lawmaking, you are employed to protect your principal, its mission, livelihoods of its personnel, and wellbeing of its customers and owners. Let us begin our training in executive agency lawmaking by outlining its similarities and differences from legislative advocacy.

SIMILARITIES AND DIFFERENCES BETWEEN LEGISLATIVE AND REGULATORY PROCESSES

How different, if at all and how much, is regulatory agency advocacy from legislative advocacy? From our perspective, both forms of lobbying are *conceptually* quite similar: legislative advocacy is lobbying for or against legislation at the legislative branch, while regulatory advocacy is lobbying for or against regulations at the executive branch.

And as to *lobbying practice*, the role of the lobbyist also is similar in both. For example, your best lobbyist will have subject matter expertise regarding the regulations in question, as for example that which Chris possesses in tax related matters; he or she will have important contacts and trust-based relationships with key agency and legislative personnel; and, he or she will possess solid advocacy skills, both written and verbal.

However, despite similarities of concepts and practice, there are huge differences[7] between the *formal processes* of enacting legislation versus adopting regulations as illustrated by this chart.

Process Distinctions: Legislative vs. Regulatory

LEGISLATIVE	REGULATORY
Designed for political, policy solutions	Designed to implement statutes, technical solutions
Limited by Constitutions, leadership, politics, state revenues, maybe Governor, seldom courts	Limited by Constitutions; authorizing & enabling laws, APA; Governor, legislature, appropriations, judicial & administrative courts
Actions often irrational, unpredictable, technically fact-free, politically logical	Actions rational, predictable, predicated on law, facts, policy
Politics at every level, except non-political chamber staff	Politics at top managers, legislative liaisons
Liable to voters, caucus, donors, Governor, seldom courts	Liable to legislature, Governor, courts
Longevity: to next election	Longevity: career civil service are job tenured; non-civil service at pleasure of Governor
Driven by self-interest, party & personal politics, biases, hidden & overt agendas, available revenue, supporters, donors, interest groups	Driven by agency mission, public strategic plan, technical & legal experts, facts, law & budget, best technical practices, biases
Lawmakers motivated by what they hear and feel, less what they read; often scant legislative record.	Agencies motivated by what they read, less by what they hear; extensive rulemaking record.

The impacts of politics also are quite different between the legislature and agencies. Legislative lobbying is greatly influenced by politics and political players. For example, in the legislature, a lobbyist is no better than the principal(s) he or she represents. Or a lobbyist might leverage being the chair's "drinking buddy" into defeating or unfavorably amending a bill. And taking a client to dinner with a lawmaker is a "wow" factor that clients will pay for. (The ins and outs of contract lobbyists and optimizing their services are discussed in detail in *Winning with Lobbyists, Professional edition*, book five in the *Insiders Talk* series.)

Much less so in the agency. Agency staff are interested mainly in the facts and law necessary to achieve the agency's mission statement. And the career civil service system, which covers most agency employees, is intended in part to keep politics out of agency decisions. This system ensures that agency staff seldom lose their jobs even for cause.

Agencies do not care about whose clients are whose, who lobbyists drink with, or having supper with lobbyists or their clients. And few lobbyists have backgrounds sufficient to discourse with an agency Ph.D., for example, as to how many microcuries of radium per liter of water is safe to drink. Politically, procedurally, and technically the legislature and agencies are very different environments. To illustrate, in chapter 2 you will read of the agency staffer who told Bob that if his principal makes a bad product then it just needs to go out of business. Annoying as that staffer's dismissal of 1,300 jobs was, in agency thinking, he was fully correct in his statement.

WHY RULEMAKING IS IMPORTANT

The easiest way to look at it is that, when a statute has been enacted, it does not mean the lawmaking battle is over. In fact, the statute is more like the starter's gun in an agency rulemaking marathon. It is a race that offers participants opportunities to kill, amend, limit, or expand the impact of a legislatively mandated regulatory scheme, albeit one yet to be developed. Moreover, if you were successful in getting your statute enacted, you now have to refight your legislative opposition to keep it from using agency inaction, unfavorable rulemaking, or hostile administrative adjudication to take away your legislative win and give it to your opponents.

Inaction happens but infrequently. Realistically, the agency has two ways to affect your statute: quasi-judicially and quasi-legislatively. "Quasi" means that the judicial branch can undo executive agency judicial or legislative action. *Quasi-judicial* means an agency by its own decree can interpret and enforce laws under its jurisdiction (i.e., they are acting like a judicial branch). *Quasi-legislative* means an agency can adopt or amend regulations (i.e., they are acting like the legislative branch). The topic of agency judicial decrees is the subject of administrative law taught in many law schools. The practice of making administrative rules is the topic of this manual.

Similar to the rules for the legislative process, a state's regulatory process is a world of its own with separate rules and procedures. And, just like in the legislative process, an effective regulatory advocate needs to know the rules and the players. The players likely will be the same as those you encountered in the legislature, friends and foes. They will petition the agency hoping it will give them more or take away what the legislature gave you.

Key differences between legislative branch lawmaking and executive agency legislating are that with agencies: generally there are fewer players, more rules formal and informal, and—as the last step in the regulatory process—agencies, not lawmakers, are first in importance to regulated entities.

OVERVIEW OF CHAPTERS TO COME

Chapter 1, *Policy: Constitutional Foundations of U.S. Agencies and the Administrative Process* overviews the legal system which you will navigate, explains the political philosophy and necessity behind executive branch agencies, and touches upon dangers that the administrative state poses to American constitutional protections.

Although regulations in a sense are inferior to statutes in terms of hierarchy of laws, rules and regulations are nonetheless laws themselves. *Inferiority* stems in part from agencies not at this time having prison or the death penalty in their catalogue of agency-imposed punishments. Only statutory violations prosecuted by the attorney general include these. In most cases in our view that inferiority of distinction is not meaningful.

Chapter 2, *The Agency Model* summarizes agency organization, power and actions and first introduces the reader to agency rulemaking starting with a state's Administrative Procedure(s) Act (APA) that guides the rulemaking process.

Chapter 3, *Administrative Procedure(s)Act* discusses in detail the *Revised Model State Administrative Procedures Act*[8] (RMSAPA). The RMSAPA is the template for most basic state administrative procedures and several states have adopted it as their APA. Advocates should be aware of the nuances of their state's APA guaranteeing opportunities to be informed, observe, and participate in agency rulemaking activities. Application of the APA will be discussed in detail in Chapter 6.

Chapter 4, *Setting the Stage for Executive Agency Lobbying* starts you on a credibility building offensive with agency staff. If staff trust you, they may listen to you. And, if they listen to you, they may come to understand you. And, if they come to understand you, they may become more inclined to do what you want. The trust and the credibility that follow are foundational to working successfully with both the legislature and with agencies.

Chapter 5, *Lobbying Internal and External Influences on the Rulemaking Proceeding,* especially section, "Who Are the Influencers That Advocates May Enlist in Affecting Rulemaking?" discusses 16 potential influencers you may have to contact in your lobbying campaign. Section, "Lobbying Staff Checklist" guides you in implementing an effective lobbying visit with staff.

Chapter 6, *Rule Adoption,* the longest chapter in the book, details the formal rulemaking process and your participation in it. The rule adoption process discussed in Chapter 6 proceeds along the path outlined in Chapter 3. The APA directs each procedural step an agency must take in the rulemaking process beginning with public notice of the proposed rulemaking.

Chapter 7, *Post-Rulemaking* describes administratively challenging an unfavorable rule. Section, "The Process Is the Punishment" describes agency use, and at times abuse, of power against regulated parties who challenge them administratively or judicially.

Chapter 8, *What You Should Learn, Accept and Challenge on Agency Regulatory Enforcement and Adjudications* offers advice on responding to agency prosecutions such as those described in Chapter 7. While Chris and Bob have little meaningful experience litigating administrative matters, we strongly believe that advocates should know enough about the topic to offer their principals good initial cautionary advice. The chapter is guest written by a multi-state administrative litigator with decades of legal experience having challenged hundreds of government actions at the state, federal, and international levels. Some *Insiders Talk* contributors risk professional and personal repercussion making necessary his anonymity.

With this introduction answering the *why* of this practice manual and overview of the chapters that follow, we launch into establishing you as an effective influencer in the agency rulemaking process. Our first building block is Chapter 1, *Policy: Constitutional Foundations of U.S. Agencies and the Administrative Process*. It gives you the big picture of agency powers, how agencies use them including delegated legislative authority, and the reach of the administrative state.

===== CHAPTER 1 =====

POLICY: CONSTITUTIONAL FOUNDATIONS OF U.S. AGENCIES AND THE ADMINISTRATIVE PROCESS

The Founders knew that a strong national government was necessary to the success of their proposed democratic republic. But to convince the newly independent former colonies to freely join the new republic, they had to assure them that their Constitutionally created United States of America would not become a new, homegrown tyrant. To defuse their own and the states' wariness of federal despotism, the drafters adopted into the Constitution the doctrine of *separation of powers,* a doctrine by which they divided power among three coequal branches each having its unique role in the administratively supreme national government.

Division of political power among coequal branches each with its own unique role would restrain federal despotism and hopefully persuade the states to willingly unite themselves under a single, national political super entity. Of course, their efforts were successful with the birth of the United States of America.

Separation of powers. To contain the inevitable *tendency toward federal despotism*, the Founders delegated to each of three coequal branches of the federal government specific, limited powers each of which was appropriate to that branch's designated governmental function: legislative, executive, and judicial. The plan was a system to foster *conflict not cooperation* among the branches expecting each branch would *by the nature of power itself* seek to increase the breadth of its own authority by diminishing the influence of the other two branches. Intra-governmental struggles for dominance, the Founders' thinking went, would lead to each branch keeping the other two branches in check. This concept became known as the system of *checks and balances.*

This untidy power-sharing is supposed to avoid what founding father James Madison called "the very definition of tyranny"— all power in one set of hands. That means we give ambitious politicians tools that bring them into conflict as a way of limiting the power of any one person or branch.

The Constitution and its separation of powers is not a clean division of labor, but what scholar Edward S. Corwin dubbed an "invitation to struggle," where elected officials protect their branches—and themselves—by meddling, being alert and, where necessary, confrontational.[9]

When the governor is fighting the legislature about which branch has the authority to adopt a policy, or the legislature is threatening to defund the courts in order to curtail judicial overreach, or the courts have nullified as unconstitutional an action by either of the other two branches, that is how the Founders intended their system of checks and balances to work.[10] *Separation of powers* works because only a coequal branch of government has sufficient political power to limit another branch.

Pure separation of powers in easier said than done. The U.S. and 40 state constitutions[11] achieve separation of powers by specifying that government be divided into three branches: legislative, executive, and judicial. California not only sets the three branches of government in three separate articles of its state constitution, but also it specifies the separation of powers doctrine in Article III, Section 3 of the state constitution. Section 3 provides: "The powers of state government are legislative, executive, and judicial. Persons charged with the exercise of one power may not exercise either of the others except as permitted by this Constitution."[12]

Despite the constitutional ideal of separation of core powers of government, in practice some overlap is unavoidable as each branch checks and balances the others. For example, while the legislative branch is empowered to enact laws, the executive branch signs or vetoes those measures. While the separation of powers doctrine states each branch is to be sovereign in its constitutionally specified jurisdiction, in actual application of authority separation can "blur."[13] Consider the potential for overlap when all three branches of state government make laws: legislative laws are called statutes; gubernatorial laws are called orders or decrees; judicial laws are called decisions or case law.

As this book develops, we will focus on a *fourth* lawmaking body, *executive branch agencies* also called *administrative agencies*. The state legislature and the judiciary have delegated or ceded to the executive branch limited legislative, executive, and judicial powers to govern a sphere of defined activity. This book focuses on agency *legislated administrative laws* called rules or regulations.

The constitutional branches at times participate in enacting laws as when, for example, the legislative and executive branches jointly develop the state budget.[14] Or the legislature writes and passes a bill and the Governor signs or vetoes the same bill. And, as applied in some jurisdictions, in the veto process the Governor may rewrite the bill. The courts can validate or overturn constitutionally impermissible laws. And, finally, after the legislative, executive, and judicial branches have settled on a law, executive agencies effect application of the law by how they execute or administer it. And, as you will see, those who administer a law define it by how they administer it. Thus, *"Last in time becomes first in authority."*

Pure separation of powers is easier said than done.

CONSTITUTIONAL AND PRACTICAL DANGERS OF ONE BODY OF MAGISTRATES HAVING LEGISLATIVE, EXECUTIVE, AND JUDICIAL POWERS

The Founders were schooled in English parliamentary government.[15] James Madison in Federalist 47 disavowed the English system writing, "When the legislative and executive powers are united in the same person or body," says he [Montesquieu], "there can be no liberty, because apprehensions may arise lest THE SAME monarch or senate should ENACT tyrannical laws to EXECUTE them in a tyrannical manner." (Emphases in Madison's original) In simpler words and as applied to agencies, in Madison's view, *tyranny will result when a government agency can enforce the laws it enacts.* This will become an important theme as you read on.

Tyranny happens not because of any individual's character failure, but because of human nature itself. Professor Zephyr Teachout writes,

> Madison and other Framers . . . believed themselves open-eyed and resigned to the fact that "man in his deepest natures was selfish and corrupt; that blind ambition most often overcomes even the most clear-eyed rationality; and that the lust for power was so overwhelming that no one should ever be entrusted with unqualified authority." They sought to design a system that could withstand the moral failings of normal humans, instead of one that could only be managed by angels. But with a few exceptions, they did not discount the importance of virtue—at least "virtue enough for success."[16]

Corruption covered a broad category of activities characterized by abuse of power rather than criminality. "Moreover, the activities included could be legal or illegal, so corruption is clearly not attached to a set of violations of criminal law . . . the corruption concern encompassed lawful abuses of power, not merely unlawful abuses or 'usurpations.'"[17] As is discussed in Chapter 7, *Post-Rulemaking,* section, "The Process Is the Punishment" agencies know *the process is the punishment,* and they have been known to use lawful processes to harass or break the resolve or bank account of a regulated party they consider a threat to their implementing the agency's mission.

And, although executive agencies as we know them did not exist at the time of writing the Constitution, the Founders foresaw *non-elected* government officials exercising government power, "The delegates believed that non-elected citizens wielding or attempting to influence public power can be corrupt and that elite corruption is a serious threat to a polity."[18]

Professor Teachout's final sentence is key to understanding contemporary executive agencies, the powers that these agencies have, and the dangers they pose to the U.S. form of constitutional government, as well as to individuals or organizations regulated or governed by them. Professor Teachout continues,

> Like the separation-of-powers principle the anti-corruption principle is a fundamental, structural commitment embodied in the Constitution, and despite the absence of any single expression along the lines of the First Amendment, it is so deeply tied to the ways in which the clauses were meant to be interpreted that to ignore it is to misread the Constitution.[19]

Executive agencies and their employees can act corruptly simply by their lawful abuse of legislative, executive and, as we will see in the next section, judicial powers. Yes, executive branch agencies exercise all three forms of government power thereby inviting the above style of corruption that the Founders feared.

HOW ADMINISTRATIVE AGENCIES USE COMBINED LEGISLATIVE, EXECUTIVE, AND JUDICIAL POWERS

The Founders' dread that the normal human "lust for power was so overwhelming that no one should ever be entrusted with unqualified authority,"[20] the dread which led them to insist on the *separation of powers*, is forced to life in administrative agencies. This is because Congress and states have united in one body of magistrates, that is, *agencies*, all three constitutional powers—legislative, executive, and judicial. Let us take a quick look at how they exercise the three powers.

Legislative. To carry out statutory law[21], that is, the *"enabling"* or *"original"* legislation, administrative agencies promulgate *administrative laws—rules* or *regulations*. Agency authority to adopt rules to implement statutes is found via Article I, Section 8 of the U. S. Constitution known as the "Necessary and Proper Clause."

Persons, corporate or natural, subject to agency laws are called *regulated parties* or *entities*. Agency lawmaking itself is *quasi-legislative*; *quasi* because, unlike the legislative branch which is coequal with the other two branches, agency lawmaking and application thereof is reviewable and reversible by the courts. This stems from the judiciary's role of keeping each branch of government within its own constitutionally assigned limits.[22]

Executive. Exercising its constitutional duty to faithfully execute the legislature's instructions as found in *statutory law*, an agency promulgates and enforces its own laws, that is, *rules* or *regulations*. An agency can make rules under the doctrine of *delegated legislative authority* which for now means the legislature transfers some of its lawmaking powers to an agency of the executive branch in order to promulgate agency laws to implement the legislature's statutes.

Judicial. An agency operates its own adjudicatory system parallel with, but subject to, the judicial branch of government. Agency staff (like police officers) allege infractions (charges) against regulated parties (defendants) with non-compliance (violations) with its rules. Its staff (like state attorneys) prosecute defendants in the agency's own administrative courts presided over by its own administrative law judges, agency employees or other state staff.[23]

If the defendant does not dispute an agency action, then the process goes to the penalty phase. If the defendant disputes facts or law, the case goes to adjudication (i.e., the agency-run court). Defendants may employ their own legal counsel or represent themselves—*pro se* defendants. The agency is presumed to have acted correctly, which the defendant must rebut in order to be successful.

Finally, even if you have a strong case, the agency can bleed you to death financially and emotionally so that you will give up by their design. We discuss this further in Chapter 7, *Post-Rulemaking*, section, "The Process Is the Punishment."

THE CREATION OF AGENCIES AND DELEGATED LEGISLATIVE AUTHORITY

Administrative agencies are creations of either the constitution, legislature, Governor, as authorized by a constitution[24], or voter initiative.[25] Irrespective of their genesis, dozens to hundreds of agencies are required to implement laws enacted by the legislature or constitution.[26] For example, in the State of California, there are more than 200 agencies, departments, boards, and commissions that have some form of rulemaking authority. The agencies do this in accord with policies of the executive and his or her political appointees.

Administrative agencies are not specified in the U.S. Constitution, nor are they found explicitly in most state constitutions. Rather, the founding document provides that the U.S. government shall assist the executive, that is, the President, in the discharge of his or her duties.

The United States Constitution does not provide specific and direct authority for the establishment of executive agencies or the appointment of Cabinet members. However, Article II, section 2, of the Constitution states that the president may "require the Opinion, in writing, of the principal Officer in each of the executive Departments, upon any Subject relating to the Duties of their respective Offices." As the government grew larger, executive agencies developed as a way to help the president discharge his duties and attend to his affairs. Today, these offices engage in the day-to-day administration and enforcement of executive orders and statutes. In total, the executive agencies employ over four million people and supervise an operating budget exceeding $2.3 trillion.[27]

State constitutions, unlike the federal, specify particular offices, such as the Attorney General, or agricultural or environmental commissioner, impose specific duties upon state government such as a free public education[28], and sometimes even create and empower executive agencies.[29] A state agency itself may have within it dozens of rulemaking departments and commissions.

For example, the California Department of Consumer Affairs has within it ". . . 37 regulatory entities comprised of boards, bureaus, committees, a program, and a commission. These 37 entities set and enforce minimum qualifications for the professions and vocations they regulate, which include nearly all of California's health care fields."[30]

Agencies reporting to the Governor, that is, executive branch agencies, are our subject of study. These constitute the vast majority of government departments. They are called by titles such as *administration, authority, board, bureau, commission, council, department, district, division, office*, other. For the rest of this book, agencies under the Governor's supervision will be referred to as *executive, regulatory* or *administrative*, the terms used synonymously.

Agency Rulemaking. Agency rulemaking will become the focus of this manual after we set the foundation for agencies. For now, agencies have the *constitutional* authority to make laws because,

> Article I, Section 1, of the federal Constitution plainly states that "[A]ll legislative Powers herein granted shall be vested in a Congress of the United States," the "necessary-and-proper" clause, in the eighth section of the same article, states that Congress shall have power "[t]o make all Laws which shall be necessary and proper for carrying into Execution the foregoing Powers, and all other Powers . . . in any Department or Officer thereof." With this language, many have argued that the

Framers of the Constitution expected, indeed encouraged, the creation of powerful administrative agencies. This argument prevailed, and courts therefore have allowed the U.S. Congress—and other legislative bodies—to make laws that delegate limited lawmaking authority to administrative agencies. The substance of an administrative agency's powers must be intelligible, and a system of controls must be in place to limit those powers, but courts almost always find that administrative agencies meet these requirements.[31]

In *Mistretta v. United States* (1989), the U.S. Supreme Court applied the "intelligible principle" test. The Court deemed it "constitutionally sufficient if Congress clearly delineates the general policy, the public agency which is to apply it, and the boundaries of this delegated authority."[32]

A legislature's style of delegating its *legislative authority* to an agency falls into one of three categories as listed by the *National Conference of State Legislatures* (NCSL):

- The "strict standards and safeguards" category. States in this category permit "delegation of legislative power only if the statute delegating the power provides definite standards or procedures" to which the recipient must adhere.
- The "loose standards and safeguards" category. States in this category view delegation as acceptable "if the delegating statute includes a general legislative statement of policy or a general rule to guide the recipient in exercising the delegated power."
- The "procedural safeguards" category. States in this group "find delegations of legislative power to be acceptable so long as recipients of the power have adequate procedural safeguards in place."[33]

CLEARING THE CONFUSION AMONG THE TERMS: ADMINISTRATIVE STATE, DEEP STATE, AND BUREAUCRACY

At times, the term *administrative state*, that is the sum of administrative agencies, state and federal, is often confused with the terms *bureaucracy* and *deep state*. *Administrative state, bureaucracy*, and *deep state* are related but are not identical so we will try to clear up the confusion. Mike Lofgren writes, "I use the term [deep state] to mean a hybrid association of elements of government and parts of top-level finance and industry that is effectively able to govern the United States without reference to the consent of the governed as expressed through the formal political process."[34]

Virgil offers a similar definition. "That term [deep state] is a catch-all for the subterranean machinations of activists within the federal government, as well of closely associated contractors, consultancies, and vendors. Typically, these people stay in their jobs even when the presidency changes hands, and so over time, of course, they develop their own worldview; one might even say that they share a *class interest*, befitting people who live off of government money—and like it that way."[35]

Finally, we turn to Miriam-Webster to understand *bureaucracy*. State and federal *bureaucracies* operate their *administrative* and *deep* states.

"The English word [*bureaucracy*] can refer to an entire body of unelected government officials or to the problematic system (often filled with *red tape*) that may result from administration by bureaucrats. From its earliest appearances, *bureaucracy* has carried a distinctly negative connotation. An 1815 *London Times* article, for example, declares: ' . . . it is in this *bureaucracy*, Gentlemen, that you will find the invisible and mischievous power which thwarts the most noble views, and prevents or weakens the effect of all the salutary reforms which France is incessantly calling for.'"[36]

For purposes of this manual, we use the term *administrative state* as descriptive of function and value-neutral. As a noun, *bureaucracy* is a neutral reference to government employees collectively but in adjective form it can be slightly pejorative. *Deep state* connotes anti-constitutional political collaborations among the bureaucracy and private interests to undermine elected governments with which they disagree. *Deep state* is not used in this book.

THE MODERN ADMINISTRATIVE STATE

Understanding state administrative agencies and processes begins with understanding the U.S. Constitution's impact on agencies. It begins with agency employees, as agents of government, who are bound to uphold the federal and state constitutions and laws protecting citizens from government abuse.

State constitutions must comport with Article VI , § 2 of the U.S. Constitution, called the *Supremacy Clause*, which requires that state governments must guarantee basic rights, privileges, protections, and organizational form as established by the U.S. Constitution.[37] States may add to but not subtract from federal guarantees. By size[38] and content, the result is a wide variety of state constitutions sharing a common federal constitutional core while expanded as necessary to meet particular local needs.[39]

Legislative Branch. The legislature alone carries the purse. Constitutions grant legislatures exclusive authority to 1) enact statutes and 2) appropriate money to the executive branch for implementation of statutes. The Founders denied legislatures authority to implement anything because, following Montesquieu and their own experience with the English Parliament, they concluded that uniting legislative and executive powers in the same group of government officials would produce tyranny. Today, while agencies can promulgate rules, legislatures *alone* carry the purse thereby controlling agency budgets.

Executive Branch. The executive branch alone carries the sword. Constitutionally it is charged with implementing, that is, *executing*, the legislature's directions, as embodied in enabling (originating) legislation, both statutes and appropriations. The legislature enacts laws, but cannot implement them; the executive implements laws, but cannot enact them. That is the Founders' design but, as you will see later in this book, that is not how it works today.

Judicial Branch. Only the judiciary carries the scales of justice and, per the Founders, is supposed to protect the people from government.[40] "Our Founders envisioned a judicial system separate from the political branches of government, a system designed to fulfill the promise that this country would provide a government based on the rule of law."[41] So central is the judiciary's role that *Themis* and *Justicia*, the Greek and Roman goddesses of justice, adorn the United States Supreme Court building.[42] However, that is not how it works because executive agencies operate their own almost parallel legal systems, although executive actions may be appealed to the judiciary and to the legislature.

EVEN IF CONSTITUTIONALLY SUSPECT, THE MODERN ADMINISTRATIVE STATE IS SECURE

Executive branch administrative agencies, each within its limited bounds of subject matter jurisdiction, call to mind the Founders' fear that tyranny comes when *one body of magistrates* exercises legislative, executive and judicial powers. And, while constitutionally suspect, in a technically complex world demanding a vast volume of work the administrative state is secure because it is inevitable, indispensable, and immense in terms of staffing, money, and power. It is the Brownlow Report's *fourth branch of government.*

Technical complexity. Given the technical complexities of modern society, the need for government regulation of increasingly sophisticated and arcane technical matters, and the demand for highly educated experts to operate the systems, the modern administrative state seems secure to continue its existence.

Volume of work. A state's judicial system would collapse if, in the name of constitutional purity, it had to decide proceedings currently being adjudicated by executive agencies. While data on state administrative workload seem to be unavailable, the federal situation may be extrapolated to the states.

> The federal administrative judiciary was created out of public necessity. Article III judges will acknowledge that it is simply not possible for their courts to handle the plethora of litigation and appeals generated by administrative agencies. Of the hundreds of federal subagencies today, just three of those subagencies—the Social Security Administration, Office of Medicare Hearings and Appeals, and the U.S. Immigration Court—are reported to maintain a backlog of approximately 3 million cases. There are also thousands of other pending cases. Not only would these numbers overwhelm the Article III courts, they pose extraordinary challenges for administrative tribunals as well.[43]

"The question over whether this represents a violation of the separation of powers persists, but few answers are to be found in the Constitution and the Supreme Court seems to have accepted the realities and necessities of delegation in a technologically complex society . . . These issues represent the struggle and seemingly paradoxical desire to maintain values of democracy while realizing the need for bureaucratic expertise."[44]

SUMMARY

The foundations of U.S. agencies and the administrative state, while not set forth clearly in the federal constitution, can be found in state constitutions. Legislatures with judicial support have delegated all three constitutional powers—legislative, executive and judicial—to agencies. Like water flowing downhill under its own inertia, by nature itself agency excess as the Founders warned is inevitable. For this book our concern is with agency excess as expressed through delegated legislative authority as exercised in rulemaking.

When enforced the constitution may and administrative procedure(s) acts (APA) do limit procedurally and substantively agency excess. However, the operative phrase here is *when enforced*. Few regulated entities have resources sufficient to protect themselves against agency power used or misused under *color of authority*, that is, according to law. But by participating in rulemaking, regulated parties may yet mitigate agency excess by influencing adoption of rules by which the agency limits itself. Agency violation of its own rules is not *under color of authority* but is *ultra vires*, that is, beyond its powers. While adjudicative bodies generally defer to agencies acting *under color of authority* they will not defer when agency action is *ultra vires*. And agency staff acting outside color of authority may lose their qualified immunity leaving them legally liable, personally and individually. (Business Leaders in Christ v. Univ. of Iowa, 2021 U.S. App. LEXIS 8256 (March 23, 2021)) For reasons of self-defense and to achieve a more favorable regulatory environment, your principal must participate in rulemaking.

In our next chapter, we begin preparing you to participate effectively by giving you insights into how agencies are constructed, their employees, and their duties and powers. We begin our focus on rulemaking, that is, agency self-legislating.

CHAPTER 2

THE AGENCY MODEL

The conceptualization for the modern administrative state began 100–150 years ago among many scholars, especially Woodrow Wilson,[45] sometimes referred to as the father of the administrative state. Ideally, per their model and as it exists today, an executive agency:

- Operates on written, unambiguous rules
- Promulgates rules that are consistent, predictable, and in accord with *enabling* and *authorizing* legislation and other laws
- Keeps politics to a minimal role in decisions
- Ensures that the Agency's mission trumps private interests
- Establishes Agency personnel as experts
- Is motivated by duty and service
- Recruits managers based on qualifications
- Utilizes functional divisions of labor
- Maintains a hierarchy of tasks and people

Operates on written, unambiguous rules. Chapter 3, *Administrative Procedure(s) Acts*, section, "Protection from Agency Excess: State and Federal Constitutions and Administrative Procedure(s) Act (APA)" quotes the Florida Bar publication on the years when "unelected bureaucrats were running the state through the use of largely unknown or inconsistently applied unauthorized rules or uncirculated memoranda hidden away in bureaucrats' desk drawers."[46]

Today, both procedural and substantive agency rules are available to the public. The advocate must be familiar with them or have immediate access to legal counsel to ensure a proper understanding of these rules in order to protect yourself and your principal.

Promulgates rules that are consistent, predictable, and in accord with enabling and authorizing legislation and other laws. A rule must advance the *enabling legislation*, that is, the specific law being implemented; follow the *authorizing legislation*, that is, the statute establishing the agency and its purpose; not contradict existing law, be a logical outgrowth of the current body of law, and be supported by facts and law as found in the rulemaking record.

The weight of facts and law as found in the rulemaking record must not contradict the final rule. For this reason, an advocate wants to submit into the rulemaking record abundant information supporting your principal's position on the proposed rule. Some states allow an agency to consider information *beyond that which is contained in the rulemaking record* as long as the final decision is neither arbitrary nor capricious. "A rule is arbitrary if it is not supported by logic or the necessary facts; a rule is capricious if it is adopted without thought or reason or is irrational."[47]

Procedurally, all agency actions, including rulemaking, are subject to your state's APA which generally is discussed in Chapter 3. We will emphasize throughout this book that your or your consultant's familiarity with your state's APA is indispensable to achieving the best outcomes for your principal in any agency interaction, including rulemaking.

As an advocate, pointing out specific APA requirements may give the agency pause and provide you with leverage and respect ultimately influencing agency actions. For example, per bullet two above, approximately one hundred percent of the time you may respectfully and appropriately ask agency staff, "Could you please show me where in the enabling legislation you believe the department finds the authority to promulgate this specific provision?" Insistence on proper application of *facts and law, facts and law, facts and law* are the advocate's constant point of reference and emphasis.

Keeps politics to a minimal role in decisions. Agency career civil service staff in performance of their official duties do not and should not care who the regulated interest is. Their concerns are limited to facts and law, the agency's mission, its strategic plan, and relevant policies. In reality, however, politics sometimes plays an *unofficial* and *out of sight* role even in official agency actions.

Ensures that the Agency's missions trumps private interests. Although this was in a legislative context, when Bob told the agency manager that the department's bill could put his principal out of business, he replied, "Bob, the department doesn't get paid to keep you in business. If you have a bad product, then I guess you'll just have to go out of business."[48] Agency staff was 100% correct. Agency mission triumphs over private interests.

Establishes Agency personnel as experts. Agency staff are more educated, white-collar, and older than the private workforce in general. "University of Wisconsin-Milwaukee economics professors Keith A. Bender and John S. Heywood, assert that state and local government workers are better educated and have more work experience, on average, than do private sector workers, so it is natural that their overall average compensation would be higher."[49]

"In 2013, 51.7% of public sector workers were between the ages of 45 and 64, compared to 42.4% of full-time private sector workers."[50] Once ensconced in the state bureaucracy, career civil service employees' jobs are secure, raises and advancement almost guaranteed, and they are harder for managers to motivate[51] and manage.

Agency personnel as experts is the norm while lawmakers and their staff often have little expertise in the subject matter they are considering. Lack of expertise within the legislature fosters lawmaker and staff dependence on agency experts for technical direction. Legislators' dependence, in turn, makes agencies politically powerful players. For example, the legislative committee chair will ask the agency's legislative liaison for the department's position on a bill before the committee. Agency support may help a bill but their technical opposition likely will kill it because few staff and fewer legislators can rebut the opinion of an agency Ph.D.

As mentioned in the previous chapter, while the modern administrative state may be constitutionally doubtful, its experts keep it indispensable and thus safe. Without millions of agency employees and billions of state dollars, statutes would be dead letters, legislatures functionally meaningless, and the modern social structure would be undone.

Is motivated by duty and service. While their jobs often pay higher[52] and career security and state benefits are unbeatable compared to the private sector,[53] we have observed that most agency staff do what they do because of their strongly-held belief in public service. For example, Bob became an environmental agency pollution control inspector for love of the natural environment.

Later you will read about the Department of Children and Families social worker who risked her safety to care for children. Assume that the agency staff with whom you are working are dedicated to carrying out their agency's mission statement. Belief in their mission and, at times, their sense of having a *higher calling* affect how they go about their daily work and their attitudes toward you, your principal, and others in your principal's line of work or industry sector.

Recruits managers based on qualifications. The Civil Service System was created to promote professionalism and combat the awarding of government jobs as payback to political supporters. In addition to secure jobs without fear of political reprisals, the hallmarks of career civil service are appropriate academic credentials and work background and professional advancement within government services.[54] While the Governor's political appointees may not need specific technical expertise to temporarily direct the agency in carrying out the Governor's political and policy objectives, civil service employees provide the long-term, stable, technically founded, non-political agency process.

Utilizes functional divisions of labor. Agencies may have thousands of employees in specialized roles requiring organization in a chain of command with duties defined by job description. The following section discusses this in greater detail.

While arguable *conceptual similarities* between the legislature and executive agencies exist, the reality is wholly different. For example, *operating on written, unambiguous rules* is a hallmark of administrative theory and a statutory demand. Other the other hand, the legislature's procedural rules may be changed at any time by unanimous consent to meet the exigencies of the moment.

Maintains a hierarchy of tasks and of people. Organization and people are discussed in the following sections.

EXECUTIVE BRANCH STRUCTURE GENERALLY

The executive branch of state government has three levels:

- *Plural executives* are the *executive* constitutional offices elected statewide by voters in partisan or non-partisan races. Offices vary by state with some found in all or most states, such as Governor (50) and lieutenant Governor (45) down to controller, which is found in 19 states.[55] Some offices are infrequently created, such as state university regents who appear in four state constitutions.[56]
- *Independent agencies* are the entities that, even though they may have appointees by the Governor, serve independently from direct influence by the chief executive.[57] For example, the Florida Constitution establishes the independent Fish and Wildlife Commission, and authorizes the legislature to establish a Department of Veteran Affairs, and a Department of Elder Affairs.[58]
- *Line agencies* are the state agencies that report directly to the Governor[59], whose appointees are subject to a direct line of authority from the Governor's Office, and are nominated for confirmation by the state senate or appointed by him or her.[60]

EXECUTIVE AGENCY ORGANIZATIONAL STRUCTURE

An executive agency has a pyramid organizational structure consisting most broadly of civil service system protected and non-civil service system protected employees. Starting at the base and working up the pyramid are: career civil service technical and clerical staff, career civil service managers, non-career civil service agency managers, and political appointees. An agency may or may not have citizen advisory committees. These categories are discussed below. The following diagram illustrates the organizational structure and relative population within each category of staff.

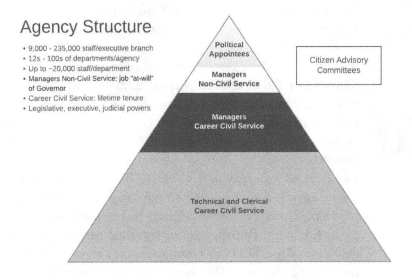

Agency Structure

- 9,000 - 235,000 staff/executive branch
- 12s - 100s of departments/agency
- Up to ~20,000 staff/department
- Managers Non-Civil Service: job "at-will" of Governor
- Career Civil Service: lifetime tenure
- Legislative, executive, judicial powers

Political Appointees

Managers Non-Civil Service

Citizen Advisory Committees

Managers Career Civil Service

Technical and Clerical Career Civil Service

Career Civil Service. Career civil service staff make up the vast majority of agency employees. "Civil service is the designation given to government employment for which a person qualifies on the basis of merit rather than political patronage of personal favor. Civil service employees, often called civil servants or public employees, work . . . for the federal, state, or local government. Legislatures establish basic prerequisites for employment such as compliance with minimum age and educational requirements and residency laws. Employees enjoy job security, promotion and educational opportunities, comprehensive medical insurance coverage, and pension and other benefits often not provided in comparable positions in private employment."[61]

For regulatory agency advocates, career civil service employees are the focus of long-term agency relationship-building activities. This is because they:

- *Provide agency continuity.* For their entire careers, they expect to be at the agency or at least work within state government given the benefits of government employment, especially members of public employee unions.[62] Depending on retirement options, their duration of state employment ranges from 20–30 years.
- *Stay at agency long after the Governor and political appointees are gone.* Top agency managers are political appointees. This means they are awarded positions in order to assist in carrying out the Governor's political agenda. They are dismissed from state service upon direction of the Governor or at the end of the Governor's term, whichever comes first. Contrast them with career civil service employees who will be at the agency for their entire careers.
- *Can wait out unpopular administrators.* Bob was meeting with a state agency over the proposed regulation of his principal's products. Governor [name deleted] had newly been elected to his first term. Perhaps sensing regulated parties' optimism over a new Republican Governor, the agency manager chairing the meeting said to us, "We here at the DEC don't like [name deleted]. We are going to sit on our hands for the next four years until [name deleted] goes away." Civil service protections and government employee unions shield state employees from losing their jobs except under the most grievous misconduct.[63]

Government employees ignoring or even undermining their managers, as above, while nothing new, recently has been termed *guerilla government.*

Rosemary O'Leary refers to as guerrilla government, or "the actions taken by career public servants who work against the wishes—either implicitly or explicitly communicated—of their superiors," is part and parcel of administration. Even though such resistance should not come as a surprise, it does generate an expected level of concern. Administrative actors are accused of undermining democratic norms when they work against their constitutional superiors, agency heads, and immediate supervisors or oppose rules, regulations, and red tape.[64]

Regulated parties should be concerned that, in taking positions strongly opposed by career civil servants, even positions which are supported by the political appointees, career staff may undermine the adoption, application, and enforcement of the rules you are promoting. Of note to private sector employees, the study did not find that the threat of job termination significantly influences guerilla government by civil servants.[65] "Managers should also be aware that the type of retribution employees may suffer does not significantly deter their decision to engage in guerrilla activities."[66]

- *Direct agency over the long term.* Promotional and educational opportunities foster longevity and rise in the organizational structure. However, a civil service employee might prefer to plateau organizationally rather than advance to an "at-will" management position.[67] (*At-will* means an employee works without guaranteed longevity.)
- *Focus of long-term agency relations.* Political appointees come and go with changing administrations. Career civil service employees are relatively permanent in government service if not at the particular agency. A cordial relationship with the bureau chief regulating your employer likely will benefit your employer more than being on a first name basis with a flash-in-the-pan agency deputy assistant secretary.

Technical and clerical staff—career civil service. They are the agency's face to the public and day-to-day operators of the agency's vast machinery of government bureaucracy. They are site inspectors, license issuers, office staff, call-center workers, lab scientists, social workers, and hundreds of other job positions. And, many of them are idealists, who work at the agency for reasons of public service. Their idealism affects how they see you and your principal relative to how they see the agency mission.

The agency mission is their first priority whether protecting the environment, collecting taxes, or helping the helpless. *Insiders Talk: Winning with Lobbyists, Professional edition* cautions,

> However, when you lobby career civil service staff, you are not necessarily dealing with people like you, and you have to adapt to them. If your principal is regulated by the agency, then you are likely dealing with people who not only are *not like you* but also *may not like you*, perhaps even having an animus toward you personally, your principal, or even your entire group or industry. Staff got their jobs to tell you what to do or to keep you from doing things. Depending on the agency, its regulatory role, and those it regulates or serves, sometimes you may encounter an "us against you" regulatory mind-set.

They can be zealous advocates for their agency's work. Some state employees are so fervent for their agency's mission and people it serves that they will endanger themselves. To illustrate, the district's Human Rights Advocacy Committee received a parents' complaint that in their view the Department of Children and Families (DCF), assisted by the county sheriff, wrongly took their toddlers into state protective custody.

The record showed that: 1) the children had been outside late on a freezing North Florida night, unsupervised, and lightly clothed; 2) parents were addicted to crack cocaine; and, 3) they were now "stalking" the DCF staffer as she drove in rural north Florida. The parents did not attend the hearing so we could not complete the case review. This young DCF employee stayed faithful to her mission to children and families despite being stalked by drug addicts. Do not expect, but do not be surprised, when you encounter zeal for their mission and dedication to their job.

32

Their focus is technical and legal, not policy. The sanitarian inspects steam tables that keep food warm to ensure food temperatures meet health codes. Trying to influence him or her with pleas that your restaurant's floor plan cannot accommodate control technology or arguing that the rule which the sanitarian is enforcing is unconstitutional will likely be futile. Agencies are technically and legally focused.

Managers—career civil service. While they direct the technical and clerical staff, advocates are concerned with them because they are long-term decision makers, the first step in agency discretion as to their area of authority, and attune to the political consequences of their section's and overall agency's actions. *Agency discretion* is a key concept for lobbyists trying to influence the agency *prior to* APA notice of proposed rulemaking. Once noticed, agency flexibility diminishes due to legal constraints in the formal APA rulemaking process.

Managers—non-career civil service. These generally are staff who have moved up and out organizationally from career civil service positions into *non-political* senior managerial positions. Not being civil service, they serve at the pleasure of the Governor and can be fired at will. The federal Senior Executive Service may be a useful analog.[68]

They implement the Governor's instructions while at the same time advancing the agency's mission. For advocates they are important because, as the interface between political appointees and the career civil service staff, they influence both policy makers and policy implementers, at times helping to harmonize internally polarized views. Having no career civil service protections, theoretically, their job tenures are uncertain. However, in practice, as long as the political appointees have confidence in them as *non-political* senior managers they keep their jobs.

Political appointees (excluding governing boards appointed by the legislature). These are top-tier agency managers nominated by the Governor, usually requiring state senate confirmation.[69] Leadership titles include secretary, commissioner, executive director; and deputies and assistants. Top agency managers are selected largely because of their political support and loyalty to the Governor, not because of expertise within the scope of agency responsibilities.

They are there to faithfully implement the Governor's political agenda, not necessarily that of agency career civil service staff. The conflict of purpose becomes acute in rulemaking when career civil service staff as technical people conflict with political appointees as policy people. Advocates may find allies in the political appointees to redirect or end an objectionable rulemaking.

Citizen advisory committees. These permanent or *ad hoc* panels may or may not exist and may have great or little influence with the agency. Group members are selected to advise the agency on matters before the agency, especially problems that may delay rulemaking or threaten agency political legitimacy.

We urge you not to solicit the *personal opinions* of agency employees on agency policy. They are paid to represent agency views, not their own. For example, a health department legislative liaison in the context of representing her agency expressed to a legislative committee considering opioid legislation her tragic story of losing her husband to opioids.

The media published two articles featuring the heart wrenching details of a well-known agency official dealing with an opioid addicted spouse. The agency fired her because her scrambling agency health policy with her personal views undermined her as a reliable impartial narrator of agency policy. (Legislative liaisons are political appointees who can be terminated at the Governor's pleasure.) She was terminated and now works as a contract lobbyist.

AGENCY TOOLS

While this manual focuses on rulemaking, for completeness sake, we must inform the reader of alternative actions that could be used to achieve your principal's objectives or may be used by the agency to elicit compliance with its directives. For example, for the former, rather than developing a new rule, you might achieve your principal's objectives via an agency declaratory order or a policy statement.

For the latter, the agency may boost a regulated party's compliance through increased site-visit monitoring rather than entering into a formal agency enforcement action. An agency's "tool set" to faithfully execute enabling statutes includes:

- Rule development
- Declaratory orders (also called declaratory statements)
- Compliance monitoring
- Enforcement of regulations, including quasi-judicial proceedings
- Administration of organizations and benefits
- Research and assistance
- Policy formulation and implementation
- Non-public procedures

Rule development (i.e., rulemaking). Starting in the next chapter, rulemaking becomes the main focus of this manual. But for now, suffice to say that your state's administrative procedures act[70] and state-specific rules implementing its APA will direct agency actions, including rulemaking, that impact the *substantial interests* of regulated parties. (Note: at its most fundamental, the term "substantial interests" means money.)

Declaratory orders (also called *declaratory statements*).[71, 72, 73] Agencies may provide official and binding statements to an interested[74] or substantially affected[75] entity defining how an agency rule or prior order affects or applies to a particular set of circumstances and parties. "A declaratory order has the same status and binding effect as any other order issued in an adjudication."[76] A favorable agency declaration could solve your principal's regulatory problem with minimal costs. It also may be precedent to apply to similarly situated parties.

To illustrate, for reasons of sanitation, food in state residential facilities must be served at a temperature prescribed by regulation. In the northern part of the state, food temperature is measured at the steam table demonstrating consistent compliance. In the southern part of the state, temperature is measured upon food being plated resulting in occasional non-compliance because, during transfer from the steam table to the plate, food cools to just below the regulatory standard.

To solve the non-compliance problem in the southern part of the state, the facilities director can seek a declaration from the agency stating that compliance with the regulation will be measured at the steam table. The declaration is a potentially quick solution to the regulatory dilemma.

Normally, the process is your legal counsel doing a dance of sorts with the agency's legal counsel trying to determine the agency's likely response to your request for a declaratory order. Because the order issued will legally bind your principal and is precedent for similarly situated parties, a regulated party wants to know *beforehand* if the order will help or harm.

Compliance Monitoring. State inspectors monitor operations reports normally required as a condition of an operating permit or license. They also conduct on-site and in the field data collection. Agencies have been known to occasionally use monitoring, especially site inspections, to harass regulated parties with whom they are having a disagreement.

More frequently, a regulated party will improve its compliance efforts knowing increased monitoring, virtually always unannounced, may reveal violations of which it is unaware and result in agency enforcement or unfavorable media coverage. State operation permits may have provisos stating that, as a condition of the permit, the permittees must allow state inspectors unrestricted access during normal business hours. Unpermitted facilities can only be inspected with a judicially issued warrant.

Enforcement of regulations, including quasi-judicial proceedings. An agency can subject a regulated party to a quasi-judicial proceeding and, if found in non-compliance, assess penalties ranging from simply fixing the problem (i.e., a "fix-it ticket" or a "right to cure" an example of which we discuss in Chapter 7 *Post-Rulemaking*, section, "That the Process *Can Be* the Punishment Does Not Mean the Process *Will Be* the Punishment") to substantial punishments such as revocation of a permit to operate a business, practice a profession (e.g., suspending a license), and fines.

Agencies generally cannot waive penalties for *adjudicated* non-compliance. However, in certain circumstances, an agency can choose *not to issue a notice of violation.* An agency enforcement officer, analogous to a police officer exercising discretion to either charge a driver for an infraction or to simply issue a warning, can seek other means of eliciting compliance short of a formal enforcement action.

Bob as a pollution control inspector would regularly instruct permittees to remediate infractions and virtually all would comply. Agency staff would regularly visit the electric utility for which Bob later in his career managed environmental compliance and inform him of deficiencies which he would ensure were fixed immediately. Agencies want compliance with agency rules, rather than to make anyone's life difficult. Permittees want to run their activities economically which fines and bad press disrupt. And, nobody wants to go to court, much less against the government with its judicial presumption of correctness, if avoidable. In many instances, minor non-compliance is handled *informally.*

However, once an agency has taken *formal action,* such as upon issuing a notice of non-compliance, the process runs according to agency rules. The regulated interest acknowledges fault by action or inaction or challenges the agency. In most cases, the respondent accepts the complaint and moves to the penalty phase.

Generally, an agency cannot waive a penalty, but it can set the penalty as just fixing the cause and effect of non-compliance. For example, a restaurant's clogged grease trap led to grease flowing across the parking lot in violation of agency rules. The agency settled the non-compliance by ordering the restaurant to clean up the grease and fix the grease trap.

A theme we repeat, in order that readers do not presume an agency is out to abuse its power, is that agencies are more interested in fulfilling the agency's mission than being punitive for innocent mistakes. Does the agency have power they can abuse? Absolutely they do and, just as the Founders feared, they at times do. But our experience is that, while they hold all the *face cards*, as long as you know that and comply with the law, abuse is unusual.

Fulfilling the agency's mission may remain more important than penalizing even egregious, but avoidable, failures. This may be especially so when the fined party provides an essential public service. For example, in the case of a sewage, "Fort Lauderdale commissioners approved a deal with state officials that would allow the city to spend more than $3 million on an environmental restoration project in lieu of paying the fine."[77]

Sewage spill control is critical for public health and environmental protections. In order to move the city to fix the problem, the city's penalty consisted of respondent city paying $5,000 in agency costs and allocating the remainder of the administrative fine to fixing the sewage problem.

Administration of organizations and benefits. Agencies operate state buildings, fleets of vehicles, hospitals, laboratories, prisons, and public housing. They purchase food, computers and supplies. They collect taxes and pay unemployment claims. They operate the administrative state.

Research and assistance. Agencies study conditions affecting their areas of legal jurisdiction and, upon identifying problems, formulate solutions, apply them and test for efficacy. They may assist regulated parties by advising them on compliance mechanisms including issuing guidance manuals.

To illustrate, agency monitoring finds that ozone concentrations in certain areas of the city exceed national ambient air quality standards during certain parts of the year. The agency proposes reducing emissions from automobiles[78] to be enforced by requiring annual state vehicle inspection. They monitor to ascertain the effectiveness of their attempted solution(s) and revise approaches to optimize efficacy.

Policy formulation and implementation. Agencies publish policies to ensure their staff uniformly apply their rules and to avoid having to go through the rigors of rulemaking. Policies are solely matters of agency discretion and may be developed without public input. However, if a policy affects a person's substantial interests (generally meaning spending money to comply) upon an affected party's legal challenge, the policy can be found to be an impermissibly adopted rule in violation of the state's administrative procedures act. An advocate should examine published agency policy to see if it might guide agency enforcement in a way beneficial to his or her principal.

Non-public procedures. Until a person's substantial interests are affected, agencies may operate internally pretty much as they choose consistent with state law. For example, they may on their own volition and for their own purposes form internal working groups to study problems and make recommendations for agency action. They may form stakeholder committees, invite persons to advise them, or create advisory committees. And they may lobby special interests for support as special interests also lobby them.

Completing this overview of agency powers, we now begin our focus on executive agency rulemaking. We start with a menu of agency rulemaking actions and proceed to considering the participants in the rulemaking process.

MENU OF AGENCY RULEMAKING ACTIONS

Agencies have a menu of possible rulemaking actions. The commonality among these options is they will be selected *when they advance the agency's interests.* A proposal that does not further their mission statement, strategic plan, or for which they do not have, or cannot get a budget appropriation, likely will be rejected. In response to your lobbying visit, the agency can:

- Decline to propose a rule
- Withdraw a proposed rule
- Propose a rule, including amending an existing rule
- Limit or expand the scope of a proposed rule

- Speed up or slow down a rule adoption proceeding
- Delay a rule adoption (such as through a study)
- Issue a policy instead of adopting a rule
- Keep or take away what the legislature gave you
- Do the same to your opponent

Decline to propose a rule. While your goal is to persuade the agency to lead enthusiastically in promulgating the rule, the agency may decline your request. In this case, you can file an administrative petition[79] requesting the agency initiate rulemaking. The (likely) agency denial of your petition will be considered a final agency action in some states in which case you can administratively appeal per your state's APA or legally challenge the inaction in court.[80]

However, upon exhaustion of the administrative remedies, you may have no judicial appeal.[81] You can lobby or formally[82] request the Governor to instruct the agency to do as you wish, or lobby the legislature to enact a statute to accomplish what you want. Expect appeal of an agency denial to be expensive in terms of time and money and have a low probability of success.

Withdraw a proposed rule. If you want an agency to withdraw a rule, the agency may decide to withdraw a rule to which you object.[83] However, once an agency has proposed a rule that it wants, the chance of getting them to withdraw it, absent strong arguments or political support, is very small. As we mention in Chapter 6, *Rule Adoption*, section, "Simplified Rule Development Process" by the time a rule is noticed per the APA, it is likely a done deal in the agency's mind.

Propose a rule, including amending an existing rule. The agency may agree that a rule is appropriate and enter into the rulemaking process, which in its entirety may take weeks for adoptions by reference to years for contentious rules.[84] This likely is the very best result for rule proponents.

Limit or expand the scope of a proposed rule (with provisions favorable to you). If rulemaking has not been publicly noticed pursuant to the APA, then changes to the conceptual internal rule development draft can be straightforward. However, if the proposed rule has been APA noticed, such that the formal rulemaking process is being followed, then the agency must treat your request the same as any other comments it receives, incorporate them into the rulemaking record, and explain its response in the next noticed version of the rule or final rule.[85]

Speed up or slow down a rule adoption proceeding. As above, prior to APA notice of formal rulemaking, the agency can adjust its own internal implementation plan (rulemaking schedule) to extend or reduce time for intra-staff deliberations, technical studies, interest group negotiations, and advisory committee discussions. However, once the proposed rule is noticed, the APA may allow[86] or disallow[87] scheduling changes.

Delay a rule adoption (such as through a study). Agencies complete technical studies *prior to filing* a rulemaking notice. They do this to ensure: 1) the technical integrity of the rule, 2) that the factual record is sufficient to defend against legal challenges claiming *arbitrary and capricious*[88] adoption, 3) affordable methods exist to enable regulated parties to comply and, 4) at times to delay the process. Both regulated parties and agencies employ delay by study, often referred to as *paralysis by analysis.*

A regulated entity might want an agency study, especially a multi-year one, in order to defer spending money on compliance or to buy time to allow it to retool its operations. Early in his career, Bob observed that an agency may delay action pending conclusions from a *privately* funded technical study.[89] That is, the agency agreed that more data were needed on which to build a rule, but the agency did not have the money to pay for the study. In such an instance, the agency may allow a private party to fund the study which the agency closely monitors.

Later, as a legislative lobbyist, action on a bill Bob was working was delayed pending a study on which study commission he served. "Finally, delay can occur simply because the agency does not want to act . . . responsible officials choose to wait, often using a study of some sort as a surrogate for action." [90] A party may convince the agency to delay action pending the results of a study, either funded by a private party, a specific legislative appropriation, or the agency itself.

Issue a policy instead of adopting a rule. Pages 43–48 of the RMSAPA discuss in detail agency adoption of policy instead of a rule.[91] In short, a policy, called in the RMSAPA a "Guidance Document," represents "mandatory instructions to agency staff members," but not legally binding on the public.[92] However, favorable policy could direct agency staff to respond more favorably to your principal.

Keep or take away what the legislature gave you. "What the legislature gives you, an executive agency can take away; and what the legislature would not give you, an executive agency might." Upon filing with the Secretary of State, and after the statutorily set time period until the law becomes effective, the agency will have determined what it intends to do with the new statute. Infrequently, an agency concludes it will not implement the law, called *recalcitrance of duty*, and let the associated appropriation revert back to the state's general fund, thereby taking away everything the legislature gave you.

Much more likely, however, the agency will develop an implementation plan in which it determines how, when, and where rules will be adopted and which subsets of regulated interests will be affected, over set periods of time. Agencies generally are given great discretion in rule implementation. For example, the agency may decide to implement section 1 this year and implement section 2 three years later. Or the rule will immediately apply to this subset of regulated interests and over a set period of time expand to other parties. The permutations of rule implementation are many and courts and legislatures generally defer to them as long as agency decisions have a rational basis in advancing the statutory scheme.

Amidst permutations of the rulemaking process, regulated interests have opportunity to lose what they have gotten or to get from the agency what the legislature would not give them. The starkest example of losing a legislative victory is the agency not adopting rules to implement your law or more likely not immediately giving you the benefits of the new law. Or the agency may promulgate rules that go far beyond the limits of the statutory language imposing extra legislatively unforeseen and costly duties.

Do the same to your opponent. What your opponent got or what you lost in the legislature can be reversed if the agency refuses to implement the objectionable legislation, or implements it in a way that you prefer to your opponent's disadvantage

MOMENTARY MUTUALISM: GIVE AND TAKE AMONG RULEMAKING PLAYERS

Agencies influence and are influenced by many of the forces listed below. In the capitol, at times political forces link: momentarily as allies, then opponents, then neutral. As in the legislature, they form ephemeral coalitions, as wary of each other as they can be interdependent. Each player calculates the impact of its participation in an immediate rulemaking on its longer-term interests.

An adopting body *composed of political appointees*, such as a regulatory commission, may be more open to some of the elements below than may civil service staff who are acting on behalf of an agency secretary or its mission. Advocates should become familiar with the symbiotic relationships driven by factors including:

- Governor's office
- Size and depth of agency resources
- Legislature
- Public
- Substantially affected interests
- Persons petitioning the legislature
- Citizen advisory and stakeholder committees
- Special interest allies
- Constituent groups
- Public employee unions
- Technical experts

- Other state and federal agencies
- Media

Governor's office. A Governor *may* influence executive agencies through appointment of agency leadership, proposed legislative agenda, annual budgeting process, and lending to the agency the authority of the Governor's office. For example, lawmakers of the same party as the Governor are predisposed to vote for whatever his or her agencies want. We say *may* because of our experiences having worked in states ranging from where the Governor's office tightly controlled agencies to states where agencies seemingly acted in a *let's keep out of each other's way* coexistence with the Governor.

The Governor's office is predisposed to support agencies when its political allies lead them and agency actions can be a political distraction or a benefit to the Governor. His or her political appointees owe their momentary jobs to the Governor so they may be willing to influence agency rulemaking that may have a political impact upon the Governor.

On the other hand, especially in difficult financial times, agency staff pay attention to the Governor who nominally controls their funding and staffing levels. Advocates should early on introduce themselves to the Governor's staff, demonstrate how their principal influences the state, mention their mutual interest coalitions, and be prepared to leverage their gubernatorial relationship. Finally, as mentioned and footnoted in Chapter 6, *Rule Adoption*, section, "Specific Steps in the Development Process" some states allow the gubernatorial veto of an agency rule which may be your quickest way to remove a rulemaking threat to your principal.

Size and depth of agency resources. 47,631[93] state agencies employ millions of people, spend billions of dollars, and enact and enforce hundreds of thousands of pages of detailed rules. A small state may have 8,000–9,000 agency employees while the largest states have 235,000+.[94] Agencies realize they influence the well-being of elected officials by how the agency impacts elected officials' constituents, political supporters, and districts' economies.

Before and during rulemaking, agency managers ask themselves if a rulemaking is worth the expenditure of physical and political assets and consider alternate ways to accomplish its goals, as for example issuing a policy rather than promulgating a rule. Before working with an agency, consider just how deeply invested it is in a particular rulemaking, what forces are motivating it to enter into this specific rulemaking, and the cost-benefit to them of expending agency resources.

Legislature. The legislature creates most agencies, either on its own initiative through a statute or by constitutional authorization.[95] It can defund an agency, reduce its authority or even abolish it. While firing agency staff is normally quite difficult, it can be done, even to a specific agency employee[96], when the legislature reduces funding to an agency.

For all practical purposes, executive agencies are technical staff to the legislature and their fact and law technical recommendations carry considerable weight with lawmakers—as long as agency staff are silent on elected officials' policy choices.

Legislators influence agencies because agencies know legislators greatly affect their pay, staffing, and economic well-being. Sometimes the influence is overt as when a lawmaker demands an executive agency political appointee to direct the department to do something for a constituent. Agencies have great discretion as to how they fulfill their duties and absent illegal action these kinds of interventions are a normal constituent service provided by lawmakers.

Legislator influence also may be just an unspoken perquisite of their power as when senior agency staff unofficially defer to a powerful lawmaker. For example, the former young agency inspector today understands why early in his career, in the parking lot and out of earshot, the deputy administrator told him it is time to get into the real world and realize that the regulated party that the idealistic inspector wanted to charge with non-compliance was an important lawmaker in determining the agency's annual budget—so drop it! Being just out of college and in a first job, the inspector did as he was told.

Finally, while career civil service staff seldom have direct official job contact with lawmakers, unofficial interactions can happen, although they should not. Shortly after the young staffer above was told by management to back off, the lawmaker himself told him that if he continued to pursue agency action, he, that is, the lawmaker himself, would run the inspector out of the job. *Ivie v. State* in the footnote suggests that a lawmaker can do just that if done correctly.

The first illustration is a common and appropriate lawmaker-agency interaction. The second, unspoken influence leading to agency deference, is just to be expected in the budgetary appropriations power dynamic. The chair of a senate appropriations committee candidly told his audience of school administrators that Bob was training that the best lawmaker they could bring with them to a meeting with agency staff is the chair of the appropriations committee.

This deference to power should not happen in an ideal world but in the normal human dynamic often it does. The final instance, that is a lawmaker threatening an agency staffer's job, is both improper and highly unlikely. Nevertheless, our experience is that all three can occur.

Advocates should know whether the legislature in its oversight function also has authority to approve or veto agency rules and the degree of symbiosis between the legislature and the particular agency. Advocates should cultivate relationships with members and staff of relevant legislative oversight, appropriations, and subject matter jurisdiction committees well before official actions against your principal begin. Assisting citizens through their contacts with agency political appointees is a normal lawmaker service.

Public. The public relies on executive agencies to protect them in areas within the agency's jurisdiction. For example, a health department citing a restaurant for food contamination can destroy a restaurant's business. On the other hand, agencies pay great attention to public support and opposition to proposed rules and permits, such as state permission to clear-cut a forest to install a solar panel farm to generate electricity. While advocates seldom want public involvement in rulemaking, the option exists.

Substantially affected interests. Regulated parties may rightly fear executive agency retribution for opposing the agency. Senate Minority Leader Chuck Schumer once commented "Let me tell you, you take on the intelligence community, they have six ways from Sunday at getting back at you."[97] While we have seen retribution *under color of law* used as a tool, its use is hardly the norm.

However, as discussed in Chapter 7, *Post-Rulemaking*, section, "The Process Is the Punishment" agencies and government employees can, and at times do, force a regulated party into a wearisome and expensive bureaucratic process that tilts very much in favor of the administrative state. Advocates should appreciate *beforehand the reprisal an agency may take against the advocate's principal* as they enter into rulemaking.

Further, agency revenge may follow an administrative or judicial rule challenge, in which if you lose, you lose and, if you win, you may also lose in a kind of pyrrhic victory.[98] Chapter 7, *Post-Rulemaking*, section, "The Process Is the Punishment" describes all too costly legal battles where even a relatively wealthy regulated party's resources were insufficient to challenge the wealthy state government or state government harassment. Chapter 8, *What You Should Learn, Accept and Challenge on Agency Regulatory Enforcement and Adjudications* will guide your thinking as you consider challenging an agency's actions.

Persons petitioning the legislature. As highlighted earlier, for all practical purposes, executive agencies are technical staff to their respective legislative committees of jurisdiction. Agency support or opposition can determine the fate of a bill. Persons petitioning the legislature cultivate positive relationships with the agency and in particular the agency's legislative liaison (agency lobbyist). On the other hand, in its own political calculus, the agency considers the potential influence of other organizations upon its own legislative agenda and appropriations requests.

Citizen advisory and stakeholder committees. Having both staffed and served as members of such committees at municipal and state levels, we have seen them influence legislative and agency processes, specifically an agency report on recommended regulatory action to the legislature.

An agency or elected body may utilize them to postpone dealing with a difficult topic or to fix rule delaying problems. If the makeup of the committee or advisory group seems favorable to your general interests, visiting with them could activate valuable political and technical support in the future.

Special interest allies. Agencies have special interest allies which lobby legislatures on behalf of shared legislative and regulatory goals. For example, a public interest group lobbies the state legislature for funding of the state agency that serves its members' interests. Or, at the urging of a special interest, an agency proposes that the state should buy a tract of land for a state park which the special interest members will frequent.

Constituent groups. A subset of special interest allies is agency constituents who generally support agency actions. These constituent groups support the agency before the legislature, in public meetings, and with the media. Agencies may be amenable to the desires expressed by friendly groups. To illustrate, Bob assisted a public interest group lobbying for a Medicaid bill. The agency welcomed us as kindred spirits. However, agency staff could barely tolerate our industry association corporate opponents largely because they found the executive director offensive. Agency support multiplied our legislative political power and agency influence.

Public employee unions. Public employee unions influence agencies on matters affecting their members including wages, benefits, working conditions, and the like. They may lobby state lawmakers on behalf of their members which can result in additional resources going to state agencies.

"State and local government workers constitute the largest subgroup (42.1 percent) of all union members in the country. Over a third (36.1 percent) of state and local government workers belong to a union, compared with just 6.5 percent of workers in the private sector nationally. This 36.1 percent share is down from the roughly 38- to 40-percent share sustained throughout the 1990s and 2000s."[99] However, public employee union membership averages vary by state. For example, over half of Illinois government employees are represented by unions.[100]

Public employee unions and agencies may cooperate for their mutual benefit. To illustrate, at a union's suggestion, the agency included funding for the hiring of more corrections officers in its budget request. The public employees' union lobbied the legislature for more money for corrections officers. Successful collaboration resulted in more public employees at the Department of Corrections and more members for the public employees' union. Advocates should examine how their issue might affect the interests of public employee unions thereby gaining an ally or heading off opposition.

Technical experts. While technical experts seldom meaningfully impact the legislature's determination of public policy, in an agency's execution of statutes, technical experts are central. Generally, agencies have more staff with advanced degrees, experience and expertise than their private sector counterparts and as experts they accord fellow experts deference. A well-credentialed expert sincerely working with the agency to follow the science and data in order to solve problems can be highly influential with the agency and positively impact your advocacy effort.

Consider this illustration of the influence of experts. Bob's Florida industry association was working with the state environmental agency to determine which of two testing methodologies was appropriate for ascertaining compliance with federal air emissions standards from power plants. The association hired as its consultant Walt Smith, formerly with USEPA, who literally wrote the book on smokestack testing. As Walt was introduced to agency staff, it just so happened that his book on testing was at that moment being referred to by staff. When his name was mentioned, staff responded almost with awe, "*Theee* Walt Smith?"

With that, he and staff collaborated effectively to settle on methodologies.[101] Experts thrive on mutual respect. Expect that full participation in agency rulemaking may require your principal hiring technical experts. If your principal does not, then a coalition of similarly affected parties should consider funding such an effort.

Other state and federal agencies. Agencies often have overlapping jurisdictions, at times uncertain as to who regulates a particular activity. For example, who controls the Right to Farm[102] disposal of food wastes on agricultural lands: Department of Environmental Regulation, Department of Health, or Department of Agriculture? All three? Chapter 8, *What You Should Learn, Accept and Challenge on Agency Regulatory Enforcement and Adjudications,* section E., "Case Study" details a success story of a citizen resolving a nuisance and environmental hazard in part by negotiating with administrative agencies having distinct but overlapping Right to Farm jurisdictions.

An advocate may locate an agency having overlapping jurisdiction willing to influence a sister agency in a matter affecting both agencies and the regulated party. To illustrate, Bob lobbied for transnational shipment of used batteries from Canada to metal recycling facilities in the United States. Transport Canada and Natural Resources Canada supported our collection, recycling, and transportation efforts with Environment Canada, the lead agency regulating transboundary matters. To influence the U.S. side of the border, earlier he had lobbied the United States Environmental Protection Agency to adopt the Universal Waste Rule.[103, 104] And, in lobbying the USEPA, Bob lobbied for state environmental agency support of the proposed rule. These lobbying efforts were successful.

A federal agency may delegate to a state agency authority and funds to enforce specific federal rules.[105] Keeping funding flowing is so important that some states exempt from APA requirements state agency applications for federal money.[106] APAs are discussed in depth in Chapter 3, *Administrative Procedures Acts.* However, motivating a federal agency to act on your principal's behalf with a state agency should be considered very unlikely.

Media. The media both influence and are influenced by executive agencies. Media may find newsworthy agencies' discoveries of wrongdoing by regulated parties, threats to the public wellbeing—even if it is just a low score from the health department—and political favoritism. Negative media publicity can undermine the public trust, harm an agency's reputation, provoke legislative oversight, and undermine the Governor's political standing. Advocates able to provide the media with a newsworthy story may covertly influence agency actions or diminish negative publicity.

SUMMARY

While we cannot knowledgeably speak about the 47,631 state agencies across the country, our experience leads to us expect:

- While numbers of agency staff range from South Dakota's 9,000 to California's 233,000 (with 24 billion dollars in annual wages)[107], our view is that most agency staff share the objectives of their agencies, whether it is protecting the vulnerable among us, safeguarding the environment, educating the populace, collecting revenues to fund government services, or any number of central public services.
- Executive agencies are organized according to a generic model that seeks to ensure transparency, accountability to the public, and protection of citizens from agency excess. This is accomplished in part by offering the public abundant opportunity to participate in agency actions generally but, most specifically, in agency rulemaking.
- Within relative limits of their respective resources, agencies have common tools and powers to implement enabling and authorizing legislation—among them is agency rulemaking, the focus of this manual.

In our next chapter we discuss the rules of the rulemaking process, that is, *Administrative Procedure(s) Acts*. Federal and state governments have enacted these laws for the specific purpose of empowering citizens to defend themselves from the excesses and abuse of the administrative state[108] of which the Founders warned. In review, from Chapter 1, section, "Constitutional and Practical Dangers of One Body of Magistrates Agency Having Legislative, Executive, and Judicial Powers" we repeat their warning,

"When the legislative and executive powers are united in the same person or body there can be no liberty, because apprehensions may arise lest THE SAME monarch or senate should ENACT tyrannical laws to EXECUTE them in a tyrannical manner." (Emphases in Madison's original)

Chapter 3 discusses in great detail the *Revised Model State Administrative Procedures Act* (RMSAPA) as it applies to standardizing rulemaking. Many states have adopted in whole or in part the RMSAPA as their *Administrative Procedures Act* (APA). However, in order to protect your employers, advocates must become thoroughly familiar with their own state's APA, as critical details vary among APAs.

CHAPTER 3

ADMINISTRATIVE PROCEDURE(S) ACT

Agencies are populated with staff who generally are zealous about fulfilling an agency's mission statement. Every mission statement we have ever read has been noble and inspiring. And agency professional staff generally know better than lawmakers and regulated interests how to fulfill the agency's mission. They create and implement technical solutions to the problems that the legislature wants to solve. Staff work at the agency to carry out the agency's and their personal missions to protect the elderly, children, save the environment, ensure public health, provide safe streets, educate the young, raise revenue, collect taxes, and pursue other critical societal interests.

To protect staff from political interference with the performance of their jobs such as illustrated in Chapter 1, the bulk of agency employees are given career civil service protections and benefits meaning they have secure jobs, guaranteed pay raises, and opportunities for professional advancement. And, when acting *under color of authority*, the state's sovereign immunity extends to them, which means they do not have any personal liability for their official actions.

Staff zeal for the agency's mission combined with job security can embolden them to stretch their authority beyond that which is seemingly reasonable in the eyes of regulated parties. Further, judicial and legislative deference to an agency's discretion in carrying out its mission aggravates a tendency to overregulate. For example, section, "Administrative Procedure(s) Act" on page 56 reprises a time when, " . . . unelected bureaucrats were running the state through the use of largely unknown or inconsistently applied unauthorized rules or uncirculated memoranda hidden away in bureaucrats' desk drawers."

Agency actions clearly beyond the limits of its statutory authority are called *ultra vires*, that is, *beyond the powers*.[109] Even productive agency actions done to further an agency's mission can be beyond its powers. For example, a *Lobby School* student told his class that the state continued to tax his principal's moth-balled industrial site as active because the tax revenue helped fund public schools. Legal abuses to further agencies' missions are not uncommon.

Agencies go beyond delegated legislative authority because their perspectives are narrow perspectives, that is, they focus on fulfilling the agency's mission. Legislatures, on the other hand, have broad perspectives because they balance competing societal interests in order to establish state regulatory policy that will be politically acceptable to the greater part of the entire society.

To safeguard citizens from agency excess, often borne from agency zeal and technical excellence, legislatures, building on the U.S. and state constitutions, have enacted statutory protections, most prominently Administrative Procedure(s) Acts. As an advocate, you must be familiar enough with your state's APA or have ready expert legal advice to help you check agency excess in the rulemaking process. Acting on your APA knowledge will help to protect your principal and perhaps even your own job.

PROTECTION FROM AGENCY EXCESS: STATE AND FEDERAL CONSTITUTIONS AND ADMINISTRATIVE PROCEDURE(S) ACTS

The Unites States Constitution's Bill of Rights and state equivalents specifically protect citizens from government abuse. For example, the Fourth Amendment to the federal Bill of Rights protects citizens against unreasonable searches and seizures of one's private property or person.

The Fourth Amendment originally enforced the notion that "each man's home is his castle," secure from unreasonable searches and seizures of property by the government. It protects against arbitrary arrests, and is the basis of the law regarding search warrants, stop-and-frisk, safety inspections, wiretaps, and other forms of surveillance, as well as being central to many other criminal law topics and to privacy law.[110]

However, when constitutional rights limit government agencies from carrying out their missions, government has been known to violate citizens' constitutional protections. To illustrate,

A citizen complained to our city's Effective Municipal Services Committee (EMSC) that while he was at his job city codes inspectors unannounced insisted upon entering his home occupied by his wife and three small daughters. The EMSC met with the head of the city inspection department to ask if inspections were occurring as the citizen described. The director confirmed the citizen's story. Asked by the committee if city inspectors informed occupants that they had the legal right to decline entry, he said staff would not inform them because if they knew their rights, they would not allow his staff into their homes. So, for purposes of departmental efficiency, staff withheld informing citizens of their right to refuse. Upon our report to the city commission and media interest, the commission ordered that future inspections would be announced in advance and notice supplied that citizens had the legal right to refuse inspector entry.

Agency staff intentionally did not inform citizens of their legal rights in order to fulfill the agency's mission to inspect homes for compliance with city codes. Laudable ends in their minds justified arguably illegal means.

The combination of agency zeal, staff unaccountability, and judicial deference to agency discretion invites agency abuse. To protect citizens from agency excess, legislatures have enacted laws. For rulemaking the state's APA is your protection *when you know how to use it.*

ADMINISTRATIVE PROCEDURE(S) ACT (APA)

Advocates should be as familiar with their states' APAs as they are with the authorizing and enabling legislation that gives rise to the agency rulemaking affecting their principals' interests. The APA's fundamental purpose is to protect regulated parties from agency abuse, no matter how well intentioned the agency is in utilizing extralegal means to fulfill its mission.

The following paragraph from the Florida Bar's "A Primer on Florida's Administrative Procedure Act" illustrates why presumably well-intentioned government employees must be forced to operate according to the APA.

> But at the time of the 1974 revisions to the APA, legislative members had become increasingly concerned that Florida was being run by a "phantom government," meaning that unelected bureaucrats were running the state through the use of largely unknown or inconsistently applied unauthorized rules or uncirculated memoranda hidden away in bureaucrats' desk drawers. Florida citizens found that they were subjected to rules which were not even written down, much less published. Legislators who worked for the defeat of a certain provision in the law often went home only to find the identical provision enacted as an administrative rule or agency memorandum a few months later. Furthermore, concerns arose about the impartiality of hearings conducted by agency employees when a citizen was accused of a rule violation. Legislators believed that a few agency administrators had in many ways usurped the authority of Florida's elected representatives, arguably giving these administrators more direct impact on the people of Florida than the officials these citizens had elected for representation.[111]

Power and certainty of one's mission are as seductive motivators today, resident in the human soul, as they were when state APAs were being enacted. This is why the Founders' distrust of power made *separation of powers* central to their new government. Thomas Jefferson noted, "Experience hath shewn, that even under the best forms of government those entrusted with power have, in time, and by slow operations, perverted it into tyranny."[112] This is not about a defect in anyone's character; it is about the human condition.

As an advocate, you must insist upon the protections provided to you and your principal by the APA. In order to do that, you must develop a basic understanding of your state's Administrative Procedures Act.[113, 114]

AGENCIES MUST STAY WITHIN PROCEDURAL AND SUBSTANTIVE LIMITS—APA AND IMPLEMENTING RULES

Thomas Jefferson observed, "The execution of laws is more important than the making of them."[115] Jefferson's statement applied to agencies means that, short of litigation, how an agency executes, that is, carries out, a statute for all practical purposes becomes the law. Thus, an agency by its practice can potentially rewrite statutes.

To protect citizens from bureaucratic overreach lawmakers have enacted substantive and procedural boundaries to limit agency actions. Violation of these restrictions may lead to adjudicative invalidation of an agency action, in whole or in part. Agency rulemaking must stay within statutory procedural and substantive limits.

Administrative Procedure(s) Act (APA). The APA's guarantee of agency transparency and public participation in rulemaking is the most important procedural tool you have to advance and protect your principal from bureaucratic abuse.[116]

Rules provide a way of informing the regulated public of how agencies intend to apply laws and deter the improper implementation of policies, thereby helping to protect the people of Florida from administrative agencies' noncompliance with legislative mandates or case-by-case decision making without regard to published policy . . . The Administrative Procedure Act serves to protect the citizens of Florida from thousands of unauthorized rules that would otherwise be in effect.[117]

An effective advocate will study and know the state's APA as both shield and sword. While laws may influence behaviors, laws seldom change hearts. The behavior the Florida Legislature was combatting in 1974 grew from unrestrained power in the hands of civil servants who sincerely believed they knew what was best for the state. This same all too human attitude remains today as, "The accumulation of all powers, legislative, executive, and judiciary, in the same hands, whether of one, a few, or many, and whether hereditary, selfappointed (sic), or elective, may justly be pronounced the very definition of tyranny."[118] The Founders then and state legislatures today guard against the abuse inevitably birthed when unaccountable power and mission combine.[119]

INSIGHTS INTO THE APA PROCESS

State APAs, which are patterned after the federal APA statute and Model State Administrative Procedure Act, set forth the rules by which the state's executive branch agencies must adopt regulations. The twin goals of the APA are to ensure, for purposes of a proposed rulemaking, notice to the public and an opportunity for the public to be heard. In that vein, the following are some insights for those who participate in the rulemaking activities of state agencies.

The defined purpose of a regulation is to "implement, interpret and make specific" a statute. Accordingly, those who submit written or verbal comments on proposed regulations to an agency should describe how a proposed regulation accomplishes one or more of these purposes (if you support the rulemaking), or why the regulation does not accomplish them (if you oppose the rulemaking).

When agencies engage in administrative rulemaking, they need to ensure that they are doing so in a manner that follows the APA requirements. For example, "clarity," or actually the lack of clarity, is one of the main reasons that an agency regulation can be overturned. Lack of clarity is usually due to ambiguous or undefined terms in the regulation. So, if the proposed regulation on which you are commenting lacks clarity, pointing that out in the rulemaking record may be your best avenue to promoting clearer rules or thwarting the adoption or ultimate approval of the regulation.

In addition, the lack of "necessity" is another common reason for the rejection of a proposed regulation. Generally, a court, for example, will look at whether the regulatory agency distinguished between the what and the why. The agency usually does a good job in explaining the "what"—what the regulation proposes to do—but not always the "why." In other words, not providing an adequate showing of "necessity" makes a rule ripe for judicial nullification.

Confusion at times arises regarding the difference between the "authority" that an agency has to adopt a rule and whether that rule is "consistent" with the authorizing statute. For example, we often hear in rulemaking proceedings that "the agency does not have the authority to adopt this regulation."

However, authority is not the right argument in this instance. Instead, the "authority" of an agency is pretty easy to determine—it is whether the agency has general or specific authority to adopt the regulation based upon the underlying statute. Almost all state agencies have explicit authority to adopt regulations. Moreover, most major agencies have general rulemaking authority, while other agencies get a specific grant of rulemaking authority (e.g., statutory language that reads, "The (agency) shall adopt regulations to implement this section.")

Often times, persons confuse these two terms—authority and consistency. When you argue that the agency does not have authority, it is not that the agency does not have the authority to adopt the regulation because almost all of them do. Instead, you should argue that the underlying statute that the agency is trying to "implement, interpret or make specific" is being improperly expanded or narrowed and, therefore, the proposed regulation is actually not consistent with the underlying statute.

REVISED MODEL STATE ADMINISTRATIVE PROCEDURES ACT (RMSAPA)

All 50 states and the District of Columbia have adopted their own Administrative Procedure(s) Acts ranging in length, complexity, state-specific details, and even titles for the legislation.[120] However, the 1946 federal *Administrative Procedure Act*[121] and *Model State Administrative Procedure Act*[122] (MSAPA) provide core administrative procedures common to state acts. The MSAPA has been adopted by 10 states and the District of Columbia.

The MSAPA also forms the core of the American Bar Association's *Model Administrative Procedure Act for Interstate Compacts* (2019) "This 'Model' Interstate Compact APA is intended for use by states for adoption by new interstate compacts/agreements, and may also be incorporated-by-reference into existing compacts."[123] Compacts govern states voluntarily collaborating when they have or want to form overlapping jurisdictions.[124]

Studying the Model Act is the beginning of your preparation for working intelligently with state executive agency rulemaking. While the Federal Administrative Procedure Act is the headwaters of state acts, the 2010 Revised Model State Administrative Procedure Act (RMSAPA)[125] synthesizes 30 years of state experiences with the 1981 MSAPA and offers suggestions to utilize technological changes occurring since then.[126]

The RMSAPA is valuable to advocates because: 1) it is found in whole in ten states and the District of Columbia and in part in others, 2) its explanatory notes provide broadly applicable reasons for its revisions, and 3) it may provide persuasive authority in your state's APA rulemaking process. While in 40 of the 50 states the RMSAPA does not replace studying your state's APA, it may give you a deeper understanding of your state's APA and an overview of many other states' administrative procedures.

To influence an agency, you must know your state's APA sufficiently and have access to APA expertise, which is often found in a law firm. You must understand the enabling legislation as well as the agency and know how both could affect your principal. And, either you or your consultant or attorney must be able to explain the facts and law behind why the agency should give you that for which you are asking.

A CONCISE SUMMARY OF RULEMAKING UNDER THE RMSAPA

Article 3, "Rulemaking: Procedural Requirements and Effectiveness of Rules" of the RMSAPA provides detailed provisions and an extensive discussion about the rulemaking process, including procedural requirements and effectiveness of rules. While practitioners must become conversant with their own states' APAs, our short summary in the foundational RMSAPA rule language and the often-extensive comments in the meanwhile will provide readers with a functional understanding of *basic* formal state rulemaking procedures. Appreciating formal administrative process is central to proceeding through the rest of this manual.

Article 3
Rulemaking: Procedural Requirements and Effectiveness of Rules
Revised Model Administrative Procedures Act (2010)

SECTION 301. RULEMAKING DOCKET. This section requires agencies to maintain a rulemaking docket that contains all of its pending rulemaking proceedings. It usually contains the following information:

1. the subject matter of the proposed rule; notices related to the proposed rule;
2. how comments on the proposed rule may be submitted;

3. the time within which comments may be submitted;
4. where comments may be inspected;
5. requests for a public hearing;
6. appropriate information concerning a public hearing, if any; and
7. the timetable for action on the proposed rule.

According to its official Comments, this section is modeled on Minn. M.S.A. Section 14.366 and is intended to state the minimum docketing and rulemaking record keeping requirements for all agencies. The Comments also explain that the current rulemaking docket is a summary list of pending rulemaking proceedings or an agenda referring to pending rulemaking.

SECTION 302. RULEMAKING RECORD. This section requires an agency to maintain a rulemaking record for each proposed rule. The rulemaking record must contain the following:

1. a copy of all publications in the [administrative bulletin] relating to the rule and the proceeding on which the rule is based;
2. a copy of any part of the rulemaking docket containing entries relating to the rule and the proceeding on which the rule is based;
3. a copy and, if prepared, an index, of all factual material, studies, and reports agency personnel relied on or consulted in formulating the proposed or final rule;
4. any official transcript of oral presentations made in the proceeding on which the rule is based or, if not transcribed, any audio recording or verbatim transcript of the presentations, and any memorandum summarizing the contents of the presentations prepared by the agency official who presided over the hearing;
5. a copy of all comments received by the agency under Section 306(a) in response to the notice of proposed rulemaking;
6. a copy of the rule and explanatory statement filed with the [publisher]; and
7. any petition for agency action on the rule.

According to the official Comments, several states have adopted this type of agency rule-making record provisions, including Arizona, Colorado, Minnesota, Mississippi, Montana, Oklahoma, and Washington. The Comments specify that the requirement of an official agency rulemaking record should facilitate a more structured and rational agency and public consideration of proposed rules. It will also aid the process of judicial review of the validity of adopted rules.

SECTION 303. ADVANCE NOTICE OF PROPOSED RULEMAKING; NEGOTIATED RULEMAKING. This section provides that an agency may gather information relevant to the subject matter of a potential rulemaking proceeding and may solicit comments and recommendations from the public by publishing an advance notice of proposed rulemaking in the [administrative bulletin] and indicating where, when, and how persons may comment.

In addition, an agency may engage in negotiated rulemaking by appointing a committee to comment or make recommendations on the subject matter of a proposed rulemaking under active consideration within the agency. A committee appointed, in consultation with one or more agency representatives, shall attempt to reach a consensus on the terms or substance of a proposed rule. This section does not prohibit an agency from obtaining information and opinions from members of the public on the subject of a proposed rule by any other method or procedure.

According to the official Comments, seeking advice before proposing a rule frequently alerts the agency to potential serious problems that will change the notice of proposed rulemaking and the rule ultimately adopted. This section is designed to encourage gathering information. This device is commonly used in federal administrative law.

Additionally, this section seeks to enable agencies to act in a fashion that will result in a balance among interested groups from whom information is received. Several states have enacted provisions of this type in their APAs. Some of them merely authorize agencies to seek informal input before proposing a rule; several of them indicate that the purpose of this type of provision is to promote negotiated rulemaking.

States include Idaho, Minnesota, Montana, and Wisconsin. Negotiated rulemaking committees are also used in federal administrative law.

SECTION 304. NOTICE OF PROPOSED RULE. This section specifies that, at least [30] days before the adoption of a rule, an agency shall file notice of the proposed rulemaking with the [publisher] for publication in the [administrative bulletin]. The notice must include the following information:

1. a short explanation of the purpose of the proposed rule;
2. a citation or reference to the specific legal authority authorizing the proposed rule;
3. the text of the proposed rule;
4. how a copy of the full text of any regulatory analysis of the proposed rule may be obtained;
5. where, when, and how a person may comment on the proposed rule and request a hearing;
6. a citation to and summary of each scientific or statistical study, report, or analysis that served as a basis for the proposed rule, together with an indication of how the full text of the study, report, or analysis may be obtained; and
7. any summary of a regulatory analysis.

According to the official Comments, many states have similar provisions to provide notice of proposed rulemaking to the public. Most states have an administrative bulletin that is published regularly. If a state does not have an administrative bulletin, it will still have to comply with the publication requirement.

This language also codifies requirements used in federal administrative law. In the federal cases, disclosure of technical information underlying a rule has been deemed essential to effective use of the opportunity to comment.

SECTION 305. REGULATORY ANALYSIS. This section requires an agency to prepare a regulatory analysis for a proposed rule that has an estimated economic impact of more than $[]. The analysis must be completed before notice of the proposed rulemaking is published. The summary of the analysis must be published with the notice of proposed rulemaking.

A regulatory analysis must contain the following information:

1. An analysis of the benefits and costs of a reasonable range of regulatory alternatives reflecting the scope of discretion provided by the statute authorizing the proposed rule; and
2. A determination whether:
   A. the benefits of the proposed rule justify the costs of the proposed rule; and
   B. the proposed rule will achieve the objectives of the authorizing statute in a more cost-effective manner, or with greater net benefits, than other regulatory alternatives.

According to the official Comments, state laws vary as to which state agency or body preparing the regulatory analysis should submit the analysis. In some states, it is the department of finance or revenue; in others it is a regulatory review agency or regulatory review committee.

In addition, regulatory analyses are widely used as part of the rulemaking process in the states. States should set the dollar amount of estimated economic impact for triggering the regulatory analysis requirement of this section at a dollar amount that they deem appropriate or by other approach make the choice to prepare regulatory analyses carefully so that the number of regulatory analyses prepared by any agency are proportionate to the resources that are available.

Agencies may rely on agency staff expertise and information provided by interested stakeholders and participants in the rulemaking process. Agencies are not required by this act to hire and pay for private consultants to complete regulatory impact analysis.

SECTION 306. PUBLIC PARTICIPATION. This section provides that an agency proposing a rule shall specify a public comment period of at least [30] days after publication of notice of the proposed rulemaking during which a person may submit information and comment on the proposed rule. The information or comment may be submitted in an electronic or written format. The agency shall consider all information and comment on a proposed rule which is submitted pursuant to this subsection within the comment period.

Unless a hearing is required by law of this state other than this [act], an agency is not required to hold a hearing on a proposed rule but may do so. A hearing must be open to the public, recorded, and held at least [10] days before the end of the public comment period. An agency representative shall preside over a hearing on a proposed rule.

According to the official Comments, state laws vary on the length of public comment periods and on whether a rulemaking hearing is required. The bracketed number of days should be interpreted to require that, if a rulemaking hearing is held, it will be held before the end of the public comment period. In that case, the minimum time period would be 50 days rather than 30 days.

In addition, this section gives discretion to the agency about whether to hold an oral hearing on proposed rules in the absence of a statutory or constitutional requirement that an oral hearing be held.

SECTION 307. TIME LIMIT ON ADOPTION OF RULE. This section specifies that an agency may not adopt a rule until the public comment period has ended. In addition, not later than [x years] after a notice of proposed rulemaking is published, the agency shall adopt the rule or terminate the rulemaking by publication of a notice of termination in the [administrative bulletin]. And, a rule is void unless it is adopted and filed within the time limits in this section.

According to the official Comments, this section codifies the final adoption and filing for publication requirements for rulemaking.

SECTION 308. VARIANCE BETWEEN PROPOSED AND FINAL RULE. This section provides that an agency may not adopt a rule that differs from the rule proposed in the notice of proposed rulemaking unless the final rule is a logical outgrowth of the rule proposed in the notice.

According to the official Comments, this section draws on provisions from several states, such as those in Mississippi and Minnesota. The variance test adopted by state and federal courts is the logical outgrowth test. If the adopted rule is a logical outgrowth of the proposed rule, no further comment period is required. If it is not a logical outgrowth, then a further comment period is required. At a minimum, the logical outgrowth test is designed to ensure fair notice to affected persons. *Long Island Care at Home Ltd. v. Coke* 551 U.S. 158 (2007).

SECTION 309. EMERGENCY RULE. This section specifies that, if an agency finds that an imminent peril to the public health, safety, or welfare or the loss of federal funding for an agency program requires the immediate adoption of an emergency rule and publishes in a record its reasons for that finding, the agency, without prior notice or hearing or on any abbreviated notice and hearing that it finds practicable, may adopt an emergency rule without complying with specified sections. The emergency rule may be effective for not longer than [180] days [renewable once for no more than [180] days].

In addition, the agency shall file with the [publisher] a rule adopted under this section as soon as practicable given the nature of the emergency, publish the rule on its Internet website, and notify persons that have requested notice of rules related to that subject matter. This section does not prohibit the adoption of a new emergency rule if, at the end of the effective period of the original emergency rule, the agency finds that the imminent peril to the public health, safety, or welfare or the loss of federal funding for an agency program still exists.

According to the official Comments, this section is taken from the Virginia Administrative Procedure Act. Many states have emergency rulemaking provisions that are based on these provisions including New York, Delaware, Utah, and Washington. Some state courts will invalidate an emergency rule when the agency has not established that there is an emergency that justifies the use of emergency rulemaking procedures.

The federal Administrative Procedure Act uses the "unnecessary, impracticable or contrary to the public interest" good cause standard for the same purposes as the imminent peril standard used in this section.

SECTION 310. DIRECT FINAL RULE. This section provides that, if an agency proposes to adopt a rule which is expected to be non-controversial, it may use direct final rulemaking authorized by this section. The proposed rule must be published in the [administrative bulletin] with a statement by the agency that it does not expect the adoption of the rule to be controversial and that the proposed rule takes effect 30 days after publication if no objection is received.

According to the official Comments, this section has been recommended by the Administrative Conference of the United States. It provides a procedure for direct final rulemaking that applies to non-controversial rules. Under this rule, when the agency is merely making a stylistic correction or correcting an error that the agency believes is noncontroversial, the rule may be adopted without full rulemaking procedures.

In order to prevent misuse of this procedural device, noncontroversial rule promulgation may be prevented by the objection of any person. The public comment period provides notice of the noncontroversial rule and the opportunity to object to the adoption of the rule. If an objection to the direct final rulemaking process is received within the public comment period, the agency must give notice of the objection and then the agency may proceed with the normal rulemaking process, including the public comment provisions.

SECTION 311. GUIDANCE DOCUMENT. This section specifies that an agency may issue a guidance document without following specified procedures. An agency that proposes to rely on a guidance document to the detriment of a person in any administrative proceeding shall afford the person an adequate opportunity to contest the legality or wisdom of a position taken in the document. The agency may not use a guidance document to foreclose consideration of issues raised in the document.

A guidance document may contain binding instructions to agency staff members if, at an appropriate stage in the administrative process, the agency's procedures provide an affected person an adequate opportunity to contest the legality or wisdom of a position taken in the document.

An agency shall maintain an index of all of its effective guidance documents, publish the index on its Internet website, make all guidance documents available to the public, and file the index [annually] with the [publisher]. The agency may not rely on a guidance document, or cite it as precedent against any party to a proceeding, unless the guidance document is published on its Internet website.

According to the official Comments, this section seeks to encourage an agency to advise the public of its current opinions, approaches, and likely courses of action by using guidance documents (also commonly known as interpretive rules and policy statements). The section also recognizes agencies' need to promulgate such documents for the guidance of both its employees and the public.

Agency law often needs interpretation, and agency discretion needs some channeling. The public needs to know the agency's opinion about the meaning of the law and rules that it administers. Increasing public knowledge and understanding reduces unintentional violations and lowers transaction costs.

This section strengthens agencies' ability to fulfill these legitimate objectives by excusing them from having to comply with the full range of rulemaking procedures before they may issue these nonbinding statements. At the same time, the section incorporates safeguards to ensure that agencies will not use guidance documents in a manner that would undermine the public's interest in administrative openness and accountability.

Four states have adopted detailed provisions regulating guidance documents in their administrative procedure acts, which are Arizona, Michigan, Virginia, and Washington. This section draws on those provisions, and also on requirements and recommendations issued by federal authorities and the American Bar Association.

Many states have recognized the need for this type of exemption for guidance documents in their administrative procedure statutes. These states have defined guidance documents—or interpretive rules and policy statements—differently from rules, and have also excused agencies creating them from some or all of the procedural requirements for rulemaking.

A guidance document, in contrast to a rule, lacks the force of law. Many state and federal decisions recognize the distinction. An integral aspect of an adequate opportunity to challenge a guidance document is the agency's responsibility to respond reasonably to arguments made against the document. Thus, when affected persons take issue with propositions expressed in a guidance document, the agency "must be prepared to support the policy just as if the [guidance document] had never been issued."

SECTION 312. REQUIRED INFORMATION FOR RULE.
This section specifies that a final rule filed by an agency with the [publisher] must contain the text of the rule and be accompanied by a record that contains the following information:

1. the date the final rule was adopted by the agency;
2. a reference to the specific statutory or other authority authorizing the rule;
3. any finding required by law as a prerequisite to adoption or effectiveness of the rule;
4. the effective date of the rule; and
5. the concise explanatory statement.

SECTION 313. CONCISE EXPLANATORY STATEMENT.
This section specifies that, when an agency adopts a final rule, the agency shall issue a concise explanatory statement that contains the following information:

1. the agency's reasons for adopting the rule, including the agency's reasons for not accepting substantial arguments made in testimony and comments;
2. the reasons for any change between the text of the proposed rule contained in the notice of proposed rulemaking and the text of the final rule; and
3. the summary of any regulatory analysis.

According to the official Comments, many states have adopted the requirement of a concise explanatory statement, such as Arkansas and Colorado. In addition, the federal Administrative Procedure Act uses equivalent terms. This provision also requires the agency to explain why it rejected substantial arguments made in comments. Such explanation helps to encourage agency consideration of all substantial arguments and fosters perception of agency action as not arbitrary.

SECTION 314. INCORPORATION BY REFERENCE. This section specifies that a rule may incorporate by reference all or any part of a code, standard, or rule that has been adopted by an agency of the United States, this state, or another state, or by a nationally recognized organization or association, if:

1. repeating verbatim the text of the code, standard, or rule in the rule would be unduly cumbersome, expensive, or otherwise inexpedient;
2. the reference in the rule fully identifies the incorporated code, standard, or rule by citation, place of inspection, and date, and states whether the rule includes any later amendments or editions of the incorporated code, standard, or rule;
3. the code, standard, or rule is readily available to the public in written or electronic form at no charge or for a reasonable charge;
4. the rule states where copies of the code, standard, or rule are available from the agency adopting the rule for a reasonable charge, if any, or where copies are available from the agency of the United States, this state, another state, or the organization or association originally issuing the code, standard, or rule; and

71

5. the agency maintains a copy of the code, standard, or rule readily available for public inspection at the principal office of the agency.

According to the official Comments, several states have provisions that require the agencies to retain the voluminous technical codes, such as Alabama, Michigan, and North Carolina. To avoid the problems created by those retention provisions, but to assure that these technical codes are available to the public, this section adopts several specific procedures.

One protection is to permit incorporating by reference only codes that are readily available from the outside promulgator, and that are of limited public interest as determined by a source outside the agency. These provisions will guarantee that important material drawn from other sources is available to the public, but that less important material that is freely available elsewhere does not have to be retained.

SECTION 315. COMPLIANCE. This section provides that an action taken under this [article] is not valid unless taken in substantial compliance with this [article].

SECTION 316. FILING OF RULE. This section requires an agency to file in written and electronic form with the [publisher] each final rule. The agency shall file the rule not later than [] days after adoption. The [publisher] shall maintain a permanent register of all filed rules and concise explanatory statements for the rules.

According to the official Comments, this section provides that the publisher is responsible for publishing the notice of adopted rules in the administrative bulletin.

SECTION 317. EFFECTIVE DATE OF RULE. This section provides that a rule becomes effective [30] days after publication of the rule [in the administrative bulletin] [on the [publisher's] Internet website]. A rule becomes effective immediately on its filing with the [publisher] or on any subsequent date earlier than that established if it is required to be implemented by a certain date by law other than this [act]. An emergency rule becomes effective on adoption by the agency. A direct final rule to which no objection is made becomes effective [30] days after publication, unless the agency specifies a later effective date.

According to the official Comments, most of the states have adopted provisions similar to these provisions, although they may differ on specific time periods. Some rules may have retroactive application or effect provided that there is express statutory authority for the agency to adopt retroactive rules.

SECTION 318. PETITION FOR ADOPTION OF RULE. This section provides that any person may petition an agency to adopt a rule. Not later than [60] days after submission of a petition, the agency shall either (1) deny the petition in a record and state its reasons for the denial; or (2) initiate rulemaking.

According to the official Comments, agency decisions that decline to adopt a rule are judicially reviewable for abuse of discretion. In addition, when an agency grants a rulemaking petition in part, and denies the petition in part, the agency should explain the partial denial.

"REGULAR" VS. "EMERGENCY" RULEMAKING

There are basically two types of rulemakings, regular and emergency, both of which are governed by the APA. The regular APA rulemaking process requires that a state agency meet public hearing and notice requirements and provide abundant opportunity for public participation. On the other hand, the general rule is that a state agency may adopt emergency regulations in response to a situation that calls for immediate action to avoid serious harm to the public peace, health, safety, or general welfare, or if a statute deems a situation to be an emergency under the APA.

Because emergency regulations are intended to avoid serious harm and require immediate action, the emergency rulemaking process is substantially abbreviated compared to the regular rulemaking process. Further, to act immediately, a Governor may precede emergency rulemaking with an emergency declaration for a short duration (e.g., 30 days) during which time the agency may provide a brief public notice comment period.

A foreseeable difficulty is not an appropriate subject for emergency rulemaking. However, given the speed at which an emergency rule can be issued, emergency rulemaking is an attractive vehicle to bypass the often long regular rulemaking process. For example, we have witnessed a court invalidate an agency emergency rule adopting a pharmaceutical formulary for Medicaid reimbursement. The state not timely adopting the formulary was indeed an emergency but it was wholly foreseeable, thus making it ineligible for emergency rulemaking.

Whether engaged in the "regular" or "emergency" rulemaking process, an agency or department follows the procedural requirements found in the APA, such as the contents of the rulemaking record, timeframes, and opportunities for public participation. As you might imagine, the vast majority of regulations adopted pursuant to the APA are submitted as "regular" rulemakings.

This comprehensive APA process is intended to further the legislature's goal of public participation in the rulemaking process. It also creates an adequate rulemaking record for oversight by designated administrative offices, such as in California the Office of Administrative Law, legislative agency oversight committees, administrative and, if necessary judicial courts.

While a prepared advocate should be aware of the permutations of process as discussed above, these situations are not frequently encountered. The normal path of rulemaking is regular as envisioned by the bulk of the content found in state administrative procedures acts. Regular rulemaking will occupy the rest of this book.

AGENCY DISCRETION AS TO GIVING APA NOTICE OF RULEMAKING

Agency discretion as a matter of practice means the legislature and the courts afford to agencies considerable leeway in carrying out the details of their duties. For example, the APA specifies timelines when the agency's duty to notice formal rulemaking begins. But it does not require that the agency announce when it is internally working on a rule, that is, what it is doing before giving APA notice and out of the public eye. As noted below and elsewhere in this book, much work goes on *before the APA notice of rulemaking* during which time the agency negotiates agreements with special interests before the public has opportunity to participate in the rule development process.

Absent specific dates in the enabling legislation or a general urgency clause in the state APA[127], or a specific set date in the statute, timing of rulemaking is a matter of agency discretion. Matters of agency discretion are generally not reviewable until they become *unreasonable*. To illustrate reasoning underlying deference given to agency timing for rulemaking,

> Turning to the merits of the case, the court notes that absent a precise statutory timetable or other factors counseling expeditious action, an agency's control over the timetable of a rulemaking proceeding is entitled to considerable deference . . . Ordering EPA to accelerate this rulemaking may not improve public health and welfare, since acceleration might come at the expense of delay of EPA action elsewhere. If anything, this rulemaking might reasonably have a lower priority than many EPA activities . . . Finally, the actual time involved in this case—less than three years and little more than a year since the close of the public comment period—is not unreasonable.[128]

Given state APA time periods as short as six months from notice to adoption within which an agency must adopt a rule (yes, APA extensions are possible) and deference to agency timing as outlined above, expect that considerable impetus exists for an agency to delay issuing its formal APA notice of proposed rulemaking until it completes drafting and negotiations with affected parties.

During the hiatus, the agency at its own pace can develop the rule to such a completed state that, upon finally noticing the rule, the agency may have little interest in rewriting it. For this reason, if you do not learn about rulemaking until it is formally noticed, then much of your opportunity to influence that rule has passed.

SUMMARY

This chapter explained the purpose and major provisions of the federal and state administrative procedure acts. After introductory comments, we examined the purpose of the APA, which is to protect the public and the regulated community from agency excess. We also emphasized that the state executive branch agencies must stay within specified procedural and substantive limits.

We extensively reviewed Article 3 of the Revised Model State Administrative Procedures Act. At the end of this chapter, we reviewed key similarities and differences between the two types of rulemaking—regular and emergency. Finally, we looked at an agency's discretion for providing notice of rulemaking activities under the APA. Agency discretion is mentioned 29 times in this manual because agencies have much deference shown to them by custom and law.

At this point Chapters 1–3 have set your foundation for agency rulemaking advocacy. In our next chapter *Setting the Stage for Executive Agency Lobbying* you begin establishing yourself as a resource for the agency by demonstrating to agency staff your credibility and utility. We will lay out how to have an effective informal meeting with them in their offices and provide tips on building beneficial relationships with key staff.

==== CHAPTER 4 ====

SETTING THE STAGE FOR EXECUTIVE AGENCY LOBBYING

Those of us having lived with executive agencies as agency staff, regulated parties, or lobbyists know that, as a practical reality, a law does not *functionally* exist until the implementing executive agency says it exists; and, no one knows what a law means until the agency says what it means, both of which agencies do via rulemaking. Agency rulemaking and enforcement are what give statutes *functional* existence, enabling legislation notwithstanding.

Some statutes start as *model legislation* drafted by national interest groups. A state bill sponsor cuts and pastes the model bill into a bill drafting request which is submitted to the chamber's bill drafting services office for introduction. The intent behind model legislation is to create a viral "copycat" effect as these same measures are introduced into other state legislatures.

Some original bills also go viral among similarly thinking legislatures. Bob devoted eight years modifying, repealing, or stopping a legislative concept birthed in Minnesota that was spreading to states on the west and east coasts, the Midwest, and Canada. His U.S. lobbying largely ended upon federal enactment of the *Mercury-Containing and Rechargeable Battery Management Act,*[129] as implemented by the *Universal Waste Rule,*[130] and state equivalent statutes.[131]

The federal law created a national regulatory scheme that preempted state regulation of his principal's products, that is, rechargeable batteries powering consumer products such as cellphones, laptop computers, and power tools. He worked the issue for another two years in Canada at the provincial and national levels. One state's concept led to a series of laws or state actions in federal, state, and international jurisdictions. Expect that the statutes and rules your state agency is being charged with implementing have histories in several other jurisdictions which records are available to you.

Further, parties to the bill-to-law process in your state, including the implementing agency's legislative liaison and technical experts, will resume their interactions in the development and promulgation of administrative rules. Well before rulemaking begins, everybody is already versed on the statute's contents, Governor's and legislature's intentions, and each group's positions.

However, statutes are broad policy directives often kept intentionally vague as a necessity to achieving legislative, political, and policy consensus. Legislatures leave to the implementing agency the job of creating a coherent regulatory scheme. It is in rulemaking where agencies make the ninety percent of law regulating your principal and which implements the legislature's ten percent of law, that is, the enabling legislation. It is in the rulemaking process that conflicts unresolved in the legislature will be revisited and you will find that indeed *the devil is in the details.*

Occasionally an athlete wins a game by preparing smarter than his or her competitors who at the same time are also getting ready for competition. Our next section will begin preparing you for an agency visit that will establish you as a participant in the rulemaking process.

STEP 1. KNOWING WHAT THE AGENCY IS PLANNING: TRACKING REGULATORY ACTIONS

The advocate must stay apprised of regulatory activities that might impact his or her principal. Tracking and analyzing proposed regulations require constant vigilance and awareness of the possible and actual rulemaking calendars of agencies exercising jurisdiction over your principal's activities, even if at the moment rule development is no more than an idea.

There are a number of tools for a lobbyist to track impending regulatory actions by the varied administrative agencies and departments in the states. These intelligence gathering opportunities are found to greater or lesser degrees in all jurisdictions. Notices may be by publication, trends, or human resources for intelligence gathering.

PUBLICATIONS FOR INTELLIGENCE GATHERING

Abundant opportunities are provided by agencies and at times by politicians, political parties, and special interests for interested parties to gather information on impending or likely agency rulemaking including the:

- Agency strategic plan
- Annual budget appropriations
- Governor's plans
- The legislature's plans
- Petitions to initiate rulemaking
- Internal Rule Development Committee docket
- Rulemaking calendars
- Freedom of Information Act (FOIA)
- Interest groups agendas
- Politicians and political parties
- Agency policy announcements
- Enforcement actions
- Agency media announcements
- Formation of citizen advisory groups and stakeholder groups
- Agency mailing lists
- Notices of rulemaking

Agency strategic plan. Agencies often issue regulatory agendas with 3–10-year horizons. Projections can be general or specific as the agency assesses problems to be solved. Longer term strategies may be little

79

more than wish lists, but shorter horizon items listed may have a realistic chance of implementation.

Annual budget appropriations. An agency can do no more than what the legislature funds and it will carry out that which has an actual appropriation. Recall from Chapter 1 the legislature's power of the purse gives it some control overs the executive branch and its agencies. Review past budget requests of the agency to the Governor, and then the Governor's incorporation or not in his or her budget proposal to the legislature, then what the legislature actually funds. Read budget rider language if any to see what directions the legislature has given the agency in implementing any specific appropriation. Rarely an agency will not spend the appropriation because all or part of the unspent funds may revert back to the general fund.

Governor's plans. The Governor's annual or biennial budget submittal to the legislature indicates the Governor's office's agenda and agency proposals which it supports.

The legislature's plans. Political parties, most importantly *the majority party*, may have a 2–4-year legislative agenda that in turn will drive the executive branch's regulatory agenda. You can interview majority party leaders to see the directions they want to take for the next 2–4 years. Majority party matters because, as an extreme example and at the moment, what Republicans want to do in Hawaii is as meaningless as what Democrats would like to do in Wyoming.

Virtually all agency actions are predicated on authorizing and enabling legislation, current or planned. This intelligence gathering should be done in conjunction with your legislative affairs department and contract lobbyist, if any. We say *should be* because we have seen larger organizations where lobbyists are dedicated to either the legislative or executive branches with one internal group seemingly not coordinating with the other. Bob has seen the same in industry associations. Yet, while lawmaking by these two branches is inextricably connected in the capitol, it may not be as connected as it should be in large, non-government organizations including associations and corporations.

Petitions to initiate rulemaking. Citizens may petition agencies to initiate rulemaking. These petitions and agency response to them indicate where the agency wants to go regarding regulating the subject or activity of the petition. In some states, the agency's refusal to enter into rulemaking is not appealable. In other states, refusal is final agency action reviewable by the courts.

Internal Rule Development Committee docket. If the agency accepts the petition above or if it is appointed by agency management to develop a rule, it will appoint an internal committee to develop the rule. We discuss this below in section, "Knowing with Whom to Build Relationships: The Internal Rule Development Committee." This docket is the first agency commitment to rule development as it enters into rulemaking. Rulemakings can take from months to years.

Rulemaking calendars. A rulemaking calendar is a common practice is many states, especially larger ones. For example, in California, there is *The California Regulatory Notice Register*, which is a weekly publication that contains notices of proposed regulatory actions and other relevant notices issued by state agencies. To assist in understanding the state's APA, interested parties can purchase from California's Office of Administrative Law (OAL) its *California Rulemaking Law under the Administrative Procedure Act*, which is an annotated compilation containing the rulemaking portion of the APA, implementing regulations and other relevant statutes.

Individuals can also request an agency's or department's rulemaking calendar, which is their annual list of projected rulemaking activities to implement statutes, and to have your name placed on their "interested parties" mailing list so that you receive ongoing regulatory updates.

Freedom of Information Act (FOIA). An FOIA request is likely to fail because FOIA "deliberative process exemptions" shield agencies from having to disclose actions surrounding *potential* rulemakings. *U.S. Fish and Wildlife Service v. Sierra Club*, 19-547 (March 4, 2021) hardened that shield.

However, in whatever state you operate, as found in all states' administrative procedures acts, is the fundamental principle to provide citizens with full notice of proposed agency actions that can affect the public and ensure full opportunity to participate in the rulemaking process.

Interest groups agendas. Your state's associated industries, chambers of commerce, leagues of cities and counties, professional associations, public interest groups, unions, and other entities have long-term legislative agendas that if enacted will lead to agency rulemaking. The Secretary of State's or similar offices publish lists of principals, their lobbyists, campaign contributions, and issues in which they are active.

Politicians and political parties. As of this writing, much of the American social consensus has frayed with radically different visions of where politicians and political parties want society to go, values they want to advance, and where their political futures lie. These trends often published in the media and party platforms may give you a level of expectation as to the direction of government in your state.

Agency policy announcements. Agencies announce to the public their views on administration and applications of their rules for purposes of information. "Such statements are often described as internal guidelines, bulletins, manuals, policy statements, directives, or instructions. The issuance of a policy statement by an agency without recourse to APA rulemaking allows the agency to retain more discretion than if it had adopted a rule for several reasons."[132] If policy statements affect substantial interests, then rulemaking must follow.

Enforcement actions. While enforcement actions are predicated on specific rules or what should be rules, enforcement or increased activity may lead to formal rulemaking.[133] The agency maintains a list of enforcement decisions and the division of administrative hearings or similar agency maintains a docket of ongoing actions, all public record.

Agency media announcements. The agency may issue announcements of projects on which it is working and may publish upper management speeches and public presentations.

Formation of citizen advisory groups and stakeholder groups. Agencies may form groups to assist them in internal, pre-APA deliberation processes. These groups may be formed for any of several reasons, but among these reasons is because the agency is considering possible rulemaking. Agencies want to avoid rule delaying problems and build consensus around proposed rules which these groups can help them achieve. Agencies " . . . strive for a result that can be embraced by the agency's external clients and constituents . . ."[134] Forming of these groups could be a rule or policy consensus building exercise.

Agency mailing lists. These lists let you know which groups, concerned over specific topics, have registered with the agency in order to receive written notification of proposed agency actions. These mailing lists also may become a roster of organizations for you to contact for information and collaboration and even as potential coalition partners. They also let you know your possible registered opponents.

Notices of rulemaking. APAs demand agencies act *in the sunshine*, that is, for all to see. Upon publication of the APA required notice of proposed rulemaking in the state register, as well as by mail to registered interested parties, the public is given an entry point to exercise its right to participate in the formal rulemaking process. The notice provides information on the substance of the rule, the rulemaking timeline, and relevant agency contacts.[135]

However, as we have noted elsewhere, when some agencies give public notice of rule development in the state register or on the agency's website, the rule may be a *done deal* in their minds. APA public procedures merely ratify what the agency has already decided to do and they have no intention of changing anything. This is the formal point of entry but it may be too late to effect anything substantive. The earlier you know, the greater impact you can have on the final rule.

HUMAN RESOURCES FOR INTELLIGENCE GATHERING

Before an agency acts, it thinks. Your best sources of pre-agency action information are those involved in the thinking, that is the earliest, stages of rule development.

Lobbyists. Lobbyists, especially former agency staff, specializing in particular agencies may have enough contacts within an agency that they may get a sense of likely agency activity before the public notice of rulemaking is made public.

Staff. Let staff know that you are interested in any agency activities affecting your interests. A good staff relationship may lead to a willingness to keep you or your lobbyist informed. While there may be no public notice at this moment, the agency deliberations are by no means to be kept secret. Staff include:

- *Agency legislative liaisons.* They are agency lobbyists who know what the agency is doing and how it may impact agency standing with the legislature.
- *Office of General Counsel.* Agency attorneys are involved in almost all agency formal actions affecting the general public and regulated parties.
- *Political appointees.* They manage the agency for the benefit of the Governor and the agency itself. Depending on their connection to the career civil service staff, they know early or later impending internal trends in rule development.

Legislature's agency oversight and subject matter jurisdiction committee(s). Members and staff can apprise you of their knowledge of agency directions and committee(s)' reactions to agency initiatives.

PREPARING FOR THE LOBBYING VISIT

The better you prepare for the lobbying visit, the more productive it will be. The following checklist will guide you in planning an effective agency meeting:

- Study how this same type of rule has developed in other jurisdictions
- Get a sense of who will be the players in the rulemaking project
- Review agency lobbyist registration and ethics rules

- Familiarize yourself with the state's APA
- Study the proposed rule in detail
- Place the proposed agency action in context of existing law
- Understand in detail the enabling legislation
- Determine what you must have out of the rule
- What do other special interests want?
- What must the agency get out of this?
- Find pressures on staff and agency
- Do not ask for something impossible:
  - legally
  - financially
  - politically
- Prepare to argue:
  - requirements of the enabling statute
  - technical and economic impacts
  - impacts of the rule upon your principal
  - impacts of the rule upon other parties, including government
  - how and why the agency can use their discretion in your favor
  - technically sound alternative positions
  - legally sound alternative positions
- Know what the agency can and cannot do
- Select the right representative(s)
- Connect with staff as fellow professionals but do not overly identify with them
- Should your consultant, lobbyist or legal counsel attend?
- Will other special interests attend the meeting?
- Suggest names of agency staff you think have knowledge useful to your position
- Request a specific amount of meeting time that fits within their schedule
- Do you represent your principal or a coalition?
- Ask to see other parties' written submissions in the rulemaking record
- Ask about *ex parte* communications
- Offer to send to staff, prior to the meeting, key information:

- your position(s) on each rule
- itemized proposed rule changes
- supporting technical materials
- experts' reports
- legal opinions

Study how this same type of rule was developed in other jurisdictions. While your state may be a state of first impression, that is, it is doing what no other state has done before, the chances of that are small. Expect that rulemaking records exist in other states that have enacted similar enabling legislation and subsequent rulemakings. This would be especially true for state implementation of model legislation.

Knowing how other states have tackled this same kind of rulemaking will be valuable to establishing your contribution to the process, credibility, and ability to influence the outcome. Expect agency staff already has developed a compendium of similar state actions including speaking with sister agencies across the country. This is public record that they may freely share with you. However, how they give access is up to them. Bob has been allowed (albeit by a former engineering school classmate who had become a top agency manager) free access to literally dig through agency files to research. But in most cases, this may require a freedom of information (FOIA) request.[136]

Get a sense of who will be the players in the rulemaking project. Players will be motivated by this principle of the rulemaking process: what the legislature gave, an executive agency can take away; and what the legislature would not give, an executive agency might. Those who got what they wanted from the legislature will participate in rulemaking trying to keep what they got and maybe hope to get more.

Those who lost in the legislature will try to get the agency to do what the legislature would not. As a simple example, an interest group failed to stop enactment of a statute. However, through rulemaking, they might be able to delay implementation of the law or portions thereof, giving them time to try again next session in the legislature to repeal the law.

Review agency lobbyist registration and ethics rules. Many states[137] require certain persons attempting to influence executive agency actions to register as lobbyists.[138, 139] Failure to register when required can lead to loss of the lobbyist's credibility, freedom to advocate, and possible legal penalties.

Familiarize yourself with the state's APA. The APA, as discussed in the previous chapter, is designed in part to protect the public from seemingly unstoppable state power wielded by state employees under the sovereign immunity doctrine while acting as "the headless fourth branch of government." You must develop enough familiarity with your state's APA to be able to discern and respond immediately when something does not seem right about what the agency is doing.

Study the proposed rule in detail. Your ability to understand what is at stake, what you need to focus upon, and how to contribute to the rulemaking process begins with a clear understanding of the proposed rule. Any hint that you do not understand what the agency is trying to do and the contents of its proposal can lead to your contributions being marginalized.

Place the proposed agency action in context of existing law. How does the proposed rule affect what you are already doing? Is it adding or subtracting a compliance burden and, if so, by how much? This will form your initial response to the proposed agency action.

Understand in detail the enabling legislation. An agency cannot legally require a regulated party to do more than that which is authorized by the enabling and authorizing statutes. Virtually 100% of the time a fully appropriate question during agency discussions is, "Can you please show me where in the enabling or authorizing legislation the department finds authority for this provision?"

Determine what you must have out of the rule. Regularly ask yourself during a rulemaking, *what needs to change to make this rule work for my principal?* Your principal's standing to challenge a rule depends upon you demonstrating in the rulemaking record its potential impact upon your principal's substantial interests. As you incrementally answer this question, the impact of the rule becomes clearer. Moreover, you should be prepared to answer agency questions regarding your anticipated costs of compliance as the agency evaluates potential supporters and opponents and degrees of interest.

What do other special interests want? Agencies, like lawmakers, hate fighting among those who they expect would have similar positions on a proposed rule. Lower the noise and confusion so the agency can hear you better by reducing the numbers of opposing parties by building *ad hoc* group consensus around common positions. Normally, the coalitions that formed during the making of the statute carry over into administrative rulemaking.

What must the agency get out of this? The agency is devoting resources to develop a rule on which it wants a favorable return on its investment. Knowing what they want and cost-benefits will help you evaluate your own potential negotiating capital.

Find pressures on staff and agency. Who is pushing for and against the rule within the agency and externally such as among special interest groups? For example, if you find that the Governor is pushing for the rule to satisfy important constituents, there is a good chance that, while the momentum may be unstoppable, amendments yet may be possible. Is this rulemaking under a mandatory time line imposed by the APA?[140]

Do not ask for something impossible legally, financially, politically. You must point to specific sections in the authorizing, enabling, and administrative statutes and rules that arguably allow the agency to do what you want. The agency must have the financial appropriation sufficient to do what you are asking. And the legislative liaison must not oppose your proposal as harmful to the agency in the legislature.

Prepare to argue. That the enabling statute demands or at least permits what you want the agency to do; the proposed rule portends technical and economic impacts upon your industry and other parties including government. You do this in order to point to the level of interest for the agency to expect; that your principal will experience substantial impacts from the rule in order to assert legal standing to challenge the rule; demonstrate that what you want the agency to do falls within the realm of agency discretion; and, offer the agency better technical and legal ways to achieve its goals and the demand of statutory requirements.

Know what the agency can and cannot do. Agencies work amidst capital politics, budgetary constraints, media and public pressures, limitations of resources, at times unclear legal authority, and internal politics especially tensions between career civil service staff and the political appointees. Before you ask them to do something apart from or beyond that in the proposed rule, know what is feasible for them legally, politically, and financially. Your analysis will help you to appear more rational and credible in a fact and law-based process.

Select the right representative(s). In the legislature, *likeability* is job number one. However, while likeability makes contrary opinions go down easier with agencies, *workability*, that is, technical competence combined with a problem-solving attitude, is more influential. He or she should be likeable, technically competent, know what an agency can and cannot do (see above), be willing to defer within reasonable interpretations of facts and law, and industriously influence agency policy and implementation to tilt the principal's way, all the while understanding rulemaking is their statutory obligation to be exercised within agency discretion.

In other words, your representative should be perceived as a problem-solving peer acting on behalf of a principal. He or she should be skilled at incorporating into their presentations Shakespeare's maxim, *brevity is the soul of wit*.[141] Finally, unless statutorily demanded, agency meetings are at the option of the agency. While an agency must respond to *written* comments, they do not necessarily have to take oral comments even at a public hearing.[142] A state may also require an agency to hold a public hearing if requested by members of the public.[143]

Connect with staff as fellow professionals but do not overly identify with them. You connect with the agency by respectfully showing yourself to be a resource who can help them do their jobs better by using your specialized knowledge and insights about what your principal, industry segment or interest group does. You can explain to staff how the proposed rule may be adjusted to meet both the agency's and your principal's objectives. However, keep in mind, agency staff are facts and law people, see your industry as a real or potential problem the legislature has told them to regulate, and they have no desire to be your friends.

In your effort to connect, do not try to overly identify with them with some disingenuous line like, *"I'm here for the same reason you're here, to* (fill in the blank with something like *fulfill the agency mission*.)" That for most regulated interests is a lie which undermines your credibility. They know you are there to protect your principal's interests, not the agency's. Be honest and be a resource.

Should your consultant, lobbyist or legal counsel attend? Only persons who can contribute to the discussion should attend, especially when the focus is on scientific or legal matters. As your technical experts may be superfluous or even distracting at a meeting to discuss the law, so too your lawyer can be distracting at a meeting to discuss technical matters. That being said, in a particular context, a person respected by the agency can greatly add to your influence with the agency.

Will other special interests attend the meeting? Ask this in order to prepare yourself for either friendly or hostile contributions. If it is a large, *publicly announced* meeting, expect varied interests to participate. Either way, contact other attendee(s) to see what your relative interests are and if any consensus among you can be achieved prior to the meeting.

Suggest names of agency staff you think have knowledge useful to your position. If another agency staffer, such as one having special insight into your operations, might be conducive to achieving mutual understanding, ask the agency contact if he or she might attend and say why.

Request a specific amount of meeting time that fits within their schedule. Agencies seldom have time to just chat and your issue is just one among many with which they are dealing at any given time. Prepare a concise meeting agenda and tailor it to fit within the requested time. Your respect for their time will be appreciated.

Do you represent your principal or a coalition? As the meeting started, the Ontario provincial ministry staffer asked Bob whom he represented. Bob answered his principal's name. The staffer, somewhat irritated, said he already knew who Bob worked for, but what he really wanted to know was who Bob represented. Was he representing only his principal or was he representing a coalition of companies? He specifically said he did not want to meet with every member of Bob's coalition. The ministry staffer wanted to know that, by satisfying Bob, he would also satisfy the group of regulated interests Bob represented. By representing a coalition, you greatly increase the interest and benefit to agency staff meeting with you.

Coalitions are time efficient, multiply influence, and get greater attention from agency staff than do individuals. Consider forming an *ad hoc* coalition to deal with this rulemaking. Again, if the same parties which collaborated in the legislature are also involved with the rulemaking, then forming a coalition should be straightforward.

Ask to see other parties' written submissions in the rulemaking record. It is all going to be public record, if it is not already, so they should have little problem letting you see comments already submitted. These submissions will let you see the direction evidence is pushing the rulemaking record.

Ask about ex parte communications. These are off-the-record, side-bar communications between an agency official involved in a rulemaking and a member of the public.[144] Ask who else they have spoken with, but do not refer to their conversations as *ex parte*, which can be a loaded legal term. *Ex parte* communications are discussed more in the next section.

Offer to send to staff, prior to the meeting, key information. Providing the following information to staff before you meet will allow focus on your issues, detailed problem-solving discussion, enable staff to think about

the issues you have raised, and be a better use of time for a more productive meeting for all parties involved. It may also provide opportunities
for you to direct the discussion thereby increasing your influence in the
outcome.

- Your position(s) on each element of the rule that is of concern
  to you. Getting this to them early gives the agency time to
  think through your concerns, develop responses and, during
  the meeting, focus on issues where they have another view.
- Itemized proposed rule changes. Written in appropriate language within the context of the proposed rule gives clearer
  meaning to your concerns and solutions.
- Supporting technical and legal materials. The rulemaking
  record is the foundation of policy and rule language chosen.
  Make the record support your position by providing your technical data, experts' reports, and legal opinions. As a result,
  all they need do is insert the information directly into the
  rulemaking record just as you provided it and without risking
  agency staff misinterpreting your presentation of facts and law.

EX PARTE COMMUNICATIONS

Per the Administrative Conference of the United States, *ex parte* communication means:

> (i) written or oral communications; (ii) regarding the substance
> of an anticipated or ongoing rulemaking; (iii) between the
> agency personnel and interested persons; and (iv) that are not
> placed in the rulemaking docket at the time they occur.[145]

In application, an *ex parte* proceeding occurs when agency staff offici-
ating over a rulemaking proceeding receive information from anyone
external to the agency rulemaking team and which information likely
influences the final rule. In rulemaking, which is a quasi-legislative proceeding, there is nothing legally inappropriate with *ex parte* communication *as long as that communication is disclosed in the rulemaking record.*

Advocates are interested in *ex parte* communications because agency rulemaking decisions have to be supported by substantial evidence found in the rulemaking record. An *ex parte* communication not disclosed in the rulemaking record "raises serious questions of fairness"[146] and is grounds for challenging the rule as invalidly adopted.

You want to know the substance of communication if the final rule affects your principal. Discovering undisclosed communications can give you some leverage to challenge the final rule. While it is unlikely that an *ex parte* communication would not be disclosed, sometimes they are not. To illustrate, Bob assisted the Florida Department of Environmental Regulation in defending a challenge to rules regulating electromagnetic fields from powerlines.[147] His piece involved an allegation by the electric utilities that a commissioner on the Florida Environmental Regulation Commission was influenced by undisclosed *ex parte* communications from her fellow environmentalists.

Ex parte communications may be welcome by some agency officials for purposes of information gathering.[148] However, other officials do not want to receive *ex parte* communications because of their concerns over litigation and because they do not want to have to recall accurately their content, and then write the discussion up to include it in the rulemaking record. It is the trouble of going through the recordation process, rather than anything nefarious, that leads to their refusal to accept *ex parte* information.

Once rulemaking has been noticed, that is, formally announced and officially begun, an agency official may cut you off midsentence, even in casual conversation, if you attempt to discuss information that should be placed into the rulemaking record. The staffer may say to you, "If you want to say it, send it to me in writing." He or she just wants to avoid the trouble of having to write it up. And, in limited instances, some agencies are prohibited from engaging in any *ex parte* communications.

EFFECTIVE MEETINGS

It is important when advocating for your position to have effective meetings with agency officials, as well as their staff. In broad terms, you should consider some of the factors that may influence these officials and their staff. There are basically two types of meetings with agency officials and their staff: relationship-building and policy.

Relationship Building Meetings. Relationship building is an important first step prior to meeting on a policy matter, such as a regulation. What are examples of relationship building?

- Taking an agency official and his or her staff for a tour of your facility
- Having an agency official write an article for your organization's newsletter
- Write an article on the agency or its officials and post it on your website
- Host an agency official for a town hall

Policy Meetings. Policy meetings are used to discuss public policy issues, specific regulations, or seek an official act. What are examples of policy "asks" for agency officials?

- Voting for or against a regulation
- Talking with other agency officials about a regulation or issue
- Getting information from or talking with a regulatory agency on your behalf

Prior to the Meeting. Prior to the meeting, you need to schedule the appointment and prepare for your meeting. This should occur a few weeks in advance. Also, determine where the meeting will occur, most often at the agency official's office.

When contacting an official's office, ask to speak with the scheduler or, if none, the staffer him or herself. And be prepared to offer several dates and times during which you can meet. Provide a list of individuals who will be attending the meeting and do not be surprised if the scheduler asks you to fax or email a formal meeting request.

Prior to the meeting, determine what specifically you are going to ask for. Asking for something specific is one of the key ways to get the attention of an official. Making a clear and concise request will help make your meeting more effective.

Determine any roles for yourself and other participants. Is everyone from the same organization? Are they from the same industry? If there are multiple persons, designate a group leader who should open and close the meeting. Then, perhaps, each person can present a key message. Agencies appreciate coalitions as they can reduce the agency's work load by resolving issues with a group's members collectively rather than having to meet with members individually.

Particularly if a group of principals' representatives is meeting with the official, then it is wise to prepare and practice for your meeting. A short "run-through" of what everyone is prepared to say is helpful. It is important for the group leader to set the tone for the meeting at the outset and ensure the meeting is on-time and progresses so that each principal represented has the opportunity to speak.

Dress appropriately for the meeting. For most lobbyists, this is a business meeting and you should dress in business attire. However, wearing distinctive clothing representative of your principal can also be an asset if it appears to be sincere and appropriate.

Be sure to confirm your meeting a day or two in advance. You certainly do not want to travel all the way to the agency office just to find out that the meeting was cancelled or re-scheduled.

During the Meeting. Always be polite in your meeting, even if you have hard feelings or are upset about a particular issue. Similarly, if you do not get the response that you desire, make sure that you engage professionally and politely. This meeting may not be successful, but hopefully your next one will be. You do not want to upset the official or the staff when you need to meet with them with your next issue or request. Keep in mind they likely do not have an APA duty to speak with you.

Always tell the *whole truth* and do not mislead or threaten anyone in a regulatory office. You want them to trust you as collaborative and a reliable source of information Any half-truth may mark the end of your meetings with officials or their staff.

When you begin your meeting, identify yourself and the organization(s) (if any) you are representing at the meeting. Explain whatever connection there is for purposes of the meeting.

Be specific in your request to the official. If your request or message is too vague, then the official or staff will likewise be general or vague in their response. To be more effective in your request, you should be specific in that request.

Try not to make more than one request per meeting. If you must bring up more than one request or message, make sure to prioritize them. Also, you may get stuck with the least controversial or easiest item instead of the more difficult request if you make multiple ones.

At the conclusion of the meeting, be sure to leave a one-three page "leave behind" with the official and make sure his or her staff get the same information. These materials need to explain your issue and what your message is. Be sure to include contact information with these materials in case anyone has follow-up questions.

After the Meeting, After the meeting, send a note thanking the official and/or his or her staff for taking the time to meet with you. As it will be a public document, be careful that what you say does not in any way compromise either your principal or the staffer. This will also provide an opportunity for you to follow-up to reiterate your message, or your request, or to just let them know you can be a resource. And be sure to acknowledge any position the official has stated.

INFLUENCING THE AGENCY AS SALES CALLS

Model your upcoming interaction with the agency as a sales call. The agency is a *potential customer*. Other special interests are your *competitors*. Your *product* is outlined by the bullets below. As a *salesperson*, your threshold question to answer is *why would the agency buy your solution rather than what your competitors are offering* or what the agency would do anyway? Agency staff will get into the right mindset to buy from you when your proposal meets these general principles:

- Solves an agency concern or problem
- Has a good technical foundation and is based on law and sound public policy
- Meets demands of the enabling statute or existing rules
- Follows APA law and rules
- Furthers the agency's mission statement
- Furthers the agency's strategic plan
- Has a funding source or line item in the budget
- Includes a rule adoption and rule implementation plan

Solves an agency concern or problem. An agency's problems stem from executing new legislation, implementing or enforcing existing legislation or rules, dealing with an entirely new crisis stemming from political pressures or unforeseen forces, or meeting goals and objectives in their strategic plan (see page 122). If you cannot help them with a specific problem, then you do not have anything to sell and they do not have anything to buy. Asking them to do something to benefit your principal that does not benefit the agency is likely to fail.

Has a good technical foundation and is based on law and sound public policy. Once a clear problem is identified, the agency will be interested when you show a feasible way to solve it, your approach comports with applicable laws, and is good public policy in that it advances the agency's mission statement, Governor's agenda, or responds to immediate political pressures.

Meets the demands of the enabling statute or existing rules. You must be able to point to chapter and verse in the statute that authorizes the agency to take the action for which you are lobbying. Or, you must be able to show the agency how your proposal enables them to do better than what they are already doing.

Follows the APA law and rules. The easier you make it for an agency to adopt your proposal, the more likely they will do it. Ensure your proposal conforms to the APA and its rules. Find an agency notice of the type you want to see in the state administrative register (or similar compendium of proposed administrative actions) and use it as a template for your proposal. Do not be generic; be specific. Later we will show you how to make your actual presentation.

Furthers the agency's mission statement. The agency's mission statement explains in the broadest terms why an agency exists. The agency will be inclined to support proposals that advance its mission and reject those contrary to it. Study their mission statement before you speak with the agency, look for examples of how they have implemented it previously, and be ready to show them how your proposal will help them achieve their mission. Mission statements normally appear in the agency's strategic plan.

Furthers the agency's strategic plan. Most agencies prepare multi-year (often 3–5 years) strategic plans that state the goals to be carried over the term of the strategic plan in order to fulfill the agency's mission. Objectives are the proposed concrete steps to be taken to meet those stated goals. You must show by specific goal and associated objective(s) how your proposal will help the agency succeed in meeting its strategic plan.

Has a funding source or line item in the budget. If there is not any budgetary authority, specifically or by a stretch of the imagination, then no matter how much agency staff like your idea, they will not be able to implement your proposal. An earlier, successful legislative lobbying campaign would have ensured both enabling legislation and specific appropriation.

Includes a rule adoption and rule implementation plan.[149] Your advocacy efforts must include an explanation to agency staff of how your proposal will be implemented and the timing, as well as how it comports with the state's APA procedures. Early in the process, it will be conceptual as the agency estimates impacts upon the agency and regulated parties. But, as the rule develops, the rule implementation plan will become more detailed and cost estimates firmer.

If the agency does not as a matter of course publish its rule implementation plans, ask staff for copies of similar plans. We have seen very sophisticated published and unpublished plans. For example, plans implementing Tennessee's Long Term Care Community Choices Act of 2008 were reviewed even though at the time they were solely intended for internal use as in-house working documents.

MOTIVATING AGENCY STAFF

Agencies staff are influenced and motivated by proposed solutions that are:

- Legally sound
- Technically optimal
- Cost-effective
- Easier to implement
- Politically less risky
- Good for the agency ("Good" according to parameters listed in the preceding section.)

Factors motivating agency staff collectively or individually include:

- Carrying out the agency's mission
- Doing their job well
- Protecting agency prerogatives and sovereignty from legislators, judges, other agencies, political appointees, and the public
- Keeping or improving budget and staff
- Expanding or reducing agency authority
- Avoiding public controversy
- Ensuring positive or not negative media coverage

- Making new allies
- Making a lasting impact on public policy and law
- Advancing individual careers (better jobs)
- Stabilizing work environments by uniform rules
- Enjoying the pure pleasure in exercising agency power

Carrying out the agency's mission. As an agency staffer, Bob lived to protect the environment—the air, surface and ground waters, natural environment, and wildlife. He observed as an industry regulatory manager that among agency staff at all levels of government *prima facie* dedication, even a zealotry, to serve the social purposes for which their agencies exist.

Many nations' equivalents to U.S. agencies are called *ministries* and officers are *ministers*. Considering the terms mission, ministry, and minister may deepen your insight into the dedication often found among agency staffs. Few agency staff will operate contrary to the mission statement, so keep it as a *first cut* guide to understanding the staff with whom you are working.

Doing their job well. As an industry regulatory compliance manager, Bob consistently found agency staff trained and fully competent to do their jobs well, often to the point of being inflexible, picky, and annoying—just like they are being paid to be.

Protecting agency prerogatives and sovereignty from legislators, judges, other agencies, political appointees, and the public. Trained zealots on a mission may develop the attitude, "Stay out of our way and keep quiet because we're the experts and we know what we are doing—and you don't." *From a technical perspective,* their attitude may be correct—they are experts who know what they are doing and, except for other experts, few fully understand what an agency is doing.

However, as to law, statutory and constitutional, agencies do not have policy sovereignty. This causes staff to struggle with the burden of appreciating that, while they may know better, they do not have the legal authority to implement their superior technical knowledge. This attitude will show itself again in the concept of *ultra vires* agency actions, which means beyond the powers provided by law. We first mentioned *ultra vires* actions in the beginning of Chapter 3, *The Administrative Procedure(s) Act.*

Keeping or improving budget and staff. This goes to self-interest as much as to mission—get more funding for the agency and get more staff to do more things. However, sometimes while an agency wants more, it resists giving up outmoded or other programs, budget, and staff in exchange. Unwillingness to give up programs leads to *program hoarding.*

Expanding or reducing agency authority. The agency has a mission to do, so it wants more authority but it is overworked or underfunded so it needs to surrender certain duties. Mission vs. money forces agencies to balance the amount of budget appropriations relative to the pressures imposed by the legislature, intra-agency goals, the Governor, or the public.

Avoiding public controversy. Governors generally want agencies to quietly and efficiently do their jobs so as not to undermine the Governor, his or her political agenda or appointees, the agency itself, or public confidence in the agency. The agency may prefer to sidestep the attention that comes with unnecessary conflict.

Ensuring positive or not negative media coverage. Agencies quietly and efficiently doing their jobs often means avoiding negative media attention. On the other hand, providing the media with a scandal, real or contrived, can motivate agencies to take action even if only for public relations purposes.

Making new allies. Staff may enlist allies to assist agencies in achieving objectives beneficial to both. For example, agency staff may induce an organization to sue the agency by offering to settle the litigation on the same day the suit is filed with terms advantageous to both. We touch upon *sue and settle* in Chapter 6, *Rule Adoption*, section, "Triggers to Motivating Agency Rulemaking."

Making a lasting impact on public policy and law.[150] Few things are more motivating for anyone involved in lawmaking, regulator or regulated, than knowing you have made a lasting impact on public policy and the law. The desire for a legacy (or conference speaker invitations) can create a certain "that rule is my baby" irrationality among rule drafters and contributors that makes it difficult to change a proposed rule *once formally noticed to the public.* This intransigence is in part why advocates want to be early, on the ground floor, assisting the agency with rule development.

Advancing individual careers (better jobs).[151] By building a record of success, agency staff can make themselves more attractive employees. For example, a successful agency staffer can move up within his or her agency, within state government, or even to the next level, such as from local to state, or state to federal. *Infrequently,* private employers will try to hire agency staff to get them on their side and, at the same time, get the staffer out of the agency making their lives difficult.

Stabilizing work environments by uniform rules.[152] By adopting rules, a predictable work environment is improved while uncertainty and stress are reduced.

Enjoying the pure pleasure in exercising agency power. Agency staff exercise government enforcement power at their choosing for noble or petty reasons. The noble normal is mentioned throughout this book. However, as the Founders knew when government exercises legislative, executive, and judicial powers, tyranny may be inevitable. As we summarized James Madison in Chapter 1, section, "Constitutional and Practical Dangers of an Agency Having Legislative, Executive, and Judicial Powers," *tyranny will result when a government agency can enforce the laws it enacts.*[153]

In Chapter 7, *Post-Rulemaking,* section, "The Process Is the Punishment" we mention how agencies can harass regulated parties into submission by just threatening to push them into the administrative enforcement process. An agency can force regulated parties into fights they do not want, cannot afford, cannot avoid, and cannot win. For example, a Florida administrative law judge noted to Bob that in his court citizens almost always lose saying, "The process is so stacked against them."

Furthermore, few private interests have the financial resources suffi-cient to resist a state agency intent on using its enforcement authority to bully a regulated party. *Lobby School* students have shared repeatedly stories of their principals collapsing under the weight of the financial burden brought on by challenging an agency. As Voltaire noted, "I was never ruined but twice: once when I lost a lawsuit, and once when I won one."[154]

Both regulator and regulated parties know *the process is the punishment*, which gives the bureaucrat almost, but not quite, unstoppable free license to do whatever he or she wants, especially on smaller matters which are not cost effective for a regulated party to fight. However, in the last section of this chapter, section, "Deference by the Other Two Branches Puts the *Almost* into Agencies Being *Almost* Unstoppable" we discuss it is only the legislature or courts that have power enough to remedy agency excess or abuse.

KNOW YOUR CUSTOMER

Good lobbyists, like good salespeople, know their customers *before they ever meet them*. By reviewing recent agency rulemaking history and inspecting the agency's organizational chart, you may be able to esti-mate the likely office(s) within an agency that will be involved in rule development and enforcement of your proposed rule.

Knowing the offices within the agency that will participate in the rulemaking, specifically the makeup of the internal rule development committee discussed below in section, "Knowing with Whom to Build Relationships: The Internal Rule Development Committee" may help you estimate which agency staffers may be involved. However, the larger the agency then the more specialized are its intra-division spe-cialties making more difficult identifying likely staff participants.

Review the history of the enabling legislation to learn what agency rep-resentatives, including technical staff, may have testified to lawmakers about the goals of the law and its implementation. Examine how the committee and members of the public responded to them and their points. Ask for a roster of committee and public participants.

Expect that a considerable rulemaking record exists for past rulemakings and that history may inform you on higher level staff with whom you may deal. Examine agency board and advisory committee minutes to see which staffers work with your issues and see how committee members responded to them.

A contract lobbyist specializing in the agency would be invaluable to explaining staff, their peculiarities, and their motivators. Other regulated parties who have participated in rulemaking topics similar to yours could provide invaluable advice about working with staff.

Go to social media, professional and personal, to learn about how they think and view the world. Before working with staff, get to know them in order to know how to frame your presentation and materials you will present to greatest effect. Get to know the agency staff who will be doing the rulemaking in order to influence them favorably toward you and by extension your issue.

BUILDING EFFECTIVE RELATIONSHIPS WITH THE AGENCY RULEMAKING TEAM

The *Insiders Talk* series of legislative lobbying manuals emphasize that effective advocates routinely work with the legislature's[155] and key lawmakers'[156] staffs. These staff draft the bills (or at least approve model or lobbyist-drafted bills if supplied ready-to-go by special interests or agencies), study bills, draft committee reports and impact statements, meet with advocates, coordinate with other lawmakers' staffs, and advise lawmakers on how to vote. *The Campaign Method for More Effective State Government Affairs* lists legislative staff as the second most important influence in getting a lawmaker's vote.[157]

Similarly, with rulemaking, agency staff are key. They draft agency regulations, do foundational research, develop the rulemaking record including APA required impact statements, meet with potentially affected parties, conduct rule workshops, negotiate deals and rule amendments, prepare the adoption hearing package, and advise rule adopters, collegial boards and agency top managers regarding how they may vote at the adoption hearing.

Legislative and executive branches' decisionmakers by their votes largely ratify rather than redo what staff has presented to them. For all practical purposes, staff write the rule and top officials sign off on it. However, beyond this similarity, the lawmaking processes, legislative and agency, diverge considerably, especially as to building relationships with staff.

DIFFICULTIES BUILDING RELATIONSHIPS WITH AGENCY RULEMAKING STAFF VS. LEGISLATIVE STAFF

While advocates building relationships with agency rulemaking and legislative staff are both quite important, building relationships with agency rulemaking staff is more difficult for many reasons, a few of which are:

- Natural tensions between regulator and regulated parties
- Legislators and legislative staffs are more open to outside influence than are command-and-control agency staffs
- Difference in size and organizational structure between legislature and agency
- Differences in ages of staff and aspirational goals
- Agency staff do not have to talk to you

Natural tensions between regulator and regulated parties. In the field, regulators and regulated know that their collaboration makes better the lives of each. Accordingly, local agency enforcement staff often have good relationships with regulated parties owing to a symbiosis developing from systematic interactions required by state law, rule, operating permits, and licensing.

However, at headquarters, where rules are written, staff have a much less collaborative attitude, are much more suspicious of regulated parties, and run on a command-and-control arms length mentality. Staff expect that regulated parties will oppose rules that add costs to their operations. And collegial relationships may be seen as *fraternizing with the enemy*.

On the other hand, legislative staff regularly cultivate relationships with any and all special interests that might affect their lawmakers' legislative and political goals. Our experience has been that in the capitol every special interest is a potential campaign donor or supporter to be courted.

Legislators and legislative staffs are more open to outside influence than are command-and-control agency staffs. Politicians' and their staffs' jobs depend on maintaining public approval which fosters openness to relationships and having civil relationships wherever possible. Their jobs depend on public approval.

Rulemaking staff on the other hand are concerned with neither the approval of regulated parties nor the public. They have little to worry about as they have secure civil service jobs. And the law presumes as to facts and law that whatever they do is correct. They have little need for outside relationships beyond special interests as clients, resources, and kindred spirits, groups discussed in the next chapter.

Difference in size and organizational structure between legislature and agency. An average state legislature has ~40 senators, ~120 house members[158], and a few hundred to low thousands of legislative staff.[159] On the other hand, executive branch agencies range from ~10,000 to ~235,000 public employees per state working for dozens to hundreds of agencies.[160]

Each agency may have within it many departments, and the departments may have within them many subdepartments, all making their own highly detailed, topic-specific rules. On the other hand, for example, the comparatively few senate and house environment committees' staff process all environmental legislation making it easy to know with whom to cultivate relationships.

Differences in ages of staff and aspirational goals. Legislative staff tend to be young and realize their careers can end at the next election. They for the most part have relatively low salaries compared to agency staff. They often spend their time hoping to get better jobs and want new relationships given the uncertainly of their employment and professional development.

On the other hand, civil service protected agency staff and managers and even non-career civil service staff tend to be middle-aged, have on average better than private sector salaries (see Chapter 2), and intend to stay at the agency until they retire. They have no job-related need of external relationships.

Agency staff do not have to talk to you. Normally, if you have something to contribute to agency rule development, staff want to speak with you. But they do not have to *if they do not want to do so.* To illustrate, Bob's colleague from another power company could be quite unmannerly with agency staff. Weary of his rudeness, staff adopted an informal policy: upon seeing him enter a public workshop, staff would fold their portfolios, collect their belongings, stand up, and as a group walk out of the room. To Bob's knowledge, agency staff only did this one time because upon learning of this, the rude colleague's management immediately removed him from agency related work. A major power company does not want to needlessly offend the agency that regulates its operations.

Staff can walk out of a meeting because, per the APA, while they have to read written materials submitted to the rulemaking record, they have no legal duty to listen to anyone speak. If they see you as a client or resource, they will want to talk to you, as we describe in the next chapter. But, if they do not want to talk to you, then they do not have to if the APA allows them to refuse.

KNOWING WITH WHOM TO BUILD RELATIONSHIPS: THE INTERNAL RULE DEVELOPMENT COMMITTEE

A generic name for the rulemaking staff that will design your rule is the *internal rule development committee* or *internal rule development team.*

Each proposed rule will have its own development team. This is necessary because, as noted above, agencies have thousands of highly detailed technical rules within dozens of departments, divisions, boards, commissions, authorities, offices, councils, bureaus, and systems, each responsible for its own specific area of regulation.[161] "On average, states have 135,000 regulatory restrictions in administrative rules, with California's regulations [395,608] more than double the national average."[162]

Like any team, while positions are consistent, individual players in those positions vary depending on subject matter under rule development. Positions may include:

- Managers of the agency subdivision affected by rulemaking
- Office of General Counsel
- Policy specialists
- Enforcement specialists
- Subject matter experts
- Drafting experts
- Economists

Knowing the person with whom to build a relationship often is uncertain because players can change. Relationships are best built on the basis of area of regulation rather than for the agency as a whole.

YOUR ASSETS IN BUILDING RULEMAKING RELATIONSHIPS

While building relationships with agency staff for the above reasons can be difficult, depending on your organization's size, you may have assets to utilize including:

- Your ability to apportion organization resources
- Activity-specific detailed information
- Your integrity and that of your principal
- Visiting to say you care about the regulator-regulated relationship.

Your ability to apportion organization resources. A common advocacy technique to maximize return on investment of resources is to divvy up lobbying responsibilities among association members. In legislative lobbying, an association member is assigned to cultivate relationships with particular lawmakers' offices. With agency lobbying, assignments can be assigned on the basis of task. For example, Bob's chief regulatory assignment was water related matters with a secondary assignment in solid waste.

Other association members were assigned to solid and hazardous waste issues, transmission line siting, and so on. This "spread the load" approach enables an association to participate in most major rulemaking activities and in the process build specific reputations and relationships with staff in each regulatory specialty. When staff repeatedly see the same face at every rulemaking meeting, familiarity develops.

Activity-specific detailed information. A defensible rulemaking record is the foundation of a rule that will be workable, respected by regulated interests and critics, and survive a legal challenge. Good technical and legal information underpin a solid rulemaking record. Agencies want good information. By providing the agency with consistently reliable information, you will build a solid relationship of trust with an agency. Staff trust can lead to unexpected opportunities to influence the agency as for example when it invites you to share your information.

Your integrity and that of your principal. As all *Insiders Talk* lobbying manuals emphasize, your integrity is the greatest asset you have, even more important than being an agency solution, as mentioned below in Chapter 5, *Lobbying Internal and External Influencers on the Rulemaking Proceeding*, section, "Face to Face Meeting with Agency Staff."

If staff trust you, they may listen to you and, if they listen to you, they might come to understand you and, if they understand you, they may incorporate your concerns into their rule. If they trust you, they will not feel the need to *initially* check the veracity of what you say. Based upon your proven reputation, they will take at face value your representations.

But if they do not trust you, they do not have to listen to a word you say. They will process your written and oral submittals to the rulemaking record, but they themselves will neither meet with nor listen to you.

Visiting to say you care about the regulator-regulated relationship. In his article "Building Effective Relationships with Regulators,"[163] Professor Norm Chap of Harvard University offers a number of techniques to build relationships with your regulators, including headquarters staff. Says Professor Champ, "I propose that you follow a strategy of constructive engagement with the regulator . . . strategies of avoidance and opposition are misguided and that constructive engagement is the only viable choice for a business seeking an effective relationship with its regulator."[164]

As in the legislature, staff are central to the rulemaking and enforcement processes. Advocates in both are well advised to build with staff trusting, mutually respectful, and reciprocally beneficial relationships.

DEFERENCE BY THE OTHER TWO BRANCHES PUTS THE *ALMOST* INTO EXECUTIVE AGENCIES BEING *ALMOST* UNSTOPPABLE

For most practical purposes, the majority of regulated parties will find agencies almost unstoppable such that, in the cost to benefit analysis, *negotiated surrender brings the most benefit.* Just give the agency what it demands and move on.

However, while a regulated party itself may be almost helpless facing an agency, the legislature and courts are not. Per the Founders' design, the only force capable of resisting one branch of government is a coequal branch of government. This is their *checks and balances* as discussed in Chapter 1.

Both or either the legislative or judicial branch can trump an agency. Legislative appeal is touched upon in Chapter 7, *Post-Rulemaking*, section, "Responding to an Unfavorable Rule." Adjudicative appeal, administrative and then judicial, is the subject of Chapter 8, *What You*

Should Learn, Accept and Challenge on Agency Regulatory Enforcement and Adjudications.

Our preference is the legislative appeal because it is potentially quicker and more economical than a judicial appeal. For example, in many states, an aggrieved party must first exhaust all of its potential administrative remedies before it can seek judicial relief. However, depending on state the process of seeking legislative relief can start instantly.

As noted earlier, both the courts and legislature give agencies considerable deference in carrying out their official duties. However, deference has its limits. This illustration from *Insiders Talk: Winning with Lobbyists, Professional edition* is worth repeating here to demonstrate that agencies are not always all powerful when facing another branch of government.

> Legislatures normally do what agencies recommend. However, if lawmakers feel the agency disrespected them, they may chastise the agency just for spite by cutting its budget, reducing its authority, or voting against it. To illustrate, the committee of subject matter jurisdiction repeatedly asked the agency for comments on my [Bob's] principal's bill. The agency repeatedly ignored the legislature's pleas for advice. The committee finally called up my bill for a final vote. As was normal procedure, the agency was invited to testify on all bills, including mine. The agency strongly objected to my bill. I feared my bill, after years of work, was going to die given agency hostility.
>
> However, much to my surprise, a committee member who generally supported the agency said to the committee, "We have for over a year repeatedly asked [name of agency] for its comments on this bill, and they for a year have ignored this committee. I propose that we in turn today ignore everything [name of agency] has said today about this bill." The committee did just that, and then favorably reported my bill which became law. My principal was the unexpected beneficiary of a political fight seemingly flowing from agency disrespect for the legislature.

The lesson here is that agencies are almost unstoppable given deference shown by the courts and legislatures. But the operative word here is *almost*.

However, as the above illustrates, there may be times when an organization's Regulatory Affairs needs Legislative Affairs more than they need their Office of General Counsel. Legislative Affairs may be able to secure from the legislature a quicker and more economical solution to an agency problem than going to court.

SUMMARY

Monitoring the agency has revealed that rulemaking affecting your principal may be or is in the works. To find out more and to establish yourself as a resource you will meet with staff to build relationships and perhaps discuss policy. Your meeting(s) will go well because you understand the agency mission, the proposed rule, and staff. You also know that the deference the legislature and courts pay to the agency means for all practical purposes they can do *almost* anything they want.

In our next chapter, *Lobbying Internal and External Influencers of the Rulemaking Proceeding,* you will begin putting this knowledge to use.

CHAPTER 5

LOBBYING INTERNAL AND EXTERNAL INFLUENCERS ON THE RULEMAKING PROCEEDING

You are now ready to put into practice the previous chapters' preparation when meeting with agency staff. However, keep in mind that, unless the APA requires otherwise, an agency has no duty to talk to, much less, meet with you. This is especially so if you are meeting during the time period between approval to enter into rule development by the internal rule development committee or similar approving entity and the time the agency notices in the state register the beginning of the official rulemaking process.

Yet, at least in our experience, the agency will meet with interested parties, especially representatives of the activities that the rule will regulate. The staff will meet for some of the following reasons:

- Information gathering
- Impact statements
- Fair play
- Avoid litigation
- Avoid delay
- Acceptance and compliance

Information gathering. While agencies are populated with experts, they are not necessarily experts in *your operations*. Your team should know more about what your principal does than they do. And, for the integ-

113

rity of their rule and to avoid rule challenges alleging *arbitrary and capricious* actions, they want reliable technical information.

Impact statements. Many APAs require agencies to complete a series of impact statements on affected parties, economic and fiscal. By knowing more about what you do, the more complete their impact statement(s) will be.

Fair play. Agency image in the eyes of the legislature and public is important for political reasons and the acceptance of their rule.

Avoid litigation. An agency does not want to expend needlessly its legal resources on rulemaking related litigation, especially litigation it could lose. Despite the general rebuttable judicial presumption that an agency is correct as to use of its powers, legal proceedings against a well-resourced, substantially affected party can be a legal, public relations, or political liability. For example, an administrative hearing officer or court may order an agency to pay a prevailing party's legal fees in the highly unlikely event that the agency should lose a rule challenge.[165] Litigation may also result in delay in rulemaking and implementation.

Avoid delay. An agency committed to rule adoption and implementation will meet with interested parties, especially those with legislative influence or financial resources, in order to avert delay stemming from avoidable litigation, public outcry, or legislative interference.

Acceptance and compliance. Agencies want those they regulate and those they serve to accept the rule as reasonable.[166] If regulated parties consider the rule unreasonable, they are less likely to comply thereby undermining the purpose of the rule and taxing agency compliance resources.

To illustrate this last bullet, USEPA, in 1979 for reasons of environmental protection, began regulating polychlorinated biphenyls (PCBs), used in many products since 1929.[167] Long-time users of PCBs dismissed the regulations saying, "I've been working with PCBs for thirty years, never saw the first bad thing about them, and they prevent fires and explosions."

Because they saw PCBs as beneficial, knew personally of no health hazards, and knew the regulations were contrary to product safety, resistance to EPA's environmental *command and control* approach delayed compliance. In the end, like mandating the end of chlorofluorocarbon production to protect the ozone layer, discontinuing production of PCBs ended PCBs use rather than acceptance among regulated parties that the regulations were indeed reasonable.

CONSENSUS IN RULEMAKING

In making laws, legislative or administrative, consensus propels and controversy kills. The rulemaking process goes better, faster, and easier when the agency and participating parties agree on a proposed course of action. *Advocates build consensus* around their preferred solutions. *Opponents build controversy* because lack of consensus or outright conflict makes an agency:

- Less willing to enter into rulemaking
- More likely to incorporate vagueness into the rule in order to get the rule into effect faster
- Prepare for rigorous enforcement
- Plan for litigation and legal delays

Agencies also experience internal conflicts, especially between the career civil service staff and the political appointees. In Chapter 2, *The Agency Model*, we first mentioned that each category of staffer has different reasons for being at the agency. Professor Cornelius Kerwin writes,

> There is another widely observed form of conflict within agencies that can delay issuance of rules. The tension between career bureaucrats and the political appointees who lead the agencies is a persistent theme in the literature of public administration. It manifests itself in rulemaking when the approach favored by the program office specialists runs afoul of the policy priorities of the political leadership . . . Policy differences aside, this type of conflict is especially damaging to timeliness when

it is not anticipated or dealt with in the rulemaking process. If the career staff develops a regulation without early input from senior agency officials there is always the chance that it will produce a rule that is not acceptable.

Political appointees may be open to assisting regulated parties because the Governor appointed them to administer the agency in order to advance or at least not get in the way of the Governor's political agenda. Their concerns are much broader than agency career civil service staff whose actions are focused more narrowly on technical implementation rather than policy.

WHO ARE THE INFLUENCERS THAT ADVOCATES MAY ENLIST IN AFFECTING RULEMAKING?

Regulatory advocates must plan how to influence other rulemaking players and their activities. While your particular rulemaking may not necessarily involve all of the influencers below, a broad list of potential contacts listed in order of importance in communicating with them includes:

- Agency constituents
- Regulated special interests
- Technical staff
- Agency legislative liaisons (agency lobbyists)
- Managers—career civil service
- Managers—non-career civil service
- Office of General Counsel
- Citizen advisory groups
- Political appointees (commissioners, secretary, top managers)
- Governor's office
- Legislators
- Legislature
- Non-government accreditation agencies and standard setting bodies
- Federal agencies
- Other state executive agencies

- Local government and agencies
- Public employee unions

Agency constituents. Agencies have allies, that is, organizations and sub-sets of people who support specific agencies and their purposes, and with whom they cultivate collaborative, mutually advantageous rela-tionships. Agencies want to keep happy:

- Supportive special interest groups. These are philosophical kindred spirits, especially with agency career civil service staff. Businesses profiting financially from an agency regulation will support agency rulemaking. They provide service and products directly to the agency, to persons regulated by the agency, or served by the agency.
- Friendly legislators. They are a subset within the legislature who generally support the agency in setting its statutory duties and appropriations.
- Governor's office. The Governor's political appointees manage the agency to advance the Governor's political agenda and who fol-low the Governor's directions. The Governor in his or her budget directly affects agency staff wages, benefits, and scope of service.
- Other agencies. Political appointees managing agencies having overlapping jurisdictional authority should be willing to collab-orate to advance the Governor's agenda.
- Federal government staff. Especially an agency that profits from delegated federal authority and funding, maintaining positive relationships with their federal counterparts is key. However, unless there is a clear federal interest, eliciting support from a federal agency is unlikely.
- Local governments. City and county officials may be kindred spirts with the agency and, either exercising their own gov-ernment's authority or that delegated by the state, administer within their jurisdictions agency rules thereby reducing an agency's enforcement burden. Local legislative delegations in the capitol may also have influence to impact agency authority, staffing, budgets, and direction.
- Media. News outlets generally have pro-regulation biases.

117

Regulated special interests. Organizations independently, as members of associations, or in coalitions of ad hoc interests can affect agencies via:

- Direct contact: permitting, enforcement, service on agency advisory committees, influencing of political appointees
- Legislature: lobbying related to an agency's budget and statutory authority
- Governor: influencing his or her directives to agencies and making political appointments
- Courts: administrative or judicial litigation, as plaintiff or intervenor
- Rulemaking: The main route interest groups have to influence agencies is by taking advantage of the extensive opportunities to participate in the rulemaking activities, especially as sources of technical information.

Most interest groups go well beyond simply participating in the rulemaking process. Groups can and often do resort to the legislative arena in order to influence rulemaking activities. Interest groups may work with the Governor as a means of pressuring state agencies to act or not act on regulations.

And, in some states, much of the rulemaking process occurs informally prior to APA-required notice of rulemaking. An agency may meet with persons likely to be affected by the proposed rule, that is, stakeholders. And, if unhappy with a final rule, interest groups can initiate administrative and judicial litigation to challenge the agency's rulemaking activities.

Advocates must keep in mind that a natural tension exists between regulator and regulated. Each pursues goals that often are at cross purposes. And each has political and financial resources that can affect the other. However, advocates who prove themselves to be collaborative, honest, and a resource can manage that tension from undermining your efforts.

Technical staff. Experts are the foundation of the rulemaking process. Their agreement or opposition greatly affects agency receptivity to

118

external influences. Agency staff must judge between persuasive arguments proffered by highly specialized proponents and opponents often with advanced degrees and experience. Support from agency technical staff for your rulemaking initiative will greatly improve your chances of success, just as their opposition could block you. Below we discuss private interests hiring private technical experts to work with agency experts.

Agency legislative liaisons (agency lobbyists). They are important to your lobbying because they:

- Predict to agency managers the likely responses to the rulemaking from lawmakers, Governor's office, affected parties, and pro and con special interests. These players collectively affect an agency's relevance, authority, funding, and staffing. They also will calculate responses from the legislature's rule oversight committees (if any).
- Protect with lawmakers the agency's political influence and credibility.
- Seek to gain chits with groups that affect the agency's influence, authority, and funding.
- May motivate agency management to suspend or shut down rulemaking that they cannot technically influence but which threatens the agency or governor politically.

Managers—career civil service. They lead their sections within the agency and have political, personnel, and perhaps technical influence with most staff reporting to them. If disposed to your point of view, they could influence staff directly working on the rulemaking.

Managers—non-career civil service. They are in a sense the link or even the mediators between career civil service employees, which often they once were, and the political appointees, which in a sense they are because their jobs, like those of political appointees, are *at will*. They more than any other group in the agency may be able to reconcile conflicting views within the department.

Office of General Counsel. The office of General Counsel (OGC) participates in rulemaking in order to apply policy and wordsmithing regulatory language. Our experience is that agency staff largely defer to the OGC such that a regulated party's positive relationship with that office may generate greater favor with the technical staff. A regulated party's negative reputation with the OGC will diminish its effectiveness with technical staff as well.

Citizen advisory groups. These may not exist but if they do an agency may refer you to a citizen advisory committee for either of two main reasons. First, in order to delay acting on a proposed rule, it may consign it to a kind of long-term limbo by referring it to an advisory committee whose members seldom agree on anything. Or second, it may want to go forward expecting the advisory committee to fix among themselves the rule delaying problems. The latter is more likely than the former, but before investing resources, advocates should determine which of the two options is at play. These committees often include experts representing wide and often conflicting interests. A stakeholder committee is a type of citizen advisory committee.

Political appointees (commissioners, secretary, top managers). Despite titles, these have varying levels of influence on agency direction and career civil service staff. When lobbying them, consider they:

- "Identify" first with fellow C-suite personalities, not mid-level staff.
- Negotiate with fellow C-suiters over broad policy.
- Could lead to incorporating external group preferences into rulemaking by involving them early in the process.
- Set agency enforcement policy to avoid conflict.
- May be able to shut down controversial rulemaking that they otherwise cannot influence as noted by Dr. Kerwin above.

Governor's office. The Governor might influence an agency because he or she:

- Nominally heads the agency via political appointees
- Appoints and removes political appointees and non-career civil service employees
- Affects the agency's budget and staffing
- Depending on his or her popularity, has variable influence with career civil service staff

He or she can exert considerable influence via his or her authority over the state budget, via the power to reorganize the executive branch, and via personal persuasion of the executive branch, as well as creating positive or negative publicity regarding the proposed rulemaking. The Governor, as head of the executive branch and nominal director of its agencies, permeates this book and accordingly is mentioned 121 times in this manual.

However, absent a well-connected lobbyist or clear political threat or damage to the Governor's agenda, do not presume his or her office will be interested enough in your particular agency activities to involve itself in rulemaking.

Legislators. Individual lawmakers:

- Have small or great influence with the agency
- Often rely and defer to agency technical advice

In many cases, the lawmakers most influential with an agency are the chairs of the appropriations or fiscal committees. Next in importance are the chairs of subcommittees having jurisdiction over specific agency budgets. Money committees have influence less for reasons of an effective regulatory program than because they determine agency funding including staff positions, programs to be funded, paychecks, and raises. A distant third in influence are the chairs of committees of *subject matter jurisdiction.* Occasionally an individual lawmaker may have disproportionate influence. For example, in Montana the agency must consult with the sponsor of the enabling legislation[168] prior to rulemaking.[169] Because of agency technical expertise, these last-mentioned committees often need the agency more than the agency needs these committees.

Legislature. Due to separation of powers as discussed in Chapter 1, legislatures have limited ability to affect specific agency acts. However, when conferring the power or authority to regulate, the Legislature can choose to grant a broad scope of authority or a very limited grant of authority. This is probably the most effective way for the legislative branch to impact a rulemaking entity. Many states give both the Governor and legislature veto authority over agency rulemaking. State legislatures can have considerable input into the pre- and post-rulemaking process.

Non-government accreditation agencies and standard setting bodies. These organizations focus on compliance methods and testing rather than on policy. However, testing methodologies are every bit as critical to compliance with government regulations by regulated parties as are government set standards themselves.

As counter intuitive as this may sound initially, your principal may be able to operate its business better under one testing methodology rather than another testing approach.[170] Standard setting and measurement protocols are long-term, highly technical, and unavailable for short-term rulemaking. These agency standards and methodologies are important to regulated interests because:

- Agencies heed standard setting or certifying bodies such as ISO, ASTM, etc.[171]
- Certification may stand in lieu of or in addition to state regulation.
- Testing and measurement protocols form the basis for determining compliance with regulations.

Federal agencies. The federal government's interest would be with how a proposed state rule would impact compliance with federal laws, delegations of federal authority or funding.

Other state executive agencies. When areas of legal jurisdiction or interests overlap creating common benefits, agencies might be able to influence one another. For example, while employed by a state university,

Bob *unsuccessfully* lobbied a state agency to include in its annual budget requested funding for specific university research. However, the university's proposal was not significant relative to the agency's own objectives and budgetary needs. Staff refused wanting no further discussion. Had Bob reviewed the agency's strategic plan *prior to visiting the agency* he might have saved everyone time, travel, and trouble. On the other hand, while lobbying in Canada, he *successfully* enlisted Transport Canada and Natural Resources Canada to support his principal's proposed transboundary administrative action pending before Environment Canada.

Local government and agencies. As state governments enforce federal laws, so too local governments with their parallel agencies enforce state law. For example, Bob was a pollution control inspector for local government which worked closely with state government. Having neither sophistication nor resources his county agency could do no more than develop piecemeal rules, so it broadly enforced state environmental laws. Further, some county and city government agencies are large and well-funded such that the state is glad to have them take the lead on regulation. Accordingly, these agencies have collaborative, mutually influential relationships.

Public employee unions. Chapter 2, *The Agency Model* noted that public employees' unions may collaborate with an agency to lobby the legislature to increase agency budget appropriations, specifically to fund additional staff. The given example of a union-agency partnership between the state Department of Corrections and public employees union benefitted both the union with more members and the agency with more staff. While we do not have experience with a union influencing an agency for a third party, it is something to consider with the right mutual benefits.

AGENCY LOBBYISTS

You may be at this point feeling a bit overwhelmed by the amount of work facing you in order to successfully lobby an executive agency on behalf of your principal. If you have the resources, consider hiring an agency lobbyist. *Winning with Lobbyists, Professional edition* in regard to agency lobbyists, emphasizes their hiring criteria,

> Your agency lobbyist should intimately understand the enabling legislation and legal context in which rulemaking fits. He or she must know the minutiae of the proposed rule and be able to make useful, line-by-line, word-by-word, and calculation-by-calculation technical suggestions about the proposed rule. Your lobbyist also must intimately know the state APA or have colleagues that do. A lobbyist having worked for an agency or having an advanced technical degree and appropriate professional credentials, such as licenses and publications, has greater influence with agency technical staff and will be of greater value to you during the rulemaking process.

In addition to an agency lobbyist, expect that you likely will need one or more technical experts for your advocacy efforts.

TECHNICAL EXPERTS

Agency rulemaking is founded on the best available technical information provided by qualified technical experts, scientific and legal, and scrutinized by agency experts, many possessing advanced academic degrees and considerable experience. Our experiences—hard science-engineering (Bob) and tax, transportation, and civil justice reform (Chris)—attest that your experts, in-house and consultant, greatly affect regulator-regulated outcomes in rulemaking, post-rulemaking challenges, and enforcement. To influence agency rulemaking, you will have to hire recognized technical and legal experts.

However, make sure you hire the right technical experts because once you have tendered their names to the agency as *your experts* expect that you are stuck with them for the duration of the rulemaking proceedings, that is, pre-APA-noticed, APA-noticed, and during post-rulemaking challenges, administrative and judicial.

Your experts also know that once they are recognized as *your experts* you cannot get rid of them during the pendency of the rulemaking proceeding, even if they go bad. Consider this life-lesson about working with expert contractors, considerably shortened for this book.

Bob chaired an industry technical committee tasked with working with the Florida Department of Environmental Regulation (DER) in setting numerical secondary groundwater standards.[172] For statistical data analyses, his principal hired a prestigious consulting firm.

After a couple of months of work, the consultant sent Bob a first draft of the statistical analysis. Upon reviewing it, Bob became quite concerned about the quality of the work. For a second opinion, he secured a Ph.D. engineer who upon review of the consultant's draft had similar worries. Bob and the Ph.D. engineer then met with the prestigious consultant to clear up their concerns.

The tense meeting went from bad to worse, when the consultant informed us that he had a Masters in Statistics and we the client were not to question his work. The Ph.D., quite offended that a Master's degree consultant would tell him not to question the work, argued statistical methodologies and appropriate uses thereof. Seeing two immovable forces arguing, Bob told the consultant that given the consultant's attitude he was removing him from the project. The consultant then paused his quarreling to give Bob the best lesson ever in client-consultant relations.

Behind his big desk, in his private office, the consultant leaned back in his high-back executive office chair, folded his hands behind his head and said (almost scornfully), "Fire me? You are going to fire me? (dragging out *you* and *me* for effect)." Then, leaning forward for emphasis said, "If you fire me [i.e., the name of his prestigious firm] every bit of data collected [by powerplants from Key West to Pensacola] will now be suspect by the agency in the rulemaking."

Bob paused to mentally process the consultant's statement and then replied, "You are right. So, I'm going to pay you to attend the rule development workshop and keep your mouth shut."

Bob, this time *after checking* for client reputation, hired a University of Florida statistics professor to analyze the data, and testify at the Tallahassee workshop, with the prestigious consultant in attendance saying nothing. In the end, DER adopted a reasonable rule for Florida.[173]

As you are considering hiring an expert, consider the following employment criteria, the last one of which Bob had failed to check. Agency staff respond to experts and clients will be happier with consultants who(se):

- Have relevant advanced degrees, *earned* (e.g., Ph.D.) or *professional* (e.g., J.D.)
- Have professional certifications/licenses (e.g., Licensed Professional Geologist)
- Have a reputation for objectivity
- Are experienced in the topic at hand
- Have published in legitimate sources
- Are respected by peers in their field
- Speak and write well
- Calmly follow where data lead
- Respect and collaborate with staff
- Former clients would hire again

In Chapter 2, section, "Momentary Mutualism: Give and Take Among Rulemaking Players" we mentioned good rapport between the DER and the right consultant. Hiring the wrong consultant will needlessly cost you excess time, money, and consternation. And if agency staff doubt your consultant they may ignore his or her opinions. Hire well!

FACE TO FACE MEETING WITH AGENCY STAFF

Recall that the agency likely has no APA *legal obligation* to meet with you. However, we have never had one—federal, state, local, or in Mexico or Canada—refuse. Expecting you will meet face to face with agency staff, technical, legal, and political, it is now time to mobilize for agency interactions during which you will try to influence staff to support your rulemaking-related proposals. Within the bounds of politeness, you will lobby the agency in every interaction, including:

- Casual conversations with staff
- Citizen advisory committees
- Stakeholder meetings
- Public workshops
- Rule adoption hearings
- Rule challenge negotiations
- Wherever you get the chance

When you are a familiar face, your very presence is lobbying. Your degree of being welcome depends on how staff sees you, going from most to least attractive: solution, client, kindred spirit, or problem. You are always respectful, helpful, timely, and tasteful when seizing the opportunity to speak appropriately to them.

Staff is obligated to respond to your written comments placed in the rulemaking record, but they do not have to converse with you. As mentioned earlier in Chapter 4, section, *"Ex Parte* Communications," they may slam the door on *ex parte* communications, if only to avoid unwelcome additional administrative burdens of having to correctly summarize your conversation to the rulemaking record.

LOBBYING STAFF CHECKLIST

Building on your Chapter 4 preparations, the following checklist will help you conduct a productive meeting with staff to discuss the proposed rule.

- Make an appointment with the correct staff.
- Let staff know in advance the subject of your visit.
- Mention who else will be with you, such as:
  - other associations
  - experts and their credentials
  - lawyers
  - staff from other agencies.

- Expect to meet in the agency's offices.
- Ensure the meeting will include the right people, such as:
  - department(s) within the agency
  - staff person(s) including department and section heads.
- Arrive at the meeting room 30–45 minutes early.
- Greet staff, introduce yourself, others, and the organizations you represent.
- Briefly state what you are there to do.
- Provide extra copies of all materials.
- Go over points one at a time, calmly discussing your views.
- Technically woo staff to your side.
- Do not point out typos or small errors in agency produced documents.
- Be pleasant because the rulemaking process is heavily weighted in the agency's favor.
- Ask staff with whom they have already met.
- Offer to provide more information, as needed.
- Ask staff about their rulemaking timeline.
- Do not offer anything of value even donuts or token gifts.
- Thank staff for their time and attention and follow up with a memorandum.

Make an appointment with the correct staff. If the proposed rule has been APA noticed[174], the announcement will list the agency's main public contact who will direct you to the proper agency staff. But, if the rulemaking has not been APA-noticed and you think the agency might be working on it, then in order to locate the right staff, during your inquiries you must be ready to cite chapter and verse of the enabling legislation specifically those sections with which you are concerned. This is because, while the law provides the legislative authority to proceed with rulemaking, the agency may be working on one section of the statute but not the one in which you are interested.

The executive branch[175] or agency itself[176] may provide a schedule of rulemakings. In some states, such as California, all agencies are required to annually publish a rulemaking calendar of upcoming regulatory projects for the forthcoming year. If the agency is working on a rule, to discover the status of a rule in process, contact the internal rule development committee (IRDC), if appointed. If an IRDC has not been formed, ask the agency public information officer, Office of General Counsel, or Secretary of the agency if the committee has been formed or with whom to talk. If you think rulemaking may be at the earliest stages of being considered, contact the agency itself to ask for its *rule implementation schedule* or *plan* for a particular law or section.

Let staff know in advance the subject of your visit. Contact the correct staff to ask about rule development. Expect you will meet with technical staff, possibly legal staff, perhaps legislative liaisons, and while unlikely, political appointees. If you conclude the time is right to contribute to rule development, ask for a meeting with relevant staff to discuss where the agency is in the regulatory process emphasizing that your principal likely may be substantially affected by the rule to be adopted. Ask for only the amount of time you will need and for permission to arrive 30 minutes early to set up your presentation and for the name of a staff person with whom you can coordinate your arrival and room access.

The easier you make it for staff to just show up and listen to your presentation, the more likely they will participate. Follow up with a letter clearly stating whom you represent, why your principal could be substantially affected, what you can attest to, and why you are interested in providing information on the rulemaking as to specific chapter and verse(s). Include a proposed meeting agenda based on your conversation, as well as the names and credentials of your team members.

Mention who else will be with you. In order for staff to prepare their team to meet with your team, let them know any other parties who will be with you including associations, experts and their credentials, lawyers, and staff from other agencies.

Expect to meet in the agency's offices. It is unlikely agency staff will come to your offices as they want to be able to call upon other staff should your visit require unexpected resources or leave early if more pressing matters unexpectedly arise. Offer to send to the agency a few days before the meeting the materials you will discuss. If agreeable with the agency avoid seating in an "us against you," agency versus regulated parties with each on its own side of the table. If the agency wants sides, then ask if lawyers can sit across from lawyers, technical people across from technical people and the like. If possible you should be at the head of the table as the host. Or have a round table to avoid overt taking sides and controlling. You want to foster collegiality. Of course, it's their office so you have to do what they want.

Ensure the meeting will include the right people. A day or two before the meeting, confirm with the agency regarding the meeting time and room number and the names of their staff who are expected to attend. Confirm for yourself that you will be speaking with the right department(s) within the agency, as well as the appropriate staff person(s) including department heads.

This is important when following a lead *on possible rulemaking* not yet APA-noticed. Memorize the names and biographies of those with whom you will meet. Look them up on social media such as LinkedIn to try to know about their background and views before you meet them in person.

Arrive at the meeting room 30–45 minutes early. This will allow you to psychologically acclimate yourself to the environment, set up your equipment, if any, and use the restroom and conduct other preparation to project a calm, organized self-confidence. Neither they nor you are there to chat. You are there to make a strong, good first impression that you can be an agency *resource* on what may be a long rulemaking road together. They are there to hear and digest your presentation.

Greet staff, introduce yourself, others, and the organizations you represent. To create a collegial tone, being first in the room, you can welcome staff. Mentally note each staffer's name, especially unexpected, additional staff. Yes, you are in their offices but it is your meeting. Do not be offended if some staff arrive late or leave early. You may have all day, but they do not. As emphasized in Chapter 4, avoid if at all possible an *us versus them* seating arrangement. Have your team spread themselves out and leave open chairs for staff between your members to fill in as they arrive.

Do not be surprised if the agency is reserved rather than warm. If they do not know you, they still have to determine whether you are a resource, client, kindred spirit, or problem. Your being there forces them to deal with a party who likely does not want a new rule or, on the other hand, is proposing to add more burden to their already busy lives by pushing for a rule.

Start your meeting as scheduled, if at all possible. Going around the table, ask each person (whose name you recall from a moment earlier and earlier research) to name him or herself, job title and agency section or organization represented. Have one of your colleagues keep notes. Ask if they would be comfortable with your recording the meeting. Be prepared to end the meeting five minutes early to allow for conversation to wind down and accommodate any staffer who wants to speak longer.

Briefly state what you are there to do. You are representing a potential substantially affected party and would like to introduce yourselves as a resource to the agency as it develops a rule to implement statute (cite), revise a rule (cite) or take some other agency action.

Provide extra copies of all materials. This is a low-risk, high return-on-investment gamble. Yes, you sent the materials to the agency three days earlier. But do not expect the staff will remember to bring them. And do not be surprised if the agency roster changes to add or subtract participants. Worst case, you lose a few printing dollars in the gamble. Best case is you buy some goodwill by thoughtfully bringing extra copies.

Go over points one at a time, calmly discussing your views. You are there to impress the agency with what a solid resource you will be going forward, as the term *resource* is defined in Chapter 4, section, "Difficulties Building Relationships with Agency Rulemaking Staff vs. Legislative Staff."

This is less about technical minutiae at the moment and more about simply establishing yourselves as interested, affected, credible, and collaborative experts who would be valuable to the agency. If staff concludes you do have something to offer, they may consult with you as the process proceeds.

Technically woo staff to your side. Agency staff are educated professionals but they likely do not know your operations as well as you do nor the potential impacts of the rule upon you, your principal, and your industry or profession. They likely have to write APA mandated impact statements so they will be interested in hearing what you have to say. Your experts and their experts, your lawyers and their lawyers should develop a mutual professional respect during your brief overview of the process, facts and law. *Brevity is the soul of wit.* The less material you give them and the shorter the meeting the more they will retain, the more they will be willing to process it and faster, and the earlier you can schedule a followup meeting.

Do not point out typos or small errors in agency produced documents. We were negotiating over chemical pollutants in surface waters, the so called "free-from" rules. "Free-from" is derived from the law stating, "Waters of the state shall be *free from* (a list of named pollutants.)" An untested, new colleague, yet to prove himself to us, excitedly jumped on a "gotcha" typo revealing that "free-from" in the draft rule should read "free form." With considerable embarrassment to him, we pointed out that this was the *free-from* not the *free form* rule. Leave needing-to-prove-themselves proofreaders at the office.

Be pleasant because the rulemaking process is heavily weighted in the agency's favor. As mentioned before, unless your state Administrative Procedures Act or other law says otherwise, but for civility and image, staff does not have to talk with you any longer than they want to. They can walk out of the meeting and tell you to send your comments to them in writing. In all lobbying, the # 1 rule is, "Likeability is job number one." If they like you, they will listen to you and may want to help you. If they do not like you, your presence is counterproductive. Be pleasant, respectful, and a welcome resource in their offices.

Ask staff with whom they have already met. All of this is or will be public record, so staff should willingly disclose with whom they have met. By knowing who has visited the agency on this rule, you can gauge the level of interest, difficulty, and assets you may have to invest and the parties with whom you will become allies or opponents.

Offer to provide more information, as needed. Because agencies want to produce technically and legally sound rules, they welcome technical, legal, and policy information to assist them in their efforts. Offer to provide more information that will incline them to draft a rule favorable to your principal. Ideally, they will want more thereby setting you up as an agency resource. Their response to your offer will be a direct indicator of the success of your meeting and their view of you and interest in what you have to say.

"Your concerns have been duly noted," is agency jargon for, "we don't want to argue or discuss this point any more, so drop it." An agency petitioner might be dismissed in this way in any interaction with staff, be it in an informal meeting or in an agency workshop. Failure to understand, or even worse abide by, the dismissal can lead to subtle agency unfriendliness.

Ask staff about their rulemaking timeline. They may not have this yet but, on the other hand, they may have developed a rule implementation schedule including dates by which time they want to have sections of rulemaking completed and whether they are considering rolling out the rule in segments over time or in one comprehensive proceeding.

Perhaps surprisingly, we have inquired of some staff about the implementation schedule only to get back a blank stare indicating the staffer had little idea what we were talking about. Sometimes one part of an agency does not know what the other is doing, but expect that the schedule exists if they are far enough along in the project.

Do not offer anything of value even donuts or token gifts. Yes, it is a sweet idea, but it is bad for you. Providing anything even of minimal value to an individual agency staffer, even if given in a group situation, could run afoul of state ethics laws. Check with your lobbyist, state ethics office, or agency itself as to ethics limits on gifts of food or tokens.

Thank staff for their time and attention and follow up with a thank you letter. At the conclusion of the meeting, thank staff for their participation. Follow up a few days later with a letter thanking their immediate manager and offering to be a resource as they proceed through rulemaking. Include in the letter what you think were points of agreement and what you would like to resolve with them at your next discussion.

LOSING APPROACHES

The above outlines how to structure a productive meeting with staff concerning a noticed or under construction proposed rule. However, the above structure fueled by a poor attitude or misleading facts could lead the agency to conclude the advocate is a problem, rather than a resource, resulting in a net loss to the advocate. Losing approaches include:

- Weak technical foundation
- Questioning staff's motivation
- Attacking the agency rulemaking record without overwhelming proof
- Not helping develop a solution
- Not addressing rulemaking issues
- Asking for more than the agency has
- Legal or political threats

Weak technical foundation. The agency may discount weak factual and legal arguments in their comments on the record.[177] As long as their decisions can be arguably supported by evidence found in the rulemaking record, and their actions stay within the bounds of agency discretion, then for all practical purposes they can promulgate whatever they decide.

Questioning staff's motivation. That they may not like you is irrelevant if the rulemaking is a valid exercise of delegated legislative authority.

Attacking the agency rulemaking record without overwhelming proof. If *arbitrary and capricious* cannot be proven, then agencies have considerable latitude in rule adoption including content and timing.[178]

Not helping develop a solution. Agency staff merely need to explain in the rulemaking record why they reject or accept your comments. They neither have to convince you nor need your approval on their reasoning in order for the agency to promulgate a valid rule, that is, as long as the rule is not *arbitrary or capricious* as a matter of law. As mentioned in Chapter 8, *What You Should Learn, Accept and Challenge on Agency Regulatory Enforcement and Adjudications*, the agency "will be upheld even if most reasonable people would agree the outcome was unfair."

Not addressing rulemaking issues. Discussion not germane to the rulemaking, such as anecdotes or accusations, wastes everyone's time, discredits the advocate, and if given in bad faith may be excluded from the rulemaking record.

Asking for more than the agency has.
- Economically—if there is no fiscal appropriation, then they likely cannot afford to do it even if they like your position.
- Legally—if there is not clear authority in enabling legislation, they cannot do it legally.
- Technically—if current technology cannot do it or is too expensive for regulated parties, they will not demand it.
- Politically—if it is contrary to the legislative liaison's advice, it is not likely to happen.

Legal or political threats. Can or does your principal want to match its resources against those of the state in light of the deference adjudicative bodies generally give to an agency's discretion in implementing a statute? That conflict is likely to result in legal, political, financial, and public relations losses. And it may invite agency revenge, of course, all done *under color of authority* and with judicial deference.

NEVER MISLEAD, LIE, OR THINK YOU ARE JUST TOO CLEVER TO BE EXPOSED

As in most lobbying, regulated parties generally oppose creation of new statutes and administrative rules. Organizational operations are optimized for one set of rules which new laws alter, generally to the regulated party's financial harm. The business maxim, *It's Performance that Counts*, at times pressures advocates to mislead or lie to agencies or foolishly think themselves too clever for regulators.

However, unlike mostly technically untrained legislators who work within a system founded on trust, agency staff are technical experts often with advanced degrees who work within a system of facts and law and who are skeptical of the motives of regulated interests. They will, in time if not immediately, expose deception. When working with agencies, an advocate should:

- Admit shortcomings in your position and address them.
- Make sure data are accurate.
- If you do not know the answer, just say so.
- Not try to stall or sabotage agency action.
- Realize that once exposed trust is gone.
- Keep in mind that agencies have long memories.

These words of advice are offered because, once your lie or deception has been exposed, the trust is gone and most agencies have long memories. An advocate will have to travel a very long road to recover from a reputation of dishonesty, if ever.

Admit shortcomings in your position and address them. Your facts and law are no more "open and shut" than are the agency's. It is just that in rulemaking agencies get the benefit of the doubt with a standard that is "highly deferential, presuming the agency action to be valid and affirming the agency action if a reasonable basis exists for its decision."[179] Argue your case, but keep in mind for now the decisions are all theirs.

Make sure data are accurate. This refers to your data for reasons of maintaining agency trust. Their data must be accurate for reasons of the rule's integrity and to avoid an adjudicatory ruling of *arbitrary and capricious*. They will appreciate having obviously wrong data corrected.

If you do not know the answer, just say so. Rulemaking normally takes as much time as it needs to do it correctly. APAs provide time extensions for this reason. Except in the adoption hearing, you will not have to provide on the spot answers. It is better to say you do not know and will get back to the agency, rather than supply the wrong answer. Preserve your integrity, because it is the most important long-term asset that you have.

Do not try to stall or sabotage agency action. If you want to be known by the agency as a resource, you have to stay within the facts and rules, enabling legislation, and administrative procedures. For example, submitting voluminous, irrelevant materials into the administrative record to try to stall agency rulemaking by burdening the agency with tedious review and comment should result in the agency disallowing the material as submitted in bad faith. Their decision would likely be upheld in adjudication because, "The presiding officer may exclude evidence in the absence of an objection if the evidence is irrelevant, immaterial, unduly repetitious . . ." [180]

Once exposed, trust is gone. Dealing with an untrustworthy person consumes excess agency resources and may result in the person's oral comments being ignored, written submittals discounted, and in-person advocacy unavailable.

Agencies have long memories. Because of the personal and financial rewards[181], agency life-time employment and retirement benefits[182], many agency staff members work for the state for their entire careers—20 to 30 years or even longer. And when they retire they may tell the next crop of agency employee "lifers" about a regulated party's bad behavior, too. It is a haunting thing to have earned a bad name in the agency lore.

RULEMAKING NEGOTIATIONS

In all phases of advocacy, expect that you will negotiate. Negotiation is so important that *Insiders Talk* Manual 3, *How to Successfully Lobby State Legislatures* devotes an entire chapter to legislative negotiation.

The *Campaign Method* video series offers a 50-minute training. Live *Lobby School* seminars combine a 15-minute pre-class preparation, with a ~45-minute+ class lecture, followed by a ~60-minute+ skills-application practice session. That session focuses on legislative negotiating among special interest groups. The second day of the training adds a 20–30-minute activity focusing on regulated parties negotiating a draft of a proposed rule with agency staff. That is just how critical it is for you to have effective negotiating skills.

We will not repeat these trainings here, but we want you to know that in the rulemaking process, like in all lobbying, you will do face-to-face, make-or-break negotiating with friends and enemies. You must prepare yourself to do it well. Lots of great training is available. Karrass offers across the world a 4-day, 16-hour business, buyer-seller training that Bob has attended and highly recommends.[183] He also cites Karrass in his other books.

You will negotiate because in doing so you have at least *some control* over the outcome depending on how good you are at it. In a formal rulemaking proceeding, you are only somewhat better off than helpless. This is because, in most cases, the presiding authority has already decided what it is going to adopt. Chapter 6, *Rule Adoption*, section, "Conduct at a Hearing," subsection, "Respond if the hearing is pro-forma" gives an example of how the agency had decided the outcome of the rulemaking before they walked into the hearing room.

Expect that to get the most out of a rulemaking, prior to the adoption hearing, you must attempt to cut your best deals and settle your disagreements with others. All of the parties mentioned above are potential allies or enemies who can help or harm your efforts to advance your principal's interests.

As noted in other *Insiders Talk* books, nobody is at a negotiation to be your friend. They are there to gain advantage for their principals and at your expense, if expedient. While Bob has negotiated many times with agency staff and special interests over details in rulemaking, one experience with a USEPA administrative order of consent[184] demonstrates the importance of being prepared for the unexpected in negotiations. Many times, negotiations are not what they seem and are rife with deceptions, secret alliances, and hidden agendas.

To illustrate, USEPA notified parties that the oil recycling facility with which the parties had contracted had discharged waste oils into the environment and that they all were *potentially responsible parties* (PRPs) in a *Superfund* action in which each had joint and severable liability. At its most basic, *joint and several* means whoever has the deepest pockets may have to pay all the bills regardless of whether they had contributed negligibly or significantly.

Bob contacted other PRPs to organize their initial response to USEPA. However, at the time he was an engineer, not an attorney, and had no understanding of how some attorneys may conduct themselves business-wise especially in a high money joint and several liability project. He arrived at another PRP's attorney's office expecting to collaborate to solve some common problems. However, the supposed collaboration became a negotiation with legal counsel seemingly more interested in cultivating other PRPs as clients rather than solving problems. The lawyer succeeded with client development and skillful representation. In the end, EPA treated the parties appropriately, assessed no penalties on most of the parties, and his principal paid a *de minimis* ~$15,857.68 (yes, USEPA is just that precise) amount for its portion of the cleanup.

The point of this illustration is that, when working with agencies and affected parties whether in an enforcement action or rulemaking, you will have to negotiate with friends, foes, and agencies just doing their jobs. And, as you represent your principal, you must realize that nobody involved in the negotiation process is there to help you no matter how chummy or beguiling they are. The agency and all parties have their own agendas to benefit their principals, and again, at your expense, if expedient.

We urge you in a rulemaking to negotiate with all the parties well before the adoption hearing. And, prepare for your negotiation like you were going to be an expert witness in an administrative hearing ready to provide good technical information but with the caution and suspiciousness of a lawyer.

SUMMARY

Here we discuss lobbying internal and external influencers of the formal rulemaking proceeding and how to try and achieve consensus in rulemaking. In order to address the influencers, you have to identify those likely for and against your position. And well before the rule adoption hearing you will have to negotiate with most or all of them to achieve consensus to bring to the agency.

Agency lobbyists and technical experts play a significant role influencing agency personnel. The *Lobbying Staff Checklist* will help you to carryout your Chapter 4 preparation in the face-to-face meeting with agency staff to discuss the proposed rulemaking action.

An advocate should not undertake any losing approaches to dealing with agency staff. In particular, never mislead, lie, or think that you are simply too clever to be exposed by agency personnel. That could be the end of your agency lobbying career even though you can still submit comments to the rulemaking record. In our next chapter, we lay out in simplified form the rulemaking process in which your principal's interests will be substantially affected and show you how you can effectively participate in it.

CHAPTER 6

RULE ADOPTION

In this chapter, you assemble and apply the previous chapters to successfully influence agency rulemaking. By *successfully*, we mean to get a final rule that will benefit your principal the most or hurt it the least. Two rubrics have guided us:

1. Thomas Jefferson's, "The execution of laws is more important than the making of them."
2. "What the legislature gives you, an executive agency can take away. And what the legislature would not give you, an executive agency might." We begin by reviewing a few key points from previous chapters as they relate to the rulemaking process.

REVIEW OF THE BASIC RULEMAKING PROCESS

As discussed earlier, a *rule* is an *administrative law* created by an *executive* agency using delegated *legislative authority*.[185, 186] Unless an agency can point to chapter and verse in its *enabling* or *authorizing legislation*, it has no authority to promulgate a rule. This is why early in Chapter 2 we wrote, "Approximately one hundred percent of the time you may respectfully and appropriately ask agency staff, 'Could you please show me where in the enabling or authorizing legislation you believe the department finds the authority to promulgate this specific provision?'"

141

Before a proposed rule can become law, some states require *legislative* concurrence. This is analogous to the two chambers of a bicameral legislature having to agree on the same version of a bill before it can be sent to the Governor for final approval.[187] In several states, the Governor must approve or veto an adopted rule just as he or she must do with an enrolled bill passed by the legislature.[188]

As to the Governor's veto the administrative and legislative paths part because an agency has no authority to overcome it. The unapproved rule is therefore dead. With gubernatorial approval, the agency files its rule or enactment with the Secretary of State (SOS) in order for it to be published, a process known as *promulgation*. After a short statutorily defined waiting period, the adopted rule or enactment becomes law. The SOS then incorporates the adopted rule into the administrative code or statute into the laws of the state to become effective at a time set by the legislature.[189] As you read this chapter, several of these points will be explained.

INTRODUCTION TO KEY RULEMAKING CONCEPTS: FORCE OF LAW, GENERAL APPLICATION, SUBSTANTIAL INTERESTS, AND STANDING

While states' APA definitions of "rule" vary greatly in detail[190, 191] all include elements of *force of law, general application, substantial interests*, and *standing*. While Chapter 8, *What You Should Learn, Accept and Challenge on Agency Regulatory Enforcement and Adjudications*, goes into much greater detail, for now let us touch upon why you must keep these elements in mind throughout the rulemaking process.

Force of law means non-compliance carries a state-imposed penalty. *General application* means that, even if parties within a particular regulatory universe are few in number, everyone within that universe is regulated by the rule. Intra-sector *universality of application of the rule*, rather than numbers of persons affected by it, is the key to understanding *general application*.[192]

Substantial interests at its most primal means affecting a regulated party's finances. This includes direct or indirect dollar expenses for meeting personal, professional, or business conduct, as well as product, construction, or material standards. It also means reducing or terminating private or public funding such as losing licenses or state financial assistance. It includes the costs of completing forms, reporting regulated activities, or incurring potential non-compliance penalties.

Another benefit of your principal demonstrating its substantial interests will be affected by a rule once adopted is that it may get you a seat at the table in post-rulemaking challenge negotiations. Prior to or during litigation, the agency may try to resolve substantially affected parties' objections to the new rule. Your principal's interests have a much better chance of being considered with you at the table rather than standing outside the negotiations with the general public. And, having demonstrated your principal is a substantially affected party could gain it standing in post-rulemaking litigation.

Standing. Standing is the right to sue in a civil or administrative court. To sue an injured party (*petitioner*) must demonstrate that the agency (*respondent*) caused an injury in fact by which the plaintiff has a *justiciable stake* in the action. *Justiciable* means the court can remedy the harm. The harm must be unique and a court must have authority to remedy the harm. *Unique* means impacted differently than the general public. Disliking a law does not make it justiciable.

WHY AGENCIES DEVELOP RULES

Agencies develop rules to implement state statutes or federal requirements, to carry out federally *delegated rules*, as well as the Governor's agenda, the agency's agenda, a court order, or to respond to legislative pressure. Specifically agencies create rules to respond to:

- State statutes
- Federal requirements
- Federally delegated rules

- The Governor's agenda
- The Agency's agenda
- Court order
- Legislative pressures

State statutes. A statute is a dead letter, that is, a writing without effect, unless implemented which per the state constitution may only be done by an executive agency as discussed in Chapter 1, section, "The Modern Administrative State."

Federal requirements. The federal government via statute and administrative rules imposes regulatory obligations upon the states. Also, as mentioned in Chapter 1 the Supremacy Clause—Article VI, § 2 of the U.S. Constitution—makes federal law the supreme law of the land. State agencies develop and enforce state rules within their jurisdictions to meet federal obligations.[193] For example, "Authorized states generally implement the national laws and regulations by enacting their own legislation and issuing permits, which must be at least as stringent as the national standards of compliance established by federal law."[194]

Federally delegated rules. Federal agencies delegate federal authority and funds to state agencies to implement federal rules.

The Governor's agenda. The Governor as head of the executive branch employs executive agencies, headed by his or her political appointees (Governor appointed or nominated for state senate confirmation) to implement his or her political agenda.

The Agency's agenda. The agency's agenda is driven by its mission statement, strategic plan, and legislative budget appropriations. As stated in Chapter 2, *The Agency Model*, section, "Executive Agency Organizational Structure" you should presume staff are committed to and motivated by the agency's mission statement. Their zeal may result in ways of thinking that may make little sense to regulated interests.

Court order. Infrequently, rule development may also flow from a court order. For example, a court may find that an agency has not timely implemented a statute and the court orders the agency to initiate development of a rule. Also, an agency in order to end litigation may enter into a settlement agreement in which the content of the agreement is in effect a new rule. Called *incipient rulemaking*, it is discussed on page 154.

Legislative pressures. The legislature may demand an agency develop rules to implement agency-ignored statutes. For example, lawmakers may threaten to withhold program-specific appropriations until the agency adopts and enforces rules to make effective a specific piece of legislation. As mentioned in Chapter 1 the legislature's purse gives it at least some real control over executive branch agencies.

OVERVIEW OF AGENCY RULE DEVELOPMENT PROCESS[195]

Agencies *adopt rules* or *regulations* year-round. State APAs generally start the rulemaking clock at the initial notice of rulemaking and end it upon final adoption or rejection of the regulation. *Notice* starts the clock by officially notifying the public that the agency is proposing to revise a section of the administrative code.[196]

Adoption occurs when the agency, using its *delegated legislative authority*, completes the rule development process in accord with the APA thereby making a proposed rule into an administrative law. Between notice and adoption are many intermediate steps, which are discussed below and which must be completed within statutorily set time periods.

Once the proposed rule has been noticed, allotted times per category or rule include:

Emergency rulemaking. In response to an imminent, normally unexpected threat to vital interests, an agency may immediately adopt a short-term rule to deal with the emergency. The rule may be renewed to deal with the continuing emergency.[197, 198, 199] A variant of emergency rule is the *public necessity rule* for immediate state action not stemming from an emergency.[200]

Adoption of rule by reference. An agency may incorporate into its rules an existing law or standard by citing the rule.[201, 202] The cited rule may be that of another jurisdiction, state or federal.

Regular rulemaking. The statutorily set maximum time within which an agency must complete rule development, depending on a particular state's APA, can run from 6, 12, 18, or 24 months, and are generally renewable.[203, 204, 205, 206]

Highly contentious rule. A highly contentious rule could take years to write and then more time to fully promulgate. In order to stay within APA deadlines, an agency may:

- Negotiate with likely interested parties *before* formally noticing a proposed rule:
  - Publicly meet with a committee composed of parties representing key interests and to which the public is invited.[207]
  - Privately meet with select interests.[208]
- Roll out rulemaking in sections over an extended period of time. That is, for example, adopt rules in year one to implement section one of the rule and then in the following year(s) adopt rules to implement section two.
- Enter rulemaking, take public comment, hold a public hearing, and ignore all testimony. This will be illustrated later in this chapter. How frequently this occurs is unknown, but we have witnessed it enough times to know it happens especially when the agency has had an extended pre-APA notice period of rule drafting, perhaps including negotiations with potentially affected parties.

Specific Steps in the Rule Development Process

Rulemaking is a highly structured process governed by a state's APA statute, APA rules, agency rules, and agency policy. Readers should review Chapter 3, section, "Revised Model State Administrative Procedures Act," in conjunction with this section. In the meanwhile, these steps generally may include:

- Pre-public notice of internal agency activities
- Recommendation to initiate rulemaking
- Decision on initiating rulemaking
- Administrative oversight
- Implementation planned
- Citizen advisory committees
- Stakeholder meetings
- Notice of intent to initiate rulemaking
- Informal public workshops
- Impact statements developed
- Publication of the proposed rule
- Formal public workshops
- Staff analysis and response to comments
- Publication of the amended rule
- Adoption of rule
- Review by Governor, Legislature, Attorney General
- Effective date of rule
- Appeals, if any

Pre-public notice of internal agency activities. Occasionally, complex regulations require more time to develop than provided by the APA. As noted above, the allowed APA window to complete the entire rulemaking process can be as short as six months from notice to adoption. For this reason, out of the public eye and wholly acceptable as a matter of law, agencies may be internally drafting rules long before public notice occurs.

Agencies may form internal rule development workgroups[209] (as mentioned in Chapter 4, section, "Knowing with Whom to Build Relationships: The Internal Rule Development Committee"), meet, negotiate, and even resolve rule delaying problems with select interest groups and stakeholders, do technical and legal research, prepare impact statements on small business, local government, environment, etc. as per APA requirements.

By the time a rule is noticed in the state register, the agency may have invested many months or even years of work into the proposed regulation. They might be willing to change minor details, but not redraft provisions substantial enough to require re-notice of a significantly revised proposed rule. By the time the rule is APA-noticed, in the agency's mind at least, the rule is done and only awaits formal ratification by the agency adoption mechanism. There still will be oversight by offices external to the agency itself and, finally, filing with the Secretary of State or revisor to complete the rulemaking project. But as far as the agency is concerned their APA mandated duties are complete.

As previous chapters emphasize, you want to be included in the pre-noticed activities, that is, *at the drawing board* activities. If you showed yourself to be a *solution* rather than a *problem* in earlier meetings, you may get the chance to influence the final rule vastly more before APA notice of rulemaking than you can once the formal APA process has begun.

Do not presume you have a *right to involve yourself* in the agency's pre-notice, internal rule development, process. Check the state's APA to discover your legally established point of entry into the process.

The following is an amalgamation of state rule adoption procedures that generally describe the rulemaking process. In any particular state, some steps may be mandated, others may be optional, or others still may not occur at all. Consult your state APA for specifics. The APA is your *Magna Carta*.

As emphasized in Chapter 3, *The Administrative Procedure(s) Act*, it is written to protect you from arbitrary and capricious government behavior by clearly delineating your rights. Know them and insist upon them. If you do not protect your principal, nobody else will. The steps generally are as follow:

Recommendation to initiate rulemaking. An internal or external entity begins the rulemaking process by recommending that the administrative code be changed: 1) An intra-agency office recommends to the agency that an internal rule development committee undertake development of a specific rule, or 2) A person files a formal petition for the agency to initiate rulemaking as described by the APA.[210]

The legislature itself may create a stakeholder committee to work with an agency to report to the legislature on what the state could do regarding a cited problem. For example, Bob served on the legislatively created Illinois Battery Task Force which brought together manufacturers, retailers, and environmental groups to study and report to the legislature on battery recycling options for the state.

Decision on initiating rulemaking. The agency's internal rule screening committee reviews the department recommendation; and, it *shall consider* a citizen's APA petition to initiate rulemaking.[211] A denied *intra-agency office recommendation* is without external recourse. Within APA timelines, the petition to initiate rulemaking must be denied or approved. In either case, the petitioner is informed and, in case of denial, the agency gives its reasons. In one state, denial constitutes final agency action which is appealable administratively and then judicially.[212] In another, it is not reviewable.[213]

Administrative oversight. Depending on the particular state, a specific extra-agency executive branch office[214] reviews, approves or denies proposed rulemaking, and coordinates executive agency rulemaking proposals. Approved rulemaking is added to the agency's rulemaking calendar. The legislature's administrative agency oversight function may be activated at this point.[215]

Implementation planned. Upon administrative approval (discussed above), the agency develops its own schedule for rulemaking and execution which may be called the *rule implementation plan.* This plan is the agency's roadmap for rulemaking and implementation, which is obviously valuable to advocates in planning and locating a point of entry into the rulemaking process. The implementation plan may reveal agency rulemaking activities prior to APA notice, such as forming citizen advisory committees, stakeholder groups, and other rulemaking preliminaries.

While some states publish their implementation plans, some do not. Some staff in the agency know little or nothing about its existence. However, you may be able to get a copy from the office of general counsel, internal rule development committee, enforcement division, office within the agency charged with implementing the subject area of the rule, or from the head of the agency.

Citizen advisory committees. At its option or by state policy or law[216], an agency may refer its intention to initiate rulemaking to an existing citizen advisory committee or form an *ad hoc* advisory committee to make recommendations to the agency regarding rule specifics. We mentioned citizen advisory committees in Chapter 2, sections, "Executive Agency Organizational Structure" and "Momentary Mutualism: Give and Take Among Rulemaking Players."

Stakeholder[217] meetings. At its option, an agency may form stakeholder groups to advise the agency on its proposal. Stakeholders are parties likely to be affected, primarily financially, upon adoption of the rule. Stakeholders may form the core of a formal regulatory negotiation that will eventually take place.[218]

Notice of intent to initiate rulemaking. At its option, the agency may publish an *intent to initiate rulemaking* which makes known to the public that the agency is considering a potential new rule. It will seek comments in writing and perhaps in informal public meetings.

Informal public workshops. At its option, the agency may or, if requested, must[219] schedule public meeting(s) for citizens to voice their thoughts and concerns about a possible new rule. If the agency does not want oral public input, its only public meeting, if any, will be the adoption hearing if requested or statutorily mandated.

Based upon input from citizen committees, stakeholders, and informal workshops, the agency will decide whether to go forward with rulemaking. If it considers the information gathered does not support a new rule, or that opposition makes adoption at the moment more trouble than it is worth, then the agency may discontinue the process.

Impact statements developed. If the agency decides to go forward, it will develop APA required statements of impact, such as the likely impact on small business, the economy, the environment, the impact on local government, or whatever their APA statute requires.[220] An agency's *finding of no significant impact* can save staff work and time and speed rule adoption which may subtly incline an agency to take it as an easy way out. Advocates should not on blind faith accept conclusions of *no significant impact* but be ready to check an agency's work.

Publication of the proposed rule. The public will receive notice of the proposed rule on the agency website, in the state administrative register, or other manner as prescribed by law. Previously registered interested parties having registered their interest in the subject area will receive mail notification, if they have not already. At this point, the APA rulemaking clock begins and you have a point of *entry by right* into the rulemaking process.

Formal Public workshops. At its option, the agency may schedule formal public workshops to take citizen comments. As a general principle, agencies are not obligated to take oral comments if they prefer a *paper hearing.* In some states an agency must hold a public hearing if an interested party submits a written request for a public hearing.[221]

Staff Analysis and response to comments. Agencies must consider and respond to all relevant public comments, written or oral, *submitted as part of the rulemaking record.* The agency may revise its proposed rule based upon comments, or it can choose not to accept suggested changes. However, the agency must explain why it accepted or rejected comments submitted by interested parties.

The agency may also announce at what point the record will be closed to further comments.[222] The agency will make a good record for what it wants but, as an advocate, do not presume they will be as careful with your comments. Check and double check to make sure the record contains information that you have submitted, whether you did so orally or in writing.

Publication of the amended rule. If the proposed rule is *substantively* changed, then the amended rule must be re-noticed in the state register for an additional public comment period. Expect an agency and supportive parties will resist restarting the rulemaking process. They may argue any changes made are the *logical outgrowth* of the noticed proposed rule and as such to not require re-notice.

Adoption of rule. The APA may prescribe or make optional a formal public hearing[223] or provide for no public hearings[224] at which the agency will adopt the proposed rule into law, pending review by the Governor or legislature. Presiding at the hearing will be the *adopting authority* which, depending on the particular state, can be an appointed board, agency staff, or administrative law judge as noted below in section, "The Nature of the Presiding Authority You Will Be Addressing."

At adoptions without a hearing, the agency head or designated officer may by signature complete the rule adoption process. An adoption hearing may happen only to conform to APA procedure when, in reality, the agency had already made its decision. We illustrate this below in section, "Conduct at the Adoption Hearing," subsection, "Hearing May Be Pro-forma."

Review by Governor, Legislature, Attorney General. Forty states allow a rule to be reviewed by the Governor and legislature prior to being sent to the Secretary of State for publication. "Of these 40 states, 35 allow for some form of legislative committee review of rules, and 33 explicitly allow the legislature to suspend adoption of a rule or bar a rule from being adopted."[225]

Governors' authority to veto an agency rule is evolving.[226, 227] The agency may seek a legal opinion on the rule from the state Attorney General. A rule disapproved by the legislature or its Administrative Rules Committee, Governor, or Attorney General may be returned to the agency for revision to meet legal requirements and even political ends, such as achieving greater public consensus over the rule.

Effective date of rule. After review by intervening state officers such as the Attorney General, the adopted rule with effective date as specified in the rule or by statute[228] will be filed with the Secretary of State and legislature for incorporation into the administrative code.

Appeals, if any. Once filed, and at times amidst rulemaking, the rule may be challenged administratively and eventually in court or directly to the judicial branch when statutorily permitted.

TRIGGERS TO MOTIVATING AGENCY RULEMAKING

Any of several triggers can motivate an agency to enter into rulemaking. These include:

- On its own
- New statute requires rulemaking
- Mandatory review of existing rules
- Petition to initiate rulemaking
- Federal government demands
- Deal with emergency/catastrophe
- Sue and settle

On its own. An agency may recognize that a current rule needs to be amended or a new one created to deal with unforeseen or changed circumstances that fall within its delegated authority, but for which conditions did not exist at the time of the original rulemaking. For example, anesthesia in medical procedures had long been administered by anesthesiologists (MDs) and Certified Registered Nurse Anesthetists (CRNAs).[229] However, universities began graduating a new category of anesthesia administrators, *anesthesiologist assistants* (AAs), who are neither MDs nor CRNAs.

New rules are being developed to license anesthesia assistants beginning with their legal status which is based on delegated authority or licensing[230], followed by which agency should regulate AAs. For example, in Florida, the Board of Medicine[231] is the regulatory agency because the AA is licensed under the anesthesiologist's license while in another state it may be through the Board of Nursing.

New statute requires rulemaking. The legislature creates a new statute requiring the enforcing agency to create new regulations to implement the new law. This is the most common and frequent basis of agency rulemaking.

Mandatory review of existing rules. State law may require an agency periodically, for example after a set number of years, to review existing regulations and consider them for re-adoption.[232] "Sunset laws" found in a number of states automatically terminate statutes, administrative rules, or programs unless affirmatively reauthorized by the appropriate body.

Petition to initiate rulemaking. A corporate or natural person may request an agency to promulgate a rule.[233] For example, "Petitioner requests that a new rule be enacted by the board to define pool equipment as well as the scope of licensure of pool and spa contractors, currently defined in Section 489.103(j), (k) and (l)."[234]

Federal government demands. Under the U.S. Constitution's Supremacy Clause, federal laws are the universal law of the land. Within a state, either a state agency delegated by the federal government to enforce federal law or the federal government itself, shall enforce the law.

Deal with emergency/catastrophe. A Governor's declaration of a state of emergency is an immediate response to sudden calamity. However, when state agencies implementing the declaration take actions that meet the definition of a rule, then they must enter into emergency rulemaking.[235, 236]

Sue and settle. Rule promulgation using the courts rather than the APA has been called "incipient rulemaking"[237] or more widely "sue and settle."[238] The process occurs when a plaintiff files a lawsuit against an agency alleging the agency failed to fulfill its statutory requirements. "Rather than defend itself, the agency chooses to settle the lawsuit by putting in place the advocacy group's desired regulation. The negotiation is court-ordered; thus, it is legally binding."[239] Sue and settle may reflect collaboration between a plaintiff and the agency defendant to get a rule quickly by judicially circumventing the legislature, APA, Governor, and the public.[240]

PETITIONS TO REPEAL OR CHANGE REGULATIONS

On occasion, your principal or an interest group may want to see an administrative agency repeal one of its expired and outdated regulations or amend existing regulations that have become problematic for the regulated community. Some state rules may have been on the books for too many years, or over time they have become unnecessarily and exceedingly burdensome, or a judicial ruling has nullified their implementation.

The Federal APA[241] and RMSAPA authorize individuals or groups to seek changes to or repeal of existing state regulations.[242] Although the process is formal, it is rather simple in its application. This process is patterned after the federal Administrative Procedure Act found at 5 U.S.C. Section 553(e).[243]

Usually this means submitting a formal request, that is, a *petition to initiate rulemaking*, for an amendment to or a repeal of an existing regulation that is directed to the rulemaking entity that adopts and administers the problematic regulation.[244] It is our expectation that those that are successful are usually presented by an association representing broad interests and those groups usually submit proposed changes to the existing regulation with their suggested amendments along with a thorough explanation of why those changes are justified.

Any interested party may file a written petition with the state agency specifying the nature of the regulatory change or repeal being requested, the reason(s) for the petition request, and citing the agency's rulemaking authority to either amend or repeal the regulation. Successful written petitions state clearly and concisely the substance or nature of the amendment or repeal requested and the reason for the request. If the petitioner has supporting documentation, such as technical or engineering studies, assuming the regulation is of a technical nature, then those should also be submitted. The more thorough and persuasive the petition, the more likely it will be successful.

And, by state law, the agency is usually required to notify the party who filed the written petition and respond with any denial of the petition within [x, often 30] calendar days. The agency's denial of the petition must be in writing and it must include the reason(s) that the agency denied the petition. If there is no denial of the petition, then the state agency must schedule the item for agency action such as a public hearing to be conducted by that agency.

Some state APAs require the state agency to transmit its written decision for publication in the *Notice Register* or equivalent so that the public is aware of the agency's determination. This is an important point of entry for interested parties to try to amend or repeal an existing regulation that may have become unduly burdensome over the course of implementation or have resulted in unintended consequences that could not have been predicted at the time of the regulation's adoption.

Thereafter, the agency may hold a public hearing before it makes a determination to grant or deny the petition. The agency often considers whether alternatives exist to address the identified situation via another means. A public hearing is intended to gather input on the petitioner's proposal and reasonable alternatives. The agency is interested in not only the petitioner's comments, but also those of others who may present verbal and written remarks.

INFORMAL PUBLIC WORKSHOPS AND MEETINGS

Rules of significant impact or expected controversy may be preceded by any number of informal public workshops and meetings at which the agency explains its goals and foundations and takes public comment on the proposed rule. These workshops may be called iterative[245] in that they form a cycle of conducting public workshops, drafting and circulating conceptual rules, taking public comments, and repeating as necessary. Some agencies also conduct informational meetings with interested or impacted parties to solicit feedback on regulatory projects that the agency may be contemplating for rulemaking activities.

RULE ADOPTION HEARING

The state Administrative Procedures Act directs the *formal rule* adoption process, that is, the final step in a proposed rule becoming an administrative law. As we have mentioned, state APAs differ greatly among themselves as to the formal processes for rule adoption. For example, in one state, a public rule adoption hearing is pro forma and in another state it is procedurally substantive. In one state, rule adoption is final upon affirmative agency vote while in another state adoption only becomes final upon filing the agency approved rule with the Secretary of State.

The agency's rulemaking notice will contain an initial statement of reasons that describes the purpose and rationale of each regulation, and identifies the factual material upon which the agency relies in proposing it. Their response to comments in the final statement of reasons must demonstrate that each relevant, timely comment has been considered by the agency.

However, expect in any adoption hearing, even if the proceeding is pro forma because the votes were decided earlier, the quality of testimony is critical even if just for putting your reasoning and facts into the rulemaking record. The agency's response to your submittals in their final statement of reasons must demonstrate that each relevant, timely comment has been considered by the agency. Failure to do say may result in the rule being adjudicated as *arbitrary* or *capricious*.

ADVOCATES' TESTIMONY

Effective testimony and comments are based on an understanding of the statutes and factual material on which the agency relied in proposing the regulation, on an understanding of what the proposed regulation is intended to do, on an understanding of the standards the regulation must satisfy, and who your listeners are. The *Authority* and *Reference* citations that follow the text of each regulation section identify the statutes on which the section is based.

You testify to persuade but equally to secure and advance your principal's party status in an eventual rule challenge and to secure a seat in post-adoption negotiations. To do all well:

- Expect the unexpected regarding the attentiveness of the audience, questions, and interruptions.
- Stay on point and within the time limits given, with your presentation designed to engage the audience.
- Be honest—lies and deceit can ruin the reputation of a principal and its advocate.
- Remember that presentations are just one component of regulatory agency advocacy.

THE NATURE OF THE PRESIDING AUTHORITY YOU WILL BE ADDRESSING

The rule adoption body before whom you will speak can be populated by: executive branch staff—technical or legal, political appointees—either citizens or agency top management, or elected office holders. The character of each body must be considered in tailoring your testimony. The impact from disclosure of *ex parte* communications should be well-thought-out in case you want to meet with presiding authorities outside of the rulemaking proceeding.

Executive branch staff—technical or legal. These are facts and law executive agency professionals either working within the agency or for another executive office such as a *Division of Administrative Hearings*. They have neither duty nor need to consider testimony unrelated to the rulemaking record. Your presentation likely will be provided to the board by your technical experts because these staff are highly conversant in the subject matter under consideration and the rulemaking record.

Political appointees—citizens. They often are appointed specifically to represent designated interest groups, for example, practitioners in the subject matter area, affected parties such as persons receiving services being regulated, and laypersons. You should learn the character of each board member and tailor your comments accordingly. Expect your technical experts to be beside you because the board will have theirs.

Political appointees—agency senior staff. These are agency top management appointed to carry out the Governor's political agenda and protect his or her political standing. They are more policy than technical people. Expect their professional staff to be there ready to advise them. Political statements such as the proposed rule is needlessly politically divisive or needs more work may resonate. Tailor your statements to what they are appointed to do, that is, run the agency in a way that benefits the Governor.

Elected officials. Elected officials are the least technically oriented but most politically motivated as are most office holders subject to citizen vote. A city commissioner once explained the reason he voted against technical staff's recommendations was because, "In politics, perception is reality." Tailor your presentations to the impact that their decisions will have upon their supporters. Facts or law not supporting board members' political aspirations will be ignored. The most effective presentations will be made by their supporters.

OUR EXPERIENCE WORKING WITH PRESIDING AUTHORITIES

We have represented our principals in agency rule adoptions in which one or the other has presided. These are our general observations.

Citizen boards. These are hundreds or thousands of citizens and professionals providing their services to the state, generally with no pay beyond per diem expenses. They are appointed by agency heads or elected officials. A state may have dozens of governing and advisory boards. For example, in Minnesota, "There are over 200 Boards, Commissions, Councils, Work Groups and Task Forces that work to advise policy makers and regulate our professionals."[246] As well as 112 appointing authorities[247] and 3,578 board/commission members.[248]

For broad issues, such as the environment, which affect all citizens, presiding officers often are boards or commissions composed of citizens appointed to create a collective decision-making body. Each commissioner represents and advocates for his or her own constituency and its values.[249] Board members are very much *political appointees* with their often-unshakeable and predictable policy biases. Agency staff provide governing boards with technical information. However, expect board members to act predictably to advance the policy objectives of their constituencies.

On the other hand, for regulation and licensing of professions, the collective decision-making body consists of members appointed to safeguard the public and police the regulated profession. These boards consist mainly of practitioners and perhaps lay representatives.[250] Practicing members are responsive to their colleagues and protection of the reputation of the very profession from which they derive their livelihoods. These boards often have their own executive directors and professional staff.

Our focus is with boards and commissions having rulemaking authority. Because governing directors are volunteers and have their own outside the agency occupations and constituencies, they like legislators, rely heavily on the advice and work of their staff. For this reason, advocates should try to lobby professional staff as well as governing boards and commissioners.

Agency staff. Our experience has been that professional staff are less politically concerned (although agency management and its legislative liaison may be) but highly partisan *for the agency mission statement*. A review of the agency mission statement, strategic plan, and current budget appropriations can give insight into how a rulemaking likely will proceed.

Agency staff's reduced concern with politics may be illustrated by an agency staffer presiding at a rulemaking development meeting who said to us, "If both sides [of an issue] are beating me around my head over a proposed rule then I figure the department is doing a pretty good job."

As to agency concern with politics relative to its mission as mentioned in Chapter 1, staff at another time said, "Bob, the department doesn't get paid to keep you in business. If you have a bad product, then I guess you'll just have to go out of business."

At that time, Bob's principal *to go out of business* was the largest manufacturer in the county, paying high wages to ~1,500 employees including 1,200 union members, a subsidiary of a large national corporation, and with a lobbyist's local political connections, one of whom was with the chair of the Florida Senate Natural Resources Committee and another in party leadership in the Florida House. The staffer, as he should, just did not care about politics.

In a rulemaking presided over by agency staff, as contrasted with a citizen board, one advances the agency's strategic plan while the other advances conflicting interests of an individual board member's constituents, each decision-maker has to be lobbied in its own way.

ACTIONS FOR YOU TO TAKE BEFORE THE RULE ADOPTION HEARING

The following are the kinds of steps that you can expect surrounding the hearing. As you consider the following, keep in mind that neither presiding officer(s) nor staff have any obligation to speak with you outside of the hearing. And, it is likely they are APA-authorized to cut off your oral testimony if your comments are not contributing to the hearing process or the presiding officer wants to move on.[251]

For example, as earlier noted but worth repeating, in rulemaking, we have observed staff end an overly long advocate's effort to prove a point with this bureaucratic classic: "Your concerns have been duly noted." It is their meeting and they can do what they want.

Lobbying support staff and presiding authority. Use every opportunity to speak with agency decision makers, staff and presiding officers, *before* the rule adoption hearing. As long as the discussion is disclosed in the rulemaking record by the officer or staff, *ex parte* communications are acceptable, unless a particular agency is prohibited from doing so. Responses can vary.

The best response might be a *political appointee* board member accepting your lunch invitation before or even on the day of the hearing and letting you say what you want. However, an expected answer from professional staff is that he or she does not want to hear anything you have to say on the topic. And if you want to say something, put it in writing and submit it to the rulemaking record. Nothing personal, staff just does not want the burden of having to record your pitch for insertion into the record. We have experienced both.

Staff brief decision maker(s) before the hearing. Lobby staff before they brief the decision makers. As in the legislature, staff is highly influential with presiding officers.

Use this as another opportunity to provide input into the formal record. You want to introduce into the rulemaking record everything even remotely favorable to your principal, even if it does not seem immediately applicable at the moment. What seems to be unimportant at the moment may at a later time surprisingly and unexpectedly become critical in an adjudicatory proceeding. This is called *record padding*. You do this because the rulemaking record is your principal's foundation to establish standing and contains the evidence to legally challenge the final rule, if necessary. Do not lose potential legal benefits because you are shy. If staff considers your submittals superfluous, they will tell you.

Most decisions are made prior to the hearing. Like in the legislature, due to effective lobbying and a political appointee's goal to please his or her constituents, most votes from appointed citizen boards largely are predictable. That being said, one or more votes may not be pledged and we have seen projected votes change upon sufficient private or public pressures.

As for agency decisionmakers, after having invested months or years developing the rule and working out its political problems with affected

Insiders Talk: Guide to Executive Branch Agency Rulemaking

parties, expect most, if not all, agency decision makers, especially political appointees, have already made up their minds. We illustrate on page 167 an agency having prejudged a rule proceeding.

PARTICIPATION IN RULE ADOPTION

A hallmark of the state *Administrative Procedure(s) Acts* (APA) is *government in the sunshine* and, in our case, *rulemaking in the sunshine*, which means specifically providing for citizen participation in the adoption of administrative agency rules. The long-ago problem of agencies *adopting* rules out of the public eye and of which citizens knew nothing until they found themselves subject to an enforcement proceeding was first mentioned in Chapter 2, *The Agency Model*.

Agencies per the APA must *adopt* rules in the public eye. However, as anecdotally illustrated in the next section, and as noted above, a state APA may allow or itself even unintentionally encourage[252] *developing* rules out of sight such that *adoption* is merely ratification of what the agency had already decided to do and is not about to change. Although we do not know how often agency rule adoption in effect occurs prior to notice of rulemaking, a kind of APA *deliberative process exemption* may permit such procedures.[253, 254]

Today state APAs and rules provide abundant opportunity for the public to participate in agency rulemaking. If the issue is contentious, or several rules with significant public impact are on the adoption docket, then expect to meet in a large room or auditorium with many interested parties in attendance. On the other hand, adoption of noncontroversial routine rules may occur in the agency's offices if no petition has been made for a public hearing or a statutorily required minimum[255] of persons do not so request.

If no public hearing request has been received, the rule may simply be signed into law without any public involvement. Within time constraints, everyone will be given a chance to speak. However, larger interest groups often hire lobbyists or attorneys to make their presentations which are appreciated by the agency. On the other hand, too many speakers especially saying the same thing will provoke annoyance and even hostility from the presiding agency officials.

Your participation affirms to agency board and staff that your principal is potentially substantially affected by the proposed rule and is prepared to defend its legal rights. Agency boards are political appointees who as such take into account political considerations in their disposition of a proposed rule. Agency staff are technocrats motivated by facts and law with politics as tertiary influence. Political appointees may be impacted seeing and hearing from those who have to live with agency decisions.

Participate openly and constructively. If as in Chapter 5, section, "Lobbying Staff Checklist" you earlier demonstrated that you are a resource as discussed, this active participation will be expected and respected.

Submit your favorable information into the rulemaking record. This likely is your last chance to submit into the rulemaking record facts and law that will be useful to you in case of a challenge to the rule, either your challenge or another's. To safeguard your principal's interests in section, "The Rulemaking Record" below we advise you to *pad* it as much as is necessary.

Establish your principal's substantial interests for party status. Legal standing as a party to challenge a rule, both administratively and judicially, depends on the rulemaking record demonstrating that your principal is *substantially affected* by the rule.

Raise every issue possible. A judge may not allow a plaintiff to raise new issues not considered during the rulemaking proceedings.[256] For example in SEME Homer City Generation LP v. EPA, D.C. Cir., No. 11–1302, oral arguments, Judge Thomas Griffith of the U.S. Court of Appeals for the District of Columbia Circuit ruled that regulatory challengers may only litigate issues they brought to the agency's attention in comments.[257] Pad the record!

CONDUCT AT AN ADOPTION HEARING

Our experience has been that political appointees are most open to persuasion. Agency staff are experts and if your experts have not changed their minds by the time of the adoption hearing, expect there will be no changes. However, political appointees are appointed because they are political and more open to considerations outside of technical facts. In planning your testimony consider how to:

- Tailor your testimony to panel members
- Prepare good arguments in writing
- Have your supporters attend
- Limit supporter testimony so it is not repetitive
- Respect staff, boards, and opponents
- Leave room after the board has voted on your rule and moved on to the next item on the agenda
- Respond if the hearing is pro-forma

Tailor your testimony to panel members. A rule of all lobbying is this, "Know your customer." Research them, get to know them, then phrase your comments to cater to their biases and interests. Be ready for the kinds of questions your research suggests they may ask.

Prepare good arguments in writing. Submit these to the agency clerk either at the hearing, if not before, or as directed by agency rulemaking procedures. Let your oral testimony provide short, compassion-provoking remarks in the public hearing and leave more detailed technical and legal comments to your written submission.

Have your supporters attend. Your supporters being visible at the hearing, even without any or many addressing the rulemaking body, can make a powerful statement of public interest in the rulemaking and support for your position. To illustrate, in a large auditorium, a proposed rule affecting the agriculture industry came up on the adoption hearing docket. Upon reaching the witness dais, the farmers' legal counsel asked permission of the board to recognize his clients seated in the audience. Upon the chair's agreement, much of the auditorium stood up uniformly dressed in bib overalls and ball caps.

They made their point with their presence, psychologically reinforcing their attorney's entreaty to the board that the rule will affect a vital part of the state and its agricultural economy. When the commission took up the next item on the agenda, the farmers departed leaving an auditorium largely empty.

Limit supporter testimony. Prepare a couple of sympathetic supporters to tell a brief personal, real-life impact story or speak a few lines telling the board of the expected impact of the rule upon the speakers. Two or three moving presentations are enough to make the point. Too many repetitious or poorly done performances may provoke animosity toward you and openness to your opponents' arguments.

Respect staff, boards, and opponents. Proponent and opponent lobbyists have had several meetings with staff and one or more with board members. Staff having reviewed the rulemaking record have made its recommendations to the board. In most, but certainly not all cases, the likelihood is small that a board member has not already made up his or her mind by the time the adoption hearing takes place.

Rudeness, impudence, or disrespect from anyone associated with your principal will make your opponents look sympathetic, is not likely to change any decision makers' minds, and potentially poison your future interactions with the agency in general and specifically should a rule challenge follow.

Leave room after the board has voted on your rule and moved on to the next item on the agenda. Ask your legal counsel if, *after the agency's final recorded vote,* your agenda item may be reopened later in that same meeting. If the answer is yes, that your agenda item may be reopened, then ask if you, as a substantially affected party, are no longer at the hearing, may the board still reopen the hearing in your absence? If yes, then you may have to stay in the hearing room all day. If the answer is no, that is, the board could not reopen the rule adoption without you in the room, then you and your supporters, as in the farmer anecdote above, may leave the hearing once you have gotten what you wanted or to rethink the next step. This question must be answered by a competent attorney.

Respond if the hearing is pro-forma. Decision makers likely have already decided what they are going to do regardless of your testimony and supporters. They are just going through APA formal motions. To illustrate,

> After much lobbying, the General Assembly adopted an industry dream bill. The Department of Natural Resources as the implementing agency noticed its proposed rule to implement the legislation. From an industry view, the noticed rule did not reflect the substance of the legislation in a classic example of how in rulemaking, "what the legislature giveth an executive agency can taketh away." As the APA required, the agency received earlier written comments, specifically from us as regulated interests.

> On the day of the rule adoption hearing, several industry representatives for household name companies participated. During our testimony, agency staff visibly yawned, while regularly glancing at their watches. Finally, the agency staffer chairing the meeting said to us, "Industry, can you hurry this thing up? You see, we've already made up our minds what we are going to do. We are just going through this because the APA says we have to." Of course, after this total waste of time in which our written and spoken comments were ignored, the agency promulgated an unfavorable rule which in our minds was *ultra vires.*

> Considering the rule *ultra vires* and feeling rudely treated by DNR staff, Bob went to the state house to complain to a member of the committee that passed his group's bill. As he whined, she interrupted saying, "Bob, do you know what DNR stands for?" Of course, he replied, the "Department of Natural Resources." She said, "Not in [state name]. DNR stands for 'Damned Near Ridiculous' because that is the kind of rules,

we get out of them." At the time in this state, this agency was so powerful that the Governor was said to be unable to control them.

THE RULEMAKING RECORD

The rulemaking record (also called *docket* or *file* in some states) is the compendium of legal and factual foundations on which an agency supports to the public its rulemaking decisions; and it aids adjudicatory review, administrative and judicial, of the validity of the rule.[258] Upon rule challenge, agency rules not supported by substantial evidence as found in the rulemaking record may be found *ultra vires*, that is, beyond the powers of the agency and illegal. The rulemaking record may be the exclusive[259] or primary[260] basis for judicial review of agency action.

Advocates want to put into the rulemaking record as much information as is possible that is or could be advantageous to their position during the rulemaking and possible post-rule adoption legal challenges. This compels a party to *pad the record* with issues and documentation in anticipation of future legal proceedings.

As mentioned above, failure to do so may foreclose raising issues seemingly unimportant at the moment but which may prove critical later on. In most jurisdictions, review will be limited to what is contained in the rulemaking record, so it is critical that any relevant information and comments beneficial to your principal be submitted as part of the formal rulemaking activity.

You can be sure that the agency will make a solid rulemaking record for what it wants. But do not presume it will make a good record to support what you want despite the camaraderie you feel or perceived interests you share. It is your job to make sure the rulemaking record supports your principal's operations and protects its *substantial interests* and *standing*.

SUMMARY

In this chapter you reap the fruit of all of your work accomplished per the directions of earlier chapters some of which is repeated here for completeness sake. While the rule development process here is simplified for explanatory purposes, you will face detailed statutes and rules governing the APA process, whether it is regular or emergency rulemaking. Chapter 3 provides a good overview of the formal process. You must have access to expertise in your state's APA in order to participate effectively and protect your principal.

What goes on *prior to the APA formal notice* of rulemaking is critical to influencing the final rule before it is too late. Chapters 4 and 5 discussed in detail pre-notice activities in which interest groups may have reached agreements with the agency about the contents of the final rule. After these pre-notice activities both staff and special interests may consider the rule to be a *done deal* such that the rule adoption hearing itself is a mere formality to ratify what staff has already decided.

In this chapter, we introduced you to some central rulemaking concepts including force of law, general application, substantial interest, and standing. We also looked at why agencies develop rules, as well as several of the triggers that motivate them to enter into rulemaking.

We also covered how to conduct yourself at the rule adoption hearing and the importance of building a favorable rulemaking record with oral testimony and written submittals. Oral testimony is tailored to the nature of the presiding authority that you will be addressing. Written testimony is for the rulemaking record and should be detailed enough to advance your principal's interests. Use written testimony to pad the record for a possible rule challenge. The utility of your oral testimony depends on the nature of the presiding body.

On the other hand with political appointees you may have more opportunity to sway them toward broader ends than agency facts and law. They are called *political appointees* because they are also broad policy people.

Our next chapter, *Post-Rulemaking* discusses responding to an unfavorable agency rule, judicial presumptions of agency correctness, and that in challenging an agency action you may as a collateral experience one of an agency's most powerful tools to elicit your compliance, that is, the regulatory enforcement process.

CHAPTER 7

POST-RULEMAKING

With the rule adopted, it is now time to comply with it, fight it, or do both. In the course of your participation in the rulemaking process, with each change you estimated your principal's financial costs for recordkeeping, procedural, engineering, and operational changes, as well as time requirements. Your in-house policy question now is: do you gear up for compliance or do you not spend those resources and instead apply them to any last-ditch efforts to stop the rule from going into effect; or do you do both? If you choose to fight, then your initial steps must be APA immediate to avoid statutory limits on the timing of appeals.

The agency has incorporated into its rollout plans the time necessary for regulated parties to meet the new rule's requirements. In many instances, it has variance procedures in cases of extraordinary hardships in complying. From many years as a compliance manager in the highly regulated electric power and battery manufacturing industries, including negotiating with agency officials over engineering related compliance agreements, serving as an agency enforcement officer, and lobbying several state and federal agencies, Bob can say with some certainty that the agency will do all it can to work with a *cooperative* principal to achieve compliance. The operative word is *cooperative* especially for those who during informal and formal regulatory proceedings showed themselves to be *agency resources.*

Those who were problems or were viewed as non-cooperative may face agency revenge as described below in the section entitled, "The Process Is the Punishment."

However, there are times when the rule is simply intolerable for your principal and you are charged with changing it. The sequence of steps below intentionally starts with the easiest and then moves to the most difficult to achieve.

Responding to an Unfavorable Rule

In many of the steps below, you will have to hire professional lobbyists and attorneys, and it is going to be long and expensive, economically and politically. The agency has not spent months or years of work developing the rule and now, when facing the prospect of having to reenter into rulemaking, is unlikely to surrender easily. The suggestions below are listed in order of ease and likelihood of success:

- Lobby the Governor and political appointees
- Lobby the legislature's administrative agency oversight committee
- File with the agency a petition to initiate rulemaking to reconsider objectionable section(s) of the rule or delay their effective date(s)
- Administrative challenge
- Judicial challenge
- Lobby the legislature to amend the enabling legislation
- Lobby the federal agency to preempt state laws or regulations on the same topic
- Lobby Congress to "occupy the field"

Lobby the Governor and political appointees. A Governor may have statutory authority to veto an agency rule.[261, 262] Furthermore, nominally at least, the agency works for the Governor and the agency's top administrators are the Governor's appointees. Gubernatorial appointees could be open to persuasively made arguments, as for example, lack of societal consensus over the rule, the rule is an invalid exercise in delegated legislative authority, or the agency rule adoption process was tainted by agency bias. If the Governor will not veto the rule, then the political appointees may be open to delaying its implementation. A well-connected lobbyist may be able to do this for you quietly. If not then you may have to organize and administer a grass roots effort in addition to hiring a lobbyist.

Lobby the legislature's administrative agency oversight committee. Many legislatures have authority to veto an agency rule[263, 264] and may be open to the same arguments above. Oversight of agency rulemaking is a function of the legislature as these agencies operate under a delegation of lawmaking authority from the legislative branch of government.[265, 266] With or without veto authority, all legislatures may revise the enabling legislation to deal with your problem, as discussed below.[267]

File with the agency a petition to initiate rulemaking to reconsider objectionable section(s) of the rule or delay their effective date(s). This is an optional prior step in the *exhaustion of administrative remedies*[268], a legal doctrine which generally requires an aggrieved party in an agency action to try to solve its problems with the agency before seeking judicial relief. "The doctrine also upholds 'the basic legislative intent that full use should be made of [an] agency's specialized understanding within [a] particular area of regulation' and gives an agency 'first opportunity to discover and correct its own errors[269]'." You will need specialized legal counsel to help you with each step of the administrative appeal process and, of course, with any litigation that might be pursued.[270]

Administrative challenge. Some state APAs authorize administrative challenges to agency rules.[271] The Revised Model State Administrative Procedure Act[272] provides the elements of the adjudicatory procedure. This process can take months or years to complete.

Judicial challenge. Some state APAs[273, 274, 275] authorize *direct judicial* challenges to a rule as a contested case.[276] However in other, if not most, states prior to a judicial challenge *exhaustion of administrative remedies* as the RMSAPA[277] calls for is required. This can be an expensive and long process. A stay of application of the rule may be possible during litigation.

Lobby the legislature to amend the enabling legislation. The legislature has the constitutional authority to fix your problem by revising the enabling legislation or amending the agency budget directly or by use of a bill "rider." With the support of the Governor, especially of the same party, this will go much easier. However, this may require a multi-year legislative advocacy campaign and a significant grass roots effort.[278] The annual bill enactment rate for state legislatures averages about 25 percent while individual states' rates range from 10–90 percent.

Lobby the federal agency to preempt state laws or regulations on the same topic. The Universal Waste Rule first mentioned in Chapter 2, section, "Momentary Mutualism: Give and Take Among Rulemaking Players" exemplifies a federal agency resolving conflicts among state laws. Convincing a federal agency to do this requires demonstrating the problem is widespread, the agency has preemptive authority, and that a nationwide benefit that will come from a federal override of the rule. This, like the next step, *Lobby Congress*, is extremely difficult to accomplish.

Lobby Congress to "occupy the field." The *Mercury Containing and Rechargeable Battery Management Act* exemplifies Supremacy Clause Congressional preemption of state laws.[279] In short, by federal preemption, the act strips U.S. states of their authority to regulate the disposal of certain batteries and products containing them. The enactment rate by Congress for many years has hovered around three percent.[280]

Bob, for the Portable Rechargeable Battery Association (PRBA) and in association with the National Electrical Manufacturers Association (NEMA), over six years lobbied in Washington, D.C. for Congress to enact the law while at the same time advocating state-by-state for state support of federal preemption. PRBA's and NEMA's members are household name global manufacturers of portable battery powered products which collaboration succeeded at both levels.

Absent a gubernatorial or legislative veto, judicial stay, or the agency voluntarily holding in abeyance its rule while amending objectionable portions, expect your principal will have to expend the resources to comply with the objectionable rule.

WEIGHTS OF EVIDENCE IN A RULE CHALLENGE

Agencies normally win rule challenges for two main reasons: adjudicator deference to the agency's determination and low evidentiary threshold in support of their decisions. Administrative and civil law judges pay considerable deference to agency decisions based upon agency expertise and legislative mandate. Judges seldom will question an agency's reliance on evidence meeting the lowest level of evidentiary weight. A common theme of judicial review is, "the court shall not substitute its judgment for that of the agency as to the weight of evidence on a question of fact."[281, 282]

Agencies must demonstrate that they relied on substantial, in Florida called *competent substantial,* evidence (see discussion below) in the rulemaking record to support the rule's adoption. To a layperson or lawyer inexperienced in administrative law, the agency's factual evidence in support of a rule may appear quite flimsy.

However, even if your position was supported by a mountain of evidence the size of Mount Everest, an administrative law judge is free to rely on contrary evidence the size of a molehill . . . consider a case that boiled down to a "battle of the experts" in which an administrative law judge is going to rule based on the expert testimony found to be more credible. Even if your expert has a doctorate from an Ivy League university and has published a treatise considered to be the ultimate authority in a particular field, an administrative law judge could theoretically base findings of fact on testimony from the opposing "expert" who received a bachelor's degree last week.[283]

This may be a useful, if rough, scale[284] for understanding the relative weights of evidence and the quality of evidence on which an agency can rely. Agencies do not have to meet these levels of evidentiary weight:

- *Beyond a reasonable doubt (~99% sure).* "Proof beyond a reasonable doubt refers to the standard of proof in criminal prosecutions. The prosecutor has the duty to convince the jury by proof beyond a reasonable doubt of each and every element of the crime before a jury should convict a defendant."[285]
- *Clear and convincing (~75% sure).* "This standard requires that the evidence show that it is highly probable or probably certain that the thing alleged has occurred."[286]
- *Preponderance of evidence (~51% sure).* "This standard means that it is more likely than not that the facts are as that which one of the parties claim."[287]

Instead, agencies have to meet the lightest level of evidentiary weight:

- "Competent substantial" or "substantial" evidence which, "although items of evidence, when viewed individually, might be sufficiently questionable that they would not be relied upon by a reasonable decision maker, when viewed together those same items of evidence might become evidence a reasonable person could accept in support of a challenged finding."[288]

The party challenging an agency may have to prove the rule is "unreasonable beyond doubt."[289] Yet the agency wins with a scintilla, that is, "the least particle . . . a mere trifle of evidence." Advise those considering a challenge to weigh their small chance of winning and high attorney fees against adjudicator agency deference and an agency evidentiary weight of nothing more than a scintilla.

THE PROCESS IS THE PUNISHMENT

The conference speaker[290], an attorney defending parties administratively and civilly charged by the United States Department of Agriculture (USDA), told his audience the following story:

An unannounced USDA inspection of a USDA licensed animal trainer was initiated in response to an activist's complaint alleging the trainer's violation of agency rules[291] promulgated under authority of the Federal Animal Welfare Act.[292] The specific allegation was that the use of a training platform in the training area reduced at that spot effective fence height to less than that required by rule. Fence height complied everywhere except at the platform. (The attorney did not reveal whether the platform was mobile such that the violation was transient.)

The trainer, attempting to protect himself by documenting the USDA inspection, took out his camera to video tape the inspection. This was his legal right.

The USDA investigator, upon seeing the camera said, "If you video tape me I'll cite you for each violation I see. If you don't video [me] we'll just call them [i.e., possible violations] teachable moments." Given the choice between certain citation[293] and "teachable moments," the trainer put away his video camera.

The attorney speculated that the inspector likely did not want to cite the trainer because had he found even a minor violation then he would have had to file a report.[294] And the trainer knew he did not have the financial resources to defend against USDA charges. Both inspector and trainer knew *the process is the punishment* thereby dissuading the trainer from acting to protect himself.

Lobby School participants have related these kinds of experiences many times, for example:

- Because mounting financial costs of suing the agency were financially breaking a state association, an affiliate of a large national health care advocate, it abandoned its litigation against the state department of health. Per their employee attending Bob's class, they quit even though the association was winning the litigation "every step of the way." Their substantial resources were insufficient when matched against those of the state.

- A career college challenging a state department of education's proposed rule found the state unexpectedly change its normal pattern of annual audits to monthly audits of the college's financial records. The employee said the monthly audits, while quite annoying and disruptive, resulted in their financial records being pristine. Once the rulemaking was completed, the state returned to annual auditing.

- A regulatory agency permit processor told her class that when a permit applicant annoyed her by complaining about the slowness of the permitting process, then each time the permit application made it to the top of her inbox, for revenge sake she would put it back to the bottom.

The above activities all were conducted under *color of agency authority*. Employees of state agencies can make *the process the punishment* because:

- Agency employees face little or no personal consequences for questionable tactics in the enforcement of agency rules and policy because: employees are protected under the state sovereign immunity doctrine; the state itself or public employees' unions will pay employees' legal fees; and, even when in the wrong, their jobs are protected by civil service, public employee unions generally, and collective bargaining agreements specifically.[295]

- Should a public employee "blow the whistle" on agency misbehavior, the agency, which may not be able to fire him or her, could make the job so miserable so as to force resignation. Agency non-disclosure agreements over recent years have been voided by the courts thus freeing whistleblowers to disclose agency wrongdoing. However, costs to careers are too high for many staff to act.

- Unions have great influence with lawmakers and agency political appointees, especially when workforces are highly unionized. In some cities, up to 90 percent and, in some states, 70 percent [296] of employees are shielded by public employee unions. In certain states, union political support is an electoral necessity.
- Firing a government employee is often too much trouble and so it is "up and out" for difficult employees. That is, the easiest way to get rid of a problem government employee is to promote him or her to another job outside the section in which he or she works.
- Courts routinely defer to agency implementation of their regulations.[297]
- Agency staff know few people have the financial resources to challenge an agency determined to make life hard for someone who opposes the agency's actions.
- Even if a complainant has the resources to challenge an agency, a state agency can intimidate private attorneys to abandon or not take on the complainant as a client. For example, a state university professor suing a fellow faculty member for defamation lost her legal counsel when the state university warned the plaintiff's law firm it would get no more business from the university if the firm continued representation. The withdrawing attorney told the professor he was withdrawing because, "That's just business."

Public employees aid and abet agency harassment in egregious[298] and minor ways, as when an agency official told Bob that the agency bosses ordered him to be nasty to disfavored citizens. Agency staff do not wear body cameras to document their misbehavior. Minor abuses by public employees are so common as not worth reciting here.

When the agency decides to take heightened interest in ensuring your principal conforms to agency rules or permit conditions, be forewarned that an agency may visit frequently and choose to overcharge many infractions expecting at least some to be upheld in litigation. Getting just one charge to stick ensures the agency will prevail in an administrative or judicial proceeding. For example, the inspector alleged numerous minor violations of non-compliance. Upon reinspection, the charging inspector was on vacation. The substitute inspector commented to Bob he did not understand why his colleague wrote up so many minor infractions. However, in litigation an agency prevails if a judge upholds even one trivial charge. So for conservation of time, money and aggravation we advise at least in minor cases, do not push back, do what the inspector wants, and move on because *the process is the punishment.*

Further, the administrative law judge hearing the case may feel a sense of pressure in favor of his or her employing agency: "Many Article I judges are not afforded judicial tenure and feel pressured to decide cases in favor of their agencies."[299]

A former USEPA attorney told Bob his agency wins in court 90 percent of the time because of presumptions of agency correctness and judicial deference to agency interpretation and administration of statutory law and agency rules. A state agency's administrative law judge confided to Bob that in his court citizen defendants almost always lose saying, "The whole process is so stacked against them."

COUNT THE COST BEFORE YOU CHALLENGE AN AGENCY

Before considering challenging an agency, a regulated party should consider the direct and indirect costs of doing so. Direct outlays include attorney fees, court costs, potential fines, or suspension of permits and licenses, and excessive scrutiny and demands for compliance modifications by the agency. Indirect costs can include negative publicity, loss of community goodwill, and an on-edge workforce fearful for their own jobs and wellbeing upon becoming an object of increased agency enforcement concern.

Bob has first-hand experience with vengeful employees using an agency's anonymous tip line to get back at their employer by falsely reporting company wrongdoing. His time as an agency enforcement officer and later as a corporate regulatory compliance manager taught him that immediately doing what the agency inspector advises makes for the fastest and least complicated way to realize a favorable cost-benefit return-on-investment and to avoid *the process being the punishment.*

THAT THE PROCESS *CAN BE* THE PUNISHMENT DOES NOT MEAN THE PROCESS *WILL BE* THE PUNISHMENT

Madison and the Founders understood the human soul. As Professor Teachout, quoted in Chapter 1, wrote,

> Madison and other Framers . . . believed themselves open-eyed and resigned to the fact that "man in his deepest natures was selfish and corrupt; that blind ambition most often overcomes even the most clear-eyed rationality; and that the lust for power was so overwhelming that no one should ever be entrusted with unqualified authority." They sought to design a system that could withstand the moral failings of normal humans, instead of one that could only be managed by angels. But with a few exceptions, they did not discount the importance of virtue—at least "virtue enough for success."[300]

They saw in government at least the seeds of the administrative state. Madison wrote as we noted in Chapter 1, "When the legislative and executive powers are united in the same person or body . . . there can be no liberty, because apprehensions may arise lest THE SAME monarch or senate should ENACT tyrannical laws to EXECUTE them in a tyrannical manner." But they could not have envisioned governments spending billions of dollars annually, employing millions of job-protected experts, to fulfill mission statements written by tens of thousands of executive agencies.

We believe the testimony of Lobby School students and others to the almost unstoppable power of the *headless fourth branch of government.* On the other hand, our experience with agencies—however limited—

has been much more benign. We have found agencies much more interested in fulfilling mission statements than in punishing well-meaning regulated parties who happened to make a mistake. To illustrate,

> The technician called frantically reporting that he mistakenly turned the wrong valve thereby putting high concentration sulfuric acid[301] (H_2SO_4) into the discharge receiving creek rather than into the power plant cooling tower. The accidental discharge of highly corrosive acid created an environmental and human hazard and broke permit requirements and state law. Bob immediately reported the accident to the regulatory agency, began monitoring and guarding the slow-moving slug of H_2SO_4, and positioned downstream a tanker truck of potassium hydroxide (KOH). When the H_2SO_4 arrived, the metered release of KOH neutralized the acid. But more significant to environmental remediation was a nearby downstream sewage treatment plant's discharge of treated water into the same stream. Its flow, orders of magnitude greater than the power plant's discharge, diluted the effects of the accident to being immeasurable. But for some dead fish, the accident had no ill effect on person, property, or environment.

But what should the agency do about penalizing the utility for illegal discharges of H_2SO_4 and KOH into waters of the state? Violations of which they are aware must be prosecuted and penalized. However, they can tailor non-compliance penalties to fit the circumstances and severity of the violation.

The power company did everything right to remedy our accident including immediately reporting non-compliance to the agency. In the end, they assessed a Chapter 2, section, "Agency Tools" "fix-it ticket." The regulatory agency required reengineering of the valve system to ensure such an accident could never occur again. End of story, but not end of lesson.

Yes, agencies have the power and discretion to abuse; and they do abuse at times. Legislative and judicial deference to agencies places regulated interests in an administrative system "so stacked against them" that few organizations have the financial resources to resist government. Plus, few are going to court over agency nastiness done *under color of authority*. Under the law agencies can be quite ugly, intimidating, hostile, and demanding.

While the process *can be* the punishment, that does not mean the process *will be* the punishment. Our work with local, state, and federal agencies demonstrates that staff are usually dedicated first to carrying out their mission statements and then moving on to solve the next case of child abuse, environmental contamination, or tax evasion. They do not exist to make difficult running a business or practicing a profession as long as these activities comply with state regulations.

Our advice is to defer to agency's demands while at the same time trying to moderate them. Suggest better ways for them to achieve their goals; ways that will burden your principal less. With a good attitude, collaborate with them. And, if you cannot be a resource, at least be a client.

Behave with scrupulous honesty and adherence to the law and conditions of your permit or license. Treat them with the greatest of respect. And, it is always acceptable to ask, "Could you please show me where in the enabling legislation you believe the department has the authority to adopt this standard?"

Participate in rulemaking so as to advance their mission statement and optimize their rules to facilitate your principal's interests. Even if they do not like you, expect that they will adhere to the APA and enabling legislation. And, if you do have to fight them, then we as lobbyists recommend you look first to legislative solutions rather than judicial and to guide you along that path consider our other manuals in the *Insiders Talk* series.

SUMMARY

In this chapter we discussed what you can do once an unfavorable agency rule is promulgated, that is, comply or fight or both.

The likelihood is remote that you will reverse an agency rule judicially even with good litigation counsel, who may be already hired and ready to go. Unless you can get an immediate veto by the Governor or legislature, the rule challenge process will be costly financially and politically.

Agencies resent opposition by regulated parties and may *under the color of authority* and over the long term exact a price from your principal that is much higher than you expected, such as more frequent unannounced inspections, harassment, or audits. The next chapter discusses additional advantages of positive agency relationships in an adjudicatory setting and overviews self-defensive actions by regulated parties.

WHAT YOU SHOULD LEARN, ACCEPT AND CHALLENGE ON AGENCY REGULATORY ENFORCEMENT AND ADJUDICATIONS

Editors' note: A multi-state administrative litigator wrote this chapter. Chris and Bob have considerable rulemaking experience but little transferrable experience in adjudication. But because adjudication is often a principal's final step in effecting its regulatory environment, we requested our expert write this chapter. His guidance will enable you to give a thoughtful, initial response to your principal, association, or coalition when they solicit your views on suing an agency, administratively or judicially. In deference to this litigator, we have generally maintained his original page formatting. We are very grateful for his contribution to your education and this manual.

A. UNDERSTANDING THE HISTORY OF ADMINISTRATIVE LAW AND AGENCY ENFORCEMENT OF REGULATIONS AND ORDERS

1. HISTORY OF ADMINISTRATIVE ENFORCEMENT

Unlike most American law which dates from the founding of the republic in the late 1700s, and which imported English common law derived from the Magna Carta Libertatum ("Great Charter of Freedoms"), commonly referred to as "the Magna Carta," "administrative law" is a mostly 20th Century legal term. Every king, queen, or sovereign, including our state and federal governments, must delegate authority to get the people's business done.

"Administrative Law is therefore that part of the public law which fixes the organization and determines the competence of the administrative authorities, and indicates to the individual remedies for the violation of his rights."[302]

Of course, some abuse of authority is inevitable when ministers wielding the power of the sovereign order citizens to do something or to not do something. The great European law tradition brought to America by colonists was intensely focused on the rights of individuals to not be unfairly pushed around by monarchs. To their credit, most agencies and public servants respect the rights of citizens.

2. BALANCING THE INTERESTS OF GOVERNMENT AND ITS CITIZENRY

At the state level, we accept that public servants must make the trains and planes run, license the health care workers and hospitals, regulate commerce, and make sure our food is safe. As a result, we must defer to their judgments to a greater or lesser extent to enjoy public services and the privileges of citizenship.

However, for over 100 years of administrative law, a basic tenant is that the rights of individuals must be protected. "The chief concern of administrative law, on the other hand, as of all other branches of civil law, is the protection of private rights, and its subject-matter is therefore the nature and the mode of exercise of administrative power and the system of relief against administrative action."[303]

Each state legislature determines how to resolve the competing rights of the state, the public, and those directly impacted by administrative enforcement and adjudication. Under the due process clause of the 14th Amendment, citizens cannot be deprived of their property, professions, licenses, or freedom to ply their trades and enter into contracts for business purposes except upon due process of law. It has long been the rule that, whether "due process must be administrative process or judicial process, depends upon the character of the transaction."[304]

In order to allow deliberate balancing of the rights of the state with the rights of the individual, it is now the American administrative law tradition that the individual must seek an agency adjudication before resorting to the judiciary. This is called "administrative exhaustion" or the "exhaustion of administrative remedies," and it is a fundamental doctrine of public administration, not just a roadblock as it may often seem to litigants.

B. THE BASIC RULES OF AGENCY ENFORCEMENT AND ADJUDICATION

1. AGENCIES ARE PARTISAN POLITICAL ENTITIES, LIKE THEY ARE SUPPOSED TO BE

In carrying out their mission, agencies are supposed to be as partisan as the gubernatorial administration that appointed their highest leadership. Like the President, the 50 Governors, Congress, and the state legislatures, administrative agencies must be understood for what they are—*political bodies carrying out political promises to the voters, activists, industry, and large donors.*

You must not let an attitude of cynicism blind you to the reality that effectuating political agendas is a legitimate and necessary function in a democracy. Regulatory enforcement and agency adjudications can often be just as important as court cases. Whether to make environmental regulation more or less rigid, public benefits easier or more difficult to obtain, or increase or reduce the number of licensed lawyers, doctors and electricians, all of these are legitimate regulatory objectives.

Agencies are supposed to be zealous advocates not for the individual, company or industry, but for their agency's mission. If you are a party to an enforcement action or adjudication, it is unrealistic to expect the process to feel fair and impartial. In fact, it is an adversarial process between you and the government. You want to win, and the agency wants to win. So long as hearing officers and administrative law judges follow the law, they are acting legitimately in selecting winners and losers under regulatory regimes.

Agency hearing officers and administrative law judges normally side with the government, and unapologetically explain that the agency is an expert in the field, and its decisions are for the benefit of the public at large. However, it would be a mistake to view the process as rigged, for agency adjudications sometimes result in the agency losing, and even being reprimanded for acting arbitrarily or without the required due process of law.

2. AGENCY ADJUDICATIONS MUST ACCORD CITIZENS DUE PROCESS OF LAW UNDER THE ADMINISTRATIVE LAW STANDARD OF PROOF AND JUDICIAL REVIEW

Due process means that the basic rules of notice and opportunity to be heard and contest an agency action must be afforded to the parties in every enforcement action and adjudication. The agency must provide you with clear written notice of the time, place and issues for the adjudication. There must be an impartial hearing officer or judge whose own job duties will not be affected by the outcome.

If it is determined that the case is not frivolous, but has sufficient merit for a full hearing, then there must be an opportunity to call your own witnesses and cross examine those of the agency or other parties. You must be allowed to submit documentary evidence and have an opportunity to review the agency's documents before the hearing. The adjudication cannot be a trial by ambush or a game of hiding the ball.

Moreover, the hearing officer or administrative law judge must issue a decision in writing in which the evidence pro and con is summarized and the governing law and regulations and their application to the case are explained. The entire administrative record must be compiled and organized so as to make meaningful judicial review possible.

"Procedural due process" is not the same thing as "substantive fairness." The agency must accord you due process but, if that is accorded to you, an adjudication against you will be upheld even if most reasonable people would agree the outcome was unfair. A fundamental principle of procedural due process of law in American jurisprudence is that an unfair outcome will be upheld by the courts if reached by a lawful process. This disconcerting concept is best illustrated by the "actual innocence" rule where it is not necessarily good legal grounds to vacate a criminal conviction of innocent persons so long as due process of law was followed in convicting them.[305]

The destruction of a business or evisceration of an entire industry is not an unlawful outcome from agency rulemaking or adjudication if carried out in accordance with the law. Social injustice and economic calamity are matters for the legislature or elections, not for agency adjudications and the courts. Due process of law guarantees fair procedures, not fair outcome, whether it is in an agency adjudication or in a U.S. Supreme Court case.

3. PLAY FOR THE LONG GAME IN ENFORCEMENT ACTIONS AND ADJUDICATIONS

Agency adjudication should be approached strategically and not in an "all or nothing" fashion. The more in line your view of the law and regulations is with that of the agency, the fairer and just the process will seem. It can be a thin line between agency rulemaking and agency adjudication, especially because agencies sometimes engage in rulemaking in anticipation of adjudications and judicial review.

After all, agency adjudications have as a central purpose the enforcement of the rules that the agency itself has promulgated, and may silently advance rules the agency would soon like to adopt, or legislative initiatives in the state capitol. The more politically attuned and savvy your team, the more realistic and sophisticated your expectations will be in an adjudication or enforcement action.

The less distance between your position and that of the agency, the greater the prospects for at least a partial win. Unlike most court proceedings in which one party wins or loses completely, agency adjudications are more fertile terrain for partial wins or less than total losses. The ideal outcome of an agency adjudication is to win everything, but the practical outcome is to win something. Large industries approach agency adjudications like a football game.

While the long touchdown pass in the closing minutes of a tie game is the dream for total victory in the case before it, a partial win, or indeed simply minimizing the magnitude of the loss, moves the ball down field in small increments, case-by-case, as the industry shapes the law over a period of years.

Industry groups may have ten-year game plans for incremental gains, and they almost never are looking only at the cases immediately before them. Similarly, if you obtain a partial victory in your agency adjudication, you may be able to leverage it in future rulemaking activity or lobbying before the legislature. In short, the most successful agency adjudicators play for the long game.

C. The Advanced Rules of Agency Enforcement and Adjudication

1. Orient Your Team to a Non-adversarial Attitude in Enforcement Actions and Adjudications

Oprah Winfrey is credited with this inspirational quotation: "The greatest discovery of all time is that a person can change his future by merely changing his attitude." So, it is when coping with administrative enforcement of agency regulations and orders, whether you are trying to get the agency to act against someone else, or to not act against you.

Just as an interested party who is oriented to a "win all or nothing" approach will almost certainly earn the latter, if you regard the agency as the enemy, you can expect to be treated that way in the adjudicatory proceeding.

If you show an attitude that the agency is incompetent or corrupt, expect adverse consequences. The best attitude is one that shows respect for the agency position, but with respectful dissent and amicable efforts to move the agency viewpoint toward yours. You will be in a stronger position on judicial review if the hearing officer or administrative law judge rules that, while you lost the case overall, you won on two or three issues of regulatory law. The less the distance between your positions and the administrative order being appealed, the greater is your chance of winning something with the reviewing court.

Similarly, if you win the adjudication, you have better odds of keeping that win if the hearing officer's or administrative law judge's written decision does not begrudge your success. An aggrieved private party who appeals your win will be better positioned to reverse it if the administrative order reads like "despite their contumacious and argumentative approaches which unnecessarily delayed the adjudication, the regulated party just barely sustained its successful challenge to the agency's action."

An administrative agency needs to only show it has acted within very broad boundaries of "reasonableness" and "fairness" to win in court. Given that reality, you can lose an enforcement action even though everyone agrees your solution was fairer and more reasonable than that chosen by the agency. Your orientation and attitude, therefore, should be to try to win anything that is reasonable and fair, even if it is not what you wanted.

Never have the attitude at the start of an administrative agency matter that, if the agency rules against you, a court will see it your way. Instead, your attitude must be that, since a court is very unlikely to vacate the agency's decision, you will muster all of your persuasive will, charms and diplomacy to get the agency hearing officer or administrative law judge to at least agree with you on something, anything. That attitude is most likely to result in an outcome that feels like success.

2. SITUATIONAL AWARENESS—FEDERAL AND UNIFORM STATE STATUTES FROM SISTER STATES MAY HELP YOUR CASE

As with legislative lobbying and complex lawsuits, situational awareness is a must for maximizing short- and long-term gains or losses in an agency adjudication. Under America's federalist form of government, the state and national governments share power.[306] While federal law is "supreme" and acts of Congress can overrule or "preempt" conflicting state legislation, the U.S. Constitution imposes limits on federal sovereignty.[307] Furthermore, the states themselves are obligated to respect the laws and court judgments of sister states, called "full faith and credit."[308]

Federalism has significant impacts on administrative law. Almost every federal agency has a state counterpart and similar agency in sister states, and similar state and federal agencies often have "jurisdictional agreements" and "memoranda of understanding" with each other which themselves may have the force of law.[309] While the state agency adjudication you are facing may be the first of its kind in your state, it may well involve matters, regulations and orders issued by parallel state or federal agencies. Such orders from adjudications may constitute "persuasive authority" in your adjudicatory proceeding.[310]

Some of the most effective "national law" that is not from a federal statute results when a group of, if not all, states enact a "model" or "uniform" law. A model or uniform act establishes the same law on the same regulatory matter among the various jurisdictions.[311] These may be adopted on the premise that there is no need for every state to reinvent the wheel. A long list of uniform laws is in existence and you must determine if the law of your state is one of them. If so, then the regulations and decisions from adjudications in other states that help you may be accepted by a hearing officer or administrative law judge in your case.

Additionally, because of these common legislative regimes, common administrative law implementing them typically occurs. This means that citizen groups, activist organizations, similar businesses, and expert witnesses that are difficult to find in your state may be available to you in a nearby sister state.[312]

3. The Agency Record Will Contain Evidence that You Should Plan on Creating

The long game for agency adjudication starts well before the adjudicatory process within the agency and continues through to the end of judicial review. Skilled administrative advocates early on contemplate what kind of record an appeals court will be reviewing a year or two into the future after the hearing officer or administrative law judge issues their final decision. Every phone call you have with the agency, and every letter and email should be regarded as a potential exhibit in the record. In this sense, from day one your interactions with agency representatives constitute the start of a process of creating evidence and an administrative record that a judge may someday review. Create your evidence abundantly, wisely, and early.

D. Judicial Review and Oversight of Agencies by the Courts

Every court on judicial review of the agency action will preface its decision with words such as "we cannot substitute our judgment for that of the agency even if we would come to a different result."[313] It is not whether the reviewing court agrees with your sense of justice, but whether the court finds the agency's sense of justice to be so far out of any reasonable bounds that it cannot be accepted.

1. COURTS AFFORD AGENCIES BROAD DISCRETION IN ADMINISTERING THE STATUTES ENTRUSTED TO THEM

The state and federal Administrative Procedure Acts do not allow courts to second-guess the substantive decisions that agency adjudicators make. However, when it comes to issues over whether the agency exercised too much or too little regulatory authority, or conducted the adjudication in accordance with due process of law and prescribed procedure, courts do not hesitate to act decisively.

Effective strategy dictates that a regulated party clearly states on the agency adjudication record their objections to the scope of the agency's jurisdiction and any shortcomings in the adjudicatory procedures. You must preserve on the adjudicatory record your arguments about procedural irregularities. A party who loses on the most important substantive issues in the agency adjudication may get a do-over if a court finds that the adjudication suffered from jurisdictional or procedural defects.

2. AGENCIES ARE EXPERTS ON TECHNICAL MATTERS, BUT NOT NECESSARILY ON DUE PROCESS

Courts defer to agencies on technical matters, but not on issues of due process of law. Agencies are experts on the subject matter entrusted to them by the legislature and the executive branch. State departments of agriculture are experts on crops and livestock, departments of environmental quality are experts on water purity, and medical boards are experts on the qualifications of doctors and nurses. This expertise, however, does not necessarily carryover into agency determinations of their own jurisdiction or the required procedures and due process in their adjudications.

Just because an agency is a technical expert within a regulatory field does not mean it is a legal expert in how to administer the law or meet the requirements of due process in an adjudication. Make sure you put your objections on the record to any agency failures to afford you the procedural rights the law prescribes, no matter how minor the agency offense may seem. If you do not, you may not be allowed to bring the

194

matter up on judicial review. Courts are very inclined to closely scrutinize whether the adjudication afforded you all the procedural process protections to which you were entitled.

3. Ambiguity in the Originating Statute May Be a Feature, Not a Bug, and Opens the Door to Close Judicial Review

The "originating statute" (ed. note, *enabling legislation* in previous chapters) is the source of agency jurisdiction over regulatory issues, but the legislatures and Congress often intentionally leave ambiguity in the statutory text. This "punting" in the statutory language to a given agency and the courts is increasingly common in America's partisan divides.

Do not assume the agency wishes the statutory language was clearer—the agency itself may have authored that language to give itself maximum flexibility in rulemaking and adjudications. However, the more ambiguous a statute, the greater is the power of a court to interpret the statute for itself and to invalidate a regulation or reverse or vacate an adjudication.

4. Do Not Assume the Agency Wants to Regulate or Adjudicate Your Issue, but the Courts Might

Although it is human nature to grab power, it is also human nature to dodge responsibility for thorny matters that might cost a public servant her job or an agency its funding. Thus, despite popular myth, agencies do not always claim more jurisdiction than the legislature gave them, but often disclaim that jurisdiction or delay asserting it. Your agency adjudication may well be adversely or beneficially affected by the agency asserting it has no power to act rather than a claim that its administrative orders went too far.

If the agency's reluctance to regulate a subject matter benefits you, then you may want to encourage that position. However, reviewing courts are sensitive to situations where an agency is shirking or stalling its required regulatory enforcement, and this make courts more likely to exercise broad review powers.

5. JUDICIAL REVIEW MAY RESULT IN A MORE FAVORABLE POLITICAL ENVIRONMENT

A court decision reversing or vacating a final administrative order may allow the losing party to relitigate the substantive issues under a different and more favorable gubernatorial administration or agency director resulting from an intervening election. Sophisticated agency practitioners keep their eyes on potential changes in administrations which would result in new political appointees running the agency. Especially when a different political party takes the helm of the state government, revisions or abrogation of substantive and procedural rules, and even switching out the hearing officer or administrative law judge may result.

E. CASE STUDY

Consider the case of "The Rotting Food Was Ruining Our Lives" from Oregon. A New York family moved to a bucolic setting in southern Oregon. One day a convoy of trucks passed their quiet home and emptied food waste on the land of a neighboring cattle farmer who decided to use the waste to enrich soil and feed his animals.

The food processing companies paid the farmer per load to accept the food waste. The smell, vermin, birds, and truck noise were overwhelming to the family. After a few minutes of Google research, the family discovered that Oregon had adopted "the Right to Farm" uniform statute that shields farmers from nuisance suits over smells or noises that emanate from a farm operation that "conforms to generally accepted agricultural and management practices."[314]

The family first filed a complaint with the Oregon Department of Environmental Quality (DEQ). The DEQ told them that, because it was a farm, it fell within the jurisdiction of the Oregon Department of Agriculture (DOA). When the family objected that the food waste constituted regulated "solid waste" by the DEQ, an investigation was started. No one told the family that the DEQ and the DOA had a "Memorandum of Understanding" (MOU) for dealing with farm waste that might impact streams or rivers. As it turned out, the first line investigators and staff at the DEQ and the DOA were themselves unaware of the MOU.

After hiring experts to sample the food waste, it was discovered that some portion of it consisted of peach pits which in sufficient concentrations leaches high cyanide levels into the ground. After filing a petition for enforcement with both the DEQ and DOA, the family also filed a zoning petition with the county land-use board arguing that the property was zoned for farm use but not for solid waste disposal.

Only through extensive Google research was the family able to ascertain that each agency had some subject matter jurisdiction over the situation, but that none of the three agencies had total jurisdiction. Consequently, to some extent, all three agencies were paralyzed in exercising a regulatory power that might offend the agricultural lobby in the capitol. The family was able to get each of the agencies to issue limited "notices of proposed enforcement" against the farmer and against the national food companies that were generating the waste.

The family did the following things exactly right:

1. They worked cooperatively and respectfully with the agencies. They persuaded the regulators at each agency that under the MOU each of the agencies was shirking its legal responsibility.
2. In response to the notices of enforcement by the DEQ and the DOA, the family got signatures on a complaint from all the neighbors against the food companies. Those companies then terminated their contracts with the farmer and with the trucking company. All the companies entered into a consent order with the agencies to prevent the delivery of more food waste. But no order could be obtained to require the farmer to clean up the food waste which remained on his property.

3. Because neither the farmer nor the food or trucking companies was willing to take responsibility for the cleanup, the family filed a suit against the farmer, the food companies and the trucking company, but not against the DEQ, DOE, DOT, or land use agency. Instead, armed with the adjudicatory notices of enforcement, the family was able to argue in the lawsuit that use of such large quantities of food waste did not constitute a "traditional" farm use protected by the Right to Farm statute. While none of the agencies was willing to take a position on this issue, neither did they oppose the family. This made it possible for the family to settle the litigation.

F. Conclusion: The Fierce Politics of Judicial Review Since *Marbury v. Madison* and the Rise of the Independent Judiciary

To understand 21st Century adjudication of contested administrative law claims, as well as the role of the courts in reviewing them, *Marbury v. Madison* is a good starting point.[315] Thomas Jefferson defeated John Adams in the presidential election in 1800. Before Jefferson was inaugurated, Adams got his allies in Congress to pass a law giving the president more control over the appointment of judges. Adams and his party wanted to make things hard on Jefferson and his party by appointing 16 circuit judges and 42 justices of the peace. All that remained before these new judges could take the bench were the delivery of "commissions", pieces of paper with the United States seal simply formalizing the appointments.[316]

William Marbury was one of the frustrated new judges, and he and the other judges took their claims to the Supreme Court, arguing that they must be seated as judges because their commissions were signed, sealed, just not yet delivered. The Court agreed that Marbury and the other appointees had a vested legal right in their appointments and that the laws afforded them a remedy, presumably in a lower court.[317] The court held that the State Department and Secretary of State should deliver the commissions. But the Court refused to hear the case itself.

Marbury v. Madison is a historic example of how politics influences not only presidents and Governors, but also the agencies they use to conduct the public's business. Judicial review can itself become tainted with politics. President Adams knew that politics can be a "dog eat dog" environment against one's adversaries. Every federal and state agency knows that as well. You need to know it and understand why and how you might gain a remedy if you are wronged, just as William Marbury did.[318]

SUMMARY

We began with providing a brief history of administrative law and agency enforcement of its regulations and orders in the United States. In reviewing administrative enforcement, agencies are generally guided by their attempt to balance the interests of government and its citizenry. We then turned to looking at the basic rules of agency enforcement and adjudication and we acknowledged that agencies are partisan political entities, which means they are acting as they are supposed to be acting.

Nonetheless, agency adjudications must accord its citizens the due process of law and courts judge those agency actions based upon a standard of proof and review. Successful regulatory advocates play for the long game in these enforcement actions and adjudications.

We then examined the advanced rules of agency enforcement and adjudication and guidance to orient your team toward a non-adversarial attitude in any enforcement actions and adjudications. You should have situational awareness and know that federal and uniform state statutes from sister states adopting similar laws may help your case before a court. In your effort to lay the groundwork for a successful appeal of the regulatory action, you need to build the regulatory record and plan to help ensure relevant evidence is contained in the agency record.

Judicial review of regulatory and enforcement actions requires appropriate oversight of agencies by the courts. Keep in mind that courts afford agencies a broad amount of discretion when they administer the statutes that are entrusted to them by the legislative branch of government. This is due to the fact that these agencies are viewed as experts on technical matters.

However, this does not mean the agencies are experts on due process requirements that they must follow. Ambiguity in the originating statute (or enabling legislation) may open the door to close judicial review of your matter. And, even though the agency may not want to regulate or adjudicate your issue, the courts may be inclined to do so.

About the Authors

Chris is an experienced lobbyist, author, and attorney and Bob is former agency staff, corporate compliance manager, attorney, and lobbyist. Both are also part-time educators sharing a love for the lobbying profession and passion to improve its practice and its practitioners.

Robert L. Guyer served as Legislative Counsel for the Ralston Purina Company; Manager of Legislative Affairs for Energizer Power Systems, and Gates Energy Products, Inc.; and as a contract lobbyist, Director of Legislative and Regulatory Affairs for the Rechargeable Battery Recycling Corporation for which he lobbied internationally. He managed domestic lobbying in 20 U.S. states and Washington, D.C. Prior to becoming a lobbyist, he served as a regulatory agency field inspector and later managed regulatory compliance for an electric utility. Since 2000 he has focused on training lobbyists in skills for effective state government affairs. His live lecture <u>client list</u> speaks to the wide and diverse interest, quality, and appeal of his live training. The 15-video online series the _Campaign Method for More Effective State Government Affairs_ is similar to his other live seminars, both standard and customized.

He has authored seven books including the six-volume _Insiders Talk_ series of lobbying manuals. Thousands of individuals, associations, corporations, and universities use his materials for teaching and implementing successful advocacy. Guyer developed and taught the graduate

course *Lobbying* at Florida State University and has
lectured at Harvard University, University of Florida, University of Texas—Austin. More at lobby-
school.com.

Mr. Guyer holds Juris Doctor, Bachelor of Science
in Civil Engineering, and Bachelor of Arts degrees.
He is admitted to the practice of law in Florida and
the District of Columbia.

Chris Micheli is an attorney and lobbyist in Sacramento, California
where he regularly testifies before policy and fiscal committees of the
California Legislature, as well as a number of administrative agencies,
departments, boards, and commissions. He regularly drafts legislative
and regulatory language and is considered a leading authority on state
tax law developments and the California legislative process.

Over the last twenty years, he has published hundreds of articles and
editorials in professional journals, newspapers and trade magazines,
whose diverse subjects range from tax incentives to transportation
funding. He wrote a bi-monthly column on civil justice reform for
five years for *The Daily Recorder*, Sacramento's daily legal newspaper,
authoring over 100 columns. He has served on the editorial advisory
boards for both state and national publications.

Micheli has been an attorney of record in several key cases, having
argued before the Supreme Court of California (just two years out of
law school), as well as the Court of Appeal several times. He has filed
more than fifteen *amicus curiae* briefs in California
courts. Additionally, Micheli has been qualified
as an expert witness on California's knife laws in
superior court, and has appeared as an expert witness before the State Board of Equalization in several tax cases.

He is a graduate of the University of California,
Davis with a B.A. in Political Science—Public

Service and the University of the Pacific, McGeorge School of Law with a J.D. degree. He currently serves as an Adjunct Professor of Law at McGeorge where he teaches the course Lawmaking in California. He resides in Sacramento, California with his wife, Liza, two daughters, Morgan and Francesca, and son, Vincenzo.

ENDNOTES

1   For example, see the *Insiders Talk* series of best practices lobbying manuals and *The Campaign Method for More Effective State
Government Affairs* at www.lobbyschool.com.

2   C-suite, "[T]he group of the most important managers in a company, for example, those whose titles begin with the letter C, for
'chief.'" *The Cambridge Dictionary* (accessed December 23, 2020).

3   Due to the perception that agencies are largely unaccountable,
they have been called the "headless fourth branch of government." Verkuil, Paul R., "The Purposes and Limits of Independent Agencies," *Duke Law Journal* (1988) http://scholarship.
law. duke.edu/cgi/viewcontent.cgi?article=3032&context=dlj,
257. Professor Verkuil's footnote to the use of the term reads:
"PRESIDENT'S COMM. ON ADMIN. MANAGEMENT,
REPORT WITH SPECIAL STUDIES 37 (1937) (known as
the Brownlow Report). The 'fourth branch' image has become
the standard way of describing the bureaucracy, not just the independent agencies, in most standard textbooks as well as in judicial opinions. See, e.g., *Process Gas Producers Group v. Consumer
Energy Council of Am.*, 463 U.S. 1216, 1218-19 (1973) (White,
J., dissenting); J. ROHR, TO RUN A CONSTITUTION 153
& n.77 (1986)."

4   "States with Most Government Employees: Totals and Per Capita Rates," *Governing* (accessed July 27, 2020) https://www. governing.com/gov-data/public-workforce-salaries/states-most-government-workers-public-employees-by-job-type.html.

5   Muchmore, Lynn R. and Thad L. Beyle, eds. *Being Governor: The View from the Office* (Durham, NC: Duke University Press, 1983), 126.

6   Nussbaum, Thomas and Chris Micheli. "California State Agencies and Their Role in Public Policy," *California Globe* (September 16, 2019) https://californiaglobe.com/section-2/state-agencies-and-their-role-in-public-policy/.

7   For example, agencies must rigorously adhere to their states' administrative procedure acts while legislatures can suspend a chamber's procedural rules in the best interests of legislative efficiency.

8   "Revised Model State Administrative Procedures Act," *National Conference of Commissioners on Uniform State Laws* (July 9-16, 2010) https://www.uniformlaws.org. Henceforth, "RMSAPA."

9   Peabody, Bruce. "Separation of powers: An invitation to struggle," *The Conversation* (January 28, 2019) https://theconversation. com/separation-of-powers-an-invitation-to-struggle-110476.

10 "But as Justice Brandeis sagely observed, suggesting the value of inter-branch friction: The doctrine of the separation of powers was adopted . . . not to promote efficiency but to preclude the exercise of arbitrary power. The purpose was, not to avoid friction, but by means of the inevitable friction incident to the distribution of the governmental powers among the three departments, to save the people from autocracy." *Myers v. United States*, 272 U.S. 52 (1926) at 293 (Brandeis, J., dissenting). Michael B. Browde, "Separation of Powers in New Mexico: Item Vetoes, State Policy-Making, and the Role of State Courts," *Mitchell Hamline Law Review*: Vol. 45: Iss. 2, Article 3. (2019) https:// open.mitchellhamline.edu/mhlr/vol45/iss2/3.

11   "Separation of Powers--An Overview," *National Conference of State Legislatures* (May 1, 2019) https://www.ncsl.org/research/about-state-legislatures/separation-of-powers-an-overview.aspx. For more on California's separation of powers doctrine, see Micheli, Chris. "Separation of Powers Doctrine in California," *California Globe* (November 22, 2019): https://californiaglobe.com/section-2/separation-of-powers-doctrine-in-california/.

12   Id.

13   "While separation of powers is key to the workings of American government, no democratic system exists with an absolute separation of powers or an absolute *lack of* separation of powers. Governmental powers and responsibilities intentionally overlap; they are too complex and interrelated to be neatly compartmentalized. As a result, there is an inherent measure of competition and conflict among the branches of government. This, again, is the system of checks and balances as practically applied. Throughout American history, there also has been an ebb and flow of preeminence among the governmental branches. Such experiences suggest that where power resides is part of an evolutionary process." Id.

14   "Yet by 1987, forty-three states had instituted a budget line-item veto and ten states allowed Governors to reduce amounts of items, as well as flatly veto them. In addition, several state constitutions mandate that the Governor submit a draft budget to the legislature and that the 'executive' budget form the basis for legislative deliberations." Tarr, G. Alan, "Interpreting the Separation of Powers in State Constitutions," *NYU Annual Survey of American Law*, 59 N.Y.U. Ann. Surv. Am. L. 329 (2003-2004) https://heinonline.org/HOL/LandingPage?handle=hein.journals/annam59&div=20&id=&page=.

15   Bishop, Rob. "Federalism: The Founders' Formula for Freedom." (May 21, 2010) https://robbishop.house.gov/media/op-eds-speeches/federalism-founders-formula-freedom.

16   Teachout, Zephyr. "The Anti-Corruption Principle," 94 Cornell

L. Rev. 341 (2009), 380.

17   Id. 376.

18   Id. 374.

19   Id. 397.

20   Cornelius, Doug. "The Anti-Corruption Principle in the U.S. Constitution," *Compliance Building*, Cornell University Law School (January 16, 2009) https://www.compliancebuilding. com.

21   "Statutory Law is the term used to define written laws, usually enacted by a legislative body. Statutory laws vary from regulatory or administrative laws that are adopted by executive agencies, and common law, or the law created by prior court decisions." "Statutory Law," *HG.org* (accessed May 18,2020) https://www. hg.org/statutory-law.html. .

22   "It is far more rational to suppose, that the courts were designed to be an intermediate body between the people and the legislature, in order, among other things, to keep the latter within the limits assigned to their authority... that where the will of the legislature, declared in its statutes, stands in opposition to that of the people, declared in the Constitution, the judges ought to be governed by the latter rather than the former." Hamilton, Alexander. "The Judiciary Department," The Federalist Papers (No. 78) (May 28, 1778) https://avalon.law.yale.edu/18th_century/fed78.asp.

23   Trials may be conducted by an agency enforcement officer, by an administrative law judge employed by the agency, or by an impartial hearing officer employed by the state in a division charged with considering conflicts between agencies and regulated parties.

24   For example, "We then hold that, under Const 1963, art 5, § 2, the Governor has the authority to transfer all the authority, powers, duties, functions, and responsibilities of a legislatively

created principal department to a gubernatorially created principal department." *House Speaker v Governor*, 443 Mich. 560 (1993) 506 N.W.2d 190.

25   "California's Stem Cell Agency was created in 2004 when 59% of California voters approved Proposition 71: the California Stem Cell Research and Cures Initiative." *California Institute for Regenerative Medicine* (accessed May 15, 2020) https://www.cirm.ca.gov/about-cirm/history.

26   For example, "State Agencies, Boards, Commissions," *State of Minnesota* (accessed June 24, 2020) https://mn.gov/portal/government/state/agencies-boards-commissions/; "State Government Executive," Title 43 RCW (Revised Code of Washington) (accessed June 24, 2020) https://app.leg.wa.gov/rcw/default.aspx?cite=43.

27   "Executive Agencies," *Justia* (updated April 2018) https://www.justia.com/administrative-law/executive-agencies/.

28   Parker, Emily. "50-State Review. Constitutional obligations for public education," *Education Commission of the States* (March 2016) https://www.ecs.org/wp-content/uploads/2016-Constitutional-obligations-for-public-education-1.pdf.

29   "Whereas the Federal Constitution creates a unitary executive, most state constitutions do not. Rather, many state constitutions create several executive-branch offices, expressly grant their occupants various powers, and provide for their separate election for each office by the people. For example, as of 2002, thirty-eight states elected their Attorney General, thirty-six their secretary of state, and thirty-six their treasurer. In addition, states have constitutionalized various agencies: the Florida Constitution, for example, creates and empowers a Game and Fresh Water Fish Commission, and the Arizona Constitution, a Corporation Commission." G. Alan Tarr, Id. 338.

30   "Internal Review of Regulation Procedures," *California Department of Consumer Affairs* (March 1, 2019) https://www.dca.

ca.gov/publications/review_reg_procedures.pdf. For a listing of these 37 entities, see: https://californiaglobe.com/section-2/ boards-and-commissions-under-the-department-of-consumer-affairs/

31   "Administrative Agency - History of Administrative Agency, Federal Administrative Agencies, State and Local Administrative Agencies, Further Readings," *Law Library - American Law and Legal Information* (accessed May 7, 2020) https://law.jrank.org/pages/4066/Administrative-Agency.html.

32   Erickson, Brenda and Kae Warnock. "Separation of Powers—Delegation of Legislative Power," *National Conference of State Legislatures* (accessed June 9, 2020) https://www.ncsl.org/research/about-state-legislatures/delegation-of-legislative-power.aspx.

33   Erickson and Warnock. Their article lists numerous citations to state legislative resources and case law.

34   Lofgren, Mike. "Essay: Anatomy of the Deep State," *Moyers on Democracy* (February 21, 2014) https://billmoyers.com/2014/02/21/anatomy-of-the-deep-state/#1.

35   Virgil. "The Deep State Becomes the Obvious State," *Breitbart* (September 28, 2020) https://www.breitbart.com/politics/2020/09/28/virgil-the-deep-state-becomes-the-obvious-state/.

36   Miriam-Webster Dictionary, "Bureaucracy" (accessed January 14, 2021) https://www.merriam-webster.com/dictionary/bureaucracy#note-1.

37   "This Constitution, and the laws of the United States which shall be made in pursuance thereof; and all treaties made, or which shall be made, under the authority of the United States, shall be the supreme law of the land; and the judges in every state shall be bound thereby, anything in the Constitution or laws of any State to the contrary notwithstanding." U. S. Const. art. VI, § 2.

38 "A constitution may be long, or it may be short. The average length for state constitutions is approximately 39,000 words. By comparison, the U.S. Constitution weighs in at a relatively brief 7,591 words, including the 27 amendments." Erickson, Brenda. "Your State's Constitution - The People's Document," *National Conference of State Legislatures* (accessed June 2, 2020) https://www.ncsl.org/blog/2017/11/17/your-states-constitution-the-peoples-document.aspx. At the opposite end of the spectrum is California's Constitution, which is just short of 75,000 words.

39 "Over the last decade voters in some of these same states, and others, have decided to attach additional amendments to their state constitutions to legalize marijuana, to allow physician-assisted suicide, to ban the use of dogs in the hunting of bear and mountain lions, to protect the privilege of gathering some types of edible seaweed, to increase the share of state budgets going to education, to ban abortion, to increase cigarette taxes, to increase the minimum wage, to either limit or increase the scope of taxes and tax rates, among other things." Simon, Christopher A., et al. *State and Local Government and Politics: Prospects for Sustainability (2nd Ed.)* (Oregon State University, 2018) https://open.oregonstate.education/government/, Chapter 5: State Constitutions.

40 "'It is more rational to suppose that the courts were designed to be an intermediate body between the people and the legislature, in order to keep the latter within the limits assigned to their authority. The interpretation of the laws is the proper and peculiar province of the courts.' —*Excerpt from* Federalist Paper No. 78, *written by Alexander Hamilton and published in 1788, part of the founding era's most important documents explaining to the people the nature of the Constitution then under consideration for ratification.*" Denniston, Lyle. "Constitution Check: Was the Supreme Court only an afterthought for the Founders?" *Constitution Daily—National Constituent Center* (May 31, 2016) https://constitutioncenter.org/blog/constitution-check-was-the-supreme-court-only-an-afterthought-for-the-found.

41 McGregor, Ruth V. "Our Founding Fathers' Vision: An Endur-
    ing Rule of Law," *Institute for the Advancement of the American
    Legal System* (September 13, 2016) https://iaals.du.edu/blog/our-
    founding-fathers-vision-enduring-rule-law.

42 "Justice [the female figure] became associated with scales to rep-
    resent impartiality and a sword to symbolize power. During the
    16th century, Justice was often portrayed with a blindfold. The
    origin of the blindfold is unclear, but it seems to have been added
    to indicate the tolerance of, or ignorance to, abuse of the law by
    the judicial system." "Figures of Justice," *Office of the Curator,
    Supreme Court of the United States* (May 22, 2003) https://www.
    supremecourt.gov/about/figuresofjustice.pdf.

43 Manuel, H. Alexander. "Judges and the Administrative State,"
    ABA Journal (May 9, 2018) https://www.abajournal.com/news/
    article/judges_and_the_administrative_state.

44 "A Deseparation of Powers?" *American Bar Association* (Janu-
    ary 1, 2018) https://www.americanbar.org/groups/public_edu-
    cation/publications/insights-on-law-and-society/volume-18/
    insights-issue-1-vol-1/a-deseparation-of-powers-/.

45 "The father of the academic field of public administration is
    generally held to be Woodrow Wilson, whose 1887 article 'The
    Study of Administration' argued that 'it is the object of admin-
    istrative study to discover, first, what government can properly
    and successfully do, and, secondly, how it can do these proper
    things with the utmost possible efficiency and at the least possi-
    ble cost either of money or of energy.'" Fukuyama, Francis. "The
    Decline of American Public Administration," *The Volker Alliance*
    (August 14, 2018) https://www.volckeralliance.org/blog/2018/
    aug/decline-american-public-administration.

46 "A Primer on Florida's Administrative Procedure Act," *The Flor-
    ida Bar* (accessed June 25, 2020) https://lsg.floridabar.org/das-
    set/cmdocs/cm255.nsf/c5aca7f8c251a58d85257236004a107f/
    d1a6fef33649cc8b852581a7006523e4/$FILE/PocketGuide-
    FloridaAPA.pdf, 1.

47   Fla. Stat. § 120.57(1)(e.) 2.d. (2009) https://www.flsenate.gov/ Laws/Statutes/2009/120.57.

48   Guyer, Robert L. *How to Successfully Lobby State Legislatures: Guide to State Legislative Lobbying, 4th edition—Revised, Updated, Expanded* (Engineering THE LAW, Inc., 2020), 51.

49   Summers, Adam. "Comparing Private Sector and Government Worker Salaries," *Reason Foundation* (May 10, 2010) https:// reason.org/policy-brief/public-sector-private-sector-salary/.

50   Mayer, Gerald. "Selected Characteristics of Private and Public Sector Workers," *Congressional Research Service* (March 21, 2014) https://fas.org/sgp/crs/misc/R41897.pdf, i.

51   Lavigna, Robert. "Why Government Workers Are Harder to Motivate," *Harvard Business Review* (November 28, 2014) https://hbr.org/2014/11/why-government-workers-are-harder-to-motivate.

52   "As of May 2012, the Bureau of Labor Statistics found that on average, workers employed by federal, state and local governments made more than those employed by the private sector. Private sector employees in all industries reported an average salary of $44,600 per year. During the same period, government workers reported an average annual salary of $51,840 -- $7,240 per year more than private-sector employees." Time, Forest. "The Pay of the Average Government Employee vs. a Private Sector Employee," *Career Trend* (Updated December 31, 2018) https:// careertrend.com/about-5155433-advantages-state-employment. html. Note: the article states the type of position greatly affects individual pay scales.

53   Khan, Sohaib. "The Advantages of State Employment," *Career Trend* (Updated December 31, 2018) https://careertrend.com/ pay-average-government-employee-vs-private-sector-employee-41973.html.

54   For example, "Federal personnel management should be imple-

mented consistent with the following merit system principles: Recruitment should be from qualified individuals from appropriate sources in an endeavor to achieve a work force from all segments of society, and selection and advancement should be determined solely on the basis of relative ability, knowledge, and skills, after fair and open competition which assures that all receive equal opportunity." 5 U.S.C. § 2301 (b)(1).

55   "State executive offices," *Ballotpedia* (accessed June 22, 2020) https://ballotpedia.org/State_executive_offices. As a state example, Micheli, Chris. "Overview of California's Executive Branch of Government," *California Globe* (March 8, 2019): https://californiaglobe.com/Governor/overview-of-californi-as-executive-branch-of-government/.

56   Hebel, Sarah. "State Regents: Should They Be Elected or Appointed?" *The Chronical of Higher Education* (October 15, 2004)   https://www.chronicle.com/article/State-Regents-Should-They-Be/10597.

57   "Independent agency. Boards, commissions, authorities and other agencies and officers of the Commonwealth government which are not subject to the policy supervision and control of the Governor..." 2 Pa. Cons. Stat. § 101.

58   "Fish and wildlife conservation commission. — There shall be a fish and wildlife conservation commission, composed of seven members appointed by the Governor, subject to confirmation by the senate for staggered terms of five years. The commission shall exercise the regulatory and executive powers of the state with respect to wild animal life and fresh water aquatic life, and shall also exercise regulatory and executive powers of the state with respect to marine life, except that all license fees for taking wild animal life, fresh water aquatic life, and marine life and penalties for violating regulations of the commission shall be prescribed by general law. The commission shall establish procedures to ensure adequate due process in the exercise of its regulatory and executive functions. The legislature may enact laws

in aid of the commission, not inconsistent with this section, except that there shall be no special law or general law of local application pertaining to hunting or fishing. The commission's exercise of executive powers in the area of planning, budgeting, personnel management, and purchasing shall be as provided by law. Revenue derived from license fees for the taking of wild animal life and fresh water aquatic life shall be appropriated to the commission by the legislature for the purposes of management, protection, and conservation of wild animal life and fresh water aquatic life. Revenue derived from license fees relating to marine life shall be appropriated by the legislature for the purposes of management, protection, and conservation of marine life as provided by law. The commission shall not be a unit of any other state agency and shall have its own staff, which includes management, research, and enforcement. Unless provided by general law, the commission shall have no authority to regulate matters relating to air and water pollution. History. —Am. C.S. for H.J.R. 637, 1973; adopted 1974; Am. proposed by Constitution Revision Commission, Revision No. 5, 1998, filed with the Secretary of State May 5, 1998; adopted 1998." Art. IV, § 9, Fla. Const.

59   For example, in Florida, "Section 7. 20 DEPARTMENTS. All executive and administrative offices, boards, bureaus, commissions, agencies and instrumentalities of the executive branch (except for the office of Governor, lieutenant Governor, secretary of state, Attorney General, superintendent of public instruction, and auditor) and their respective functions, powers, and duties, shall be allocated by law among not more than 20 principal departments so as to provide an orderly arrangement in the administrative organization of state government. Temporary commissions may be established by law and need not be allocated within a department, Section 8." Art. IV, § 7, Fla. Const.

60   "Section 8. APPOINTING POWER. (1) The departments provided for in section 7 shall be under the supervision of the Governor. Except as otherwise provided in this constitution or by law, each department shall be headed by a single executive

appointed by the Governor subject to confirmation by the senate to hold office until the end of the Governor's term unless sooner removed by the Governor. (2) The Governor shall appoint, subject to confirmation by the senate, all officers provided for in this constitution or by law whose appointment or election is not otherwise provided for. They shall hold office until the end of the Governor's term unless sooner removed by the Governor." Art. IV, § 8, Mont. Const.

61   "Civil Service," *The Free Dictionary* (accessed June 23, 2020) https://legal-dictionary.thefreedictionary.com/civil+service.

62   "Workers who are union members earn 26.2 percent more than non-union workers. The difference is even greater for women and people of color. Women and African Americans represented by unions earn between 29.7 and 33.1 percent more than their non-union counterparts. And Latino workers with the union advantage make 47.1 percent more than those not represented by a union." "What is a Union?" *Local 551 American Federation of State, County and Municipal Employees, AFL–CIO* (accessed August 5, 2020) https://www.afscmemn.org/local-551-minneapolis-public-housing-authority/what-union.

63   "In all cities and states, public employees have legal rights to getting notice and the opportunity to discuss their situation before they can be fired. Things get even more complicated thanks to civil service systems, which provide specific protections like the right to multiple appeals. In union environments, the process is even more complicated. More than 35 percent of public-sector workers are in unions and contractual guarantees for organized workers provide even more potent job protections." Barrett, Katherine and Richard Greene. "'You're Fired': Ways to Get Rid of Bad Government Workers," *Governing* (September 17, 2015) https://www.governing.com/columns/smart-mgmt/gov-firing-public-employees.html.

64   Holligaugh Jr,. Gary E., et al. "Why Public Employees Rebel: Guerrilla Government in the Public Sector," *Public Adminis-*

tration Review (November 9, 2019) https://onlinelibrary.wiley. com/doi/full/10.1111/puar.13118.

65   Little fear of retribution may reflect the study participants were federal workers who are protected by civil service, and public employee unions, with little fear of job loss or even demotion.

66   Hollibaugh, Id.

67   "Service First moves a huge cohort of employees--anyone with even a remotely managerial or supervisory title--into a 'selected exempt service,' all of whom do serve at will." Harney, Sarah. "Civil Service Tsunami," *Governing* (May 2003) https://www. governing.com/topics/politics/Civil-Service-Tsunami.html.

68   "Guide to The Senior Executive Service," *United States Office of Personnel Management* (March 2017) https://www.opm.gov/policy-data-oversight/senior-executive-service/reference-materials/guidesesservices.pdf.

69   Table 4.10 - Selected State Administrative Officials: Methods of Selection, "The Book of the States 2019," *Council of State Governments* (accessed June 24, 2020) http://knowledgecenter.csg.org/kc/system/files/4.10.2019.pdf.

70   "The Administrative State," *Ballotpedia* (accessed June 25, 2020) https://ballotpedia.org/State_administrative_procedure_acts. "The Administrative State" series is invaluable for rulemaking participants and students of the fourth branch of government.

71   For example in Iowa, "Definitions. 'Declaratory order' means the department's interpretation of a statute, rule or order as applied to specified circumstances. A declaratory order is issued in response to a petition for declaratory order." 761 IAC 12.1 (17A).

72   "A declaratory statement is used to obtain an interpretation of a statute, rule, or order from a state agency as applicable to a petitioner's 'particular set of circumstances.' It is a means of resolving a controversy or addressing questions or doubts about

the applicability of statutes, rules, or agency orders." Fla. Stat. §
120.565(1) (2012).

73   See also, Dudley, Fred. "The Importance and Proper Use of
Administrative Declaratory Statements." *Florida Bar Journal*,
vol. 87, no. 3, 2013, p. 41. https://www.floridabar.org/the-flor-
ida-bar-journal/the-importance-and-proper-use-of-administra-
tive-declaratory-statements/.

74   "(a) Any interested person may petition an agency for a declaration of the applicability of any rule or prior order issued by the
agency." SECTION 203. DECLARATIONS BY AGENCY.
RMSAPA. (2005 Draft) https://rb.gy/dvcx6y.

75   "Any substantially affected person may seek a declaratory statement regarding an agency's opinion as to the applicability of a
statutory provision, or of any rule or order of the agency, as it
applies to the petitioner's particular set of circumstances." Fla.
Stat. § 120.565(1) (2009).

76   SECTION 203(e). DECLARATIONS BY AGENCY.
RMSAPA. (2005 DRAFT) https://rb.gy/dvcx6y.

77   Bryan, Susannah. "State to Fort Lauderdale: Pay record fine for
sewage spill or invest in environment," *South Florida Sun Sentinel*
(October 7, 2020) https://www.wlrn.org/2020-10-07/state-to-
fort-lauderdale-pay-record-fine-for-sewage-spills-or-invest-in-
environment.

78   "While ozone is not emitted directly from automobiles, the
unstable compound is formed in the atmosphere through a complex set of chemical reactions involving hydrocarbons, oxides
of nitrogen, and sunlight." "Cars and Air Pollution," *Arkansas
Energy and Environment* (accessed June 25, 2020) https://www.
adeq.state.ar.us/air/planning/ozone/cars.aspx.

79   "Any person may petition an agency to adopt a rule." SECTION
318. PETITION FOR ADOPTION OF RULE. RMSAPA
(2005 draft) https://rb.gy/dvcx6y.

80   For example in Arizona, "If an agency rejects a petition pursuant to subsection C of this section, the petitioner has thirty days to appeal to the council to review whether the existing agency practice or substantive policy statement constitutes a rule. The council chairperson shall place this appeal on the agenda of the council's next meeting if at least three council members make such a request of the council chairperson within two weeks after the filing of the appeal." Ariz. Rev. Stat. § 41-1033. https://www.azleg.gov/ars/41/01033.htm.

81   Benesh, W. Steve. "Texas Court of Appeals Holds There Is No Right Under the Administrative Procedure Act to Seek Judicial Review of a State Agency's Denial of a Petition for Rulemaking," *JDSupra* (July 28, 2014) https://www.jdsupra.com/legalnews/texas-court-of-appeals-holds-there-is-no-35741/.

82   "APPEAL OF DENIAL OF PETITION FOR RULEMAKING BY SAVE OUR SUMMERS, et al., RELATING TO THE ADOPTION OF WHEAT STUBBLE BURNING RFGULATIONS THAT WOULD PROTECT THE MEDICAL HEALTH AND WELFARE OF THE PUBLIC," (February 5, 2001) http://www.buffalogirlsproductions.com/dev/sos/appeal.pdf.egal.html. See also, *Recommendation from the Agricultural Air Quality Task Force to U.S. Department of Agriculture* (November 10, 1999) https://rb.gy/fc6vxg.

83   "Before the effective date specified in Section 317, the agency may withdraw the adoption of a rule by giving notice of the withdrawal to the [rules review committee] and to the [publisher] for publication in the [administrative bulletin]." SECTION 703. [RULES REVIEW COMMITTEE] PROCEDURE AND POWERS. RMSAPA.

84   "(a) At least [30] days before the adoption of a rule, an agency shall file notice of the proposed rulemaking with the [publisher] for publication in the [administrative bulletin]." SECTION 304. NOTICE OF PROPOSED RULE. RMSAPA.

85   "An agency may not adopt a rule that differs from the rule pro-

posed in the notice of proposed rulemaking unless the final rule is a logical outgrowth of the rule proposed in the notice." SECTION 308. VARIANCE BETWEEN PROPOSED AND FINAL RULE. RMSAPA.

86 "The agency may extend the time for adopting the rule once for an additional [two years] by publishing a statement of good cause for the extension but must provide for additional public participation as provided in Section 306 before adopting the rule." SECTION 307. TIME LIMIT ON ADOPTION OF RULE. RMSAPA.

87 For example in Washington state, "An agency may not modify time limits relating to rule-making procedures..." Wash. Rev. Code § 34.05.080(1). Variation from time limits.

88 "A rule is arbitrary if it is not supported by logic or the necessary facts; a rule is capricious if it is adopted without thought or reason or is irrational..." Fla. Stat. § 120.57(1)(e.) 2.d. (2009) https://www.flsenate.gov/Laws/Statutes/2009/120.57.

89 "In Florida, a statewide sulfur oxides group, funded by the state's electric and gas utility companies, has funded a large sulfur oxides study... to clarify the issues of air quality and human health in Florida, particularly related to the anticipated industrial growth and the accompanying increased use of high sulfur fuel for power production." "Statement of Sulfates Research," OFFICE OF RESEARCH AND DEVELOPMENT UNITED STATES ENVIRONMENTAL PROTECTION AGENCY WASHINGTON D.C., EPA-600/8-77-004 FEBRUARY 17, 1977, 7.

90 Kerwin, Cornelius M. and Scott R. Furlong. *Rulemaking: How Government Agencies Write Law and Make Policy*, Fifth edition (CQ Press: Thousand Oaks, California, 2019), Kindle.

91 SECTION 311. GUIDANCE DOCUMENT. RMSAPA.

92 "(a)(14) 'Guidance document' means a record of general applica-

INSIDERS TALK: GUIDE TO EXECUTIVE BRANCH AGENCY RULEMAKING

bility developed by an agency which lacks the force of law but states the agency's current approach to, or interpretation of, law, or describes how and when the agency will exercise discretionary functions." SECTION 102. DEFINITIONS. RMSAPA.

93   "We use this approach to describe and analyze the diversity in functional scale and structure among the 50 US state governments reflected in the webpages and links they have created online: 32.5 million webpages and 110 million hyperlinks among 47,631 agencies." Kosak, Stephen, et al. "Functional Structures of US State Governments," *Proceedings of the National Academy of Sciences* (November 13, 2018) https://www.pnas.org/content/115/46/11748.

94   "States with Most Government Employees: Totals and Per Capita Rates," *Governing* (accessed May 18, 2020). https://www.governing.com/gov-data/public-workforce-salaries/states-most-government-workers-public-employees-by-job-type.html.

95   For example, the Florida Constitution authorizes the legislature to create a Department Veterans Affairs (Art. IV, § 11, Fla. Const.) and Department of Elderly Affairs (Art. IV, § 12, Fla. Const.).

96   "Plaintiff Ronald Rex Ivie appeals the trial court's dismissal of his complaint against State Senator John William Hickman and State Representative Stephen H. Urquhart (Legislative Defendants). Plaintiff argues that the trial court erred in concluding that the actions of the Legislative Defendants were within the legitimate legislative sphere, and thus, they were immune from suit under the Utah Constitution. See Utah Const. art. VI, § 8 providing legislative immunity 'for words used in any speech or debate in either house'). We affirm, albeit on a different basis." *Ivie v. State*, 2004 UT App 469 https://law.justia.com/cases/utah/court-of-appeals-published/2004/ivie121604.html.

"According to Plaintiff's complaint, sometime after the budget reduction, Senator Hickman made a real or veiled threat to Department Executive Director Rod Betit, that if he did not implement the budget cuts to eliminate Plaintiff's position, Senator Hickman would push for future cuts in the Department's budget appropriations. Subsequently, Plaintiff's position was eliminated and his employment terminated. Plaintiff unsuccessfully appealed his termination to the Department head." Id.

97   "New Senate Minority Leader Charles Schumer (D-N.Y.) said Tuesday that President-elect Donald Trump is 'being really dumb' by taking on the intelligence community and its assessments on Russia's cyber activities. 'Let me tell you, you take on the intelligence community, they have six ways from Sunday at getting back at you,' Schumer told MSNBC's Rachel Maddow. 'So even for a practical, supposedly hard-nosed businessman, he's being really dumb to do this.'" Shelbourne, Mallory. "Schumer: Trump 'really dumb' for attacking intelligence agencies," *The Hill* (January 3, 2017) https://thehill.com/homenews/administration/312605-schumer-trump-being-really-dumb-by-going-after-intelligence-community.

98   "A *pyrrhic victory* is a victory that comes at a great cost, perhaps making the ordeal to win not worth it. It relates to Pyrrhus, a king of Epirus who defeated the Romans in 279 BCE but lost many of his troops." "What is a 'Pyrrhic victory'?" *Merriam-Webster* (accessed January 14, 2021) https://www.merriam-webster.com/words-at-play/pyrrhic-victory-meaning.

99   Wolfe, Julia and John Schmitt "A profile of union workers in state and local government," *Economic Policy Institute* (June 7, 2018) https://www.epi.org/publication/a-profile-of-union-workers-in-state-and-local-government-key-facts-about-the-sector-for-followers-of-janus-v-afscme-council-31/.

100   "There are 724,000 public employees in Illinois. Of those employees, 378,600, or just over half, are union members." Bauman, Naomi Lopez. "Illinois Labor-Union Membership in 10 Charts," *Illinois Policy Institute* (March 10, 2015) https://www.illinoispolicy.org/illinois-labor-union-membership-in-10-charts/.

101   "I agree that the paragraph is true. Thank you." Walt Smith, Walter Smith & Associates, Inc. email to Robert Guyer (June 25, 2020).

102   "All fifty states have enacted right-to-farm laws that seek to protect qualifying farmers and ranchers from nuisance lawsuits filed by individuals who move into a rural area where normal farming operations exist, and who later use nuisance actions to attempt to stop those ongoing operations." "States' Right-To-Farm Statutes," *National Agricultural Law Center* (accessed June 24, 2020) https://nationalaglawcenter.org/state-compilations/right-to-farm/.

103   40 CFR PART 273—STANDARDS FOR UNIVERSAL WASTE MANAGEMENT (February 19, 2021) https://www.ecfr.gov/cgi-bin/text-idx?SID=0501d91ec562faafa833c60c2404d806&mc=true&node=pt40.27.273&rgn=div5.

104   "Universal Waste," *USEPA* (accessed February 23, 2021) https://www.epa.gov/hw/universal-waste.

105   For example, "Section 112(l) of the CAA [Clean Air Act] and 40 CFR part 63, subpart E, authorizes EPA to delegate authority to any state or local agency which submits adequate regulatory procedures for implementation and enforcement of emission standards for hazardous air pollutants. The hazardous air pollutant standards are codified at 40 CFR parts 61 and 63, respectively." 83 FR 25382 (June 1, 2018) https://www.federal-register.gov/d/2018-11757/p-31, 25382-25390.

106   For example, "The Governor may exempt an agency from complying with any provision of this chapter where necessary to conform to any provisions of federal law or rules and regulations as a condition to the receipt of federal granted funds provided that…" Tenn. Code Ann. § 4-5-104.

107   "State Employment Demographics," *California State Controller's Office* (access October 2, 2020) https://www.sco.ca.gov/ppsd_empinfo_demo.html.

108   Elias, Roni A. "The Legislative History of the Administrative Procedure Act." 27 Fordham Envtl. L. Rev. 207 (2016), http://commons.law.famu.edu/cgi/viewcontent.cgi?article=1012&-context=studentworks.

109   For example, "While the term 'ultra vires' has a well-defined meaning in Latin, in the legal vernacular in Texas it is used in order to allege that public official-type folks are doing something they should not do, or refusing to do something that they should. You should not act ultra vires—you should always act intra vires. And, if you are acting ultra vires, you may be subject to a writ of mandamus or an injunction (but not money damages). That is because governmental immunity from a lawsuit applies only to claims based on actions within the scope of governmental authority; actions taken outside the scope of an official's governmental authority do not get the benefit of governmental immunity." de la Fuente, Jose E. and James Parker. "Mandamus and Ultra Vires Issues: What can happen if you go 'ultra' vires," *TCAA* [Texas City Attorneys Association] *2016 Summer Conference* (June 16, 2016) DeLaFuente_Mandamus-and-Ultra-Vires-Issues-TCAA-Summer-2016-conference.pdf.

110   "Fourth Amendment," *Cornell Law School Legal Information Institute* (accessed June 14, 2020) https://www.law.cornell.edu/constitution/fourth_amendment.

111   "A Primer on Florida's Administrative Procedure Act," Id.

112   "Tyranny Founding Fathers Quotes," *AZ Quotes* (accessed June 9, 2020) https://www.azquotes.com/quotes/topics/tyranny-founding-fathers.html.

113   Several states provide helpful guidance. For example, California's Office of Administrative Law publishes the "2020 California Rulemaking Law under the Administrative Procedure Act," https://oal.ca.gov/publications/apa_book.

114   Micheli, Chris. "Participating in California Rulemaking," *Capital Center for Law and Policy* (accessed December 28, 2020) https://

www.capimpactca.com/wp-content/uploads/sites/408/2018/01/
Participating-in-California-Rulemaking.pdf.

115 Bailey, Jeremy D. "The Execution of Laws Is More Important Than the Making of Them," *Cambridge University Press* (excerpt) (accessed July 30, 2020) http://assets.cambridge. org/97805218/68310/excerpt/9780521868310_excerpt.pdf.

116 Roni A. Elias, Id.

117 "A Primer on Florida's Administrative Procedure Act," Id., ii.

118 James Madison, Federalist 47.

119 Consider this grant of state power: "(name) has been appointed by the Governor in accordance with sect. 402.166, Florida Statutes and shall have access to all client files, reports, and records for the purpose of monitoring and investigating in any facility which is licensed, funded, or operated by DCF [Department of Children and Families] and may request copies of such records in accordance with Section 402.166, (8), F.S." [signed] Jeb Bush, Governor.

120 For example, in one state APA proper referral is the *Administrative Procedure Act*, in another it is the *Administrative Procedures Act*, in another it is *Administrative Process Act* or *(State Name) Administrative Procedure Act*, or *Uniform Administrative Procedures Act*. Despite name differences they are generically simply the *APA* and share common elements although details differ. See "State administrative procedure acts," *Ballotpedia* (accessed December 9, 2020) https://ballotpedia.org/State_administrative_procedure_acts.

121 Administrative Procedure Act, 5 U.S.C. § 555 (2006).

122 RMSAPA.

123 "Model Administrative Procedure Act for Interstate Compacts," *The American Bar Association* (January 2019) www.uniformlaws. org.

124 Bishop, Ken W. "Interstate Compacts - The Next Frontier for Administrative Procedure Rulemaking," *Council of State Governments* (accessed December 7, 2020) www.csg.org.

125 RMSAPA.

126 "There now exists a substantial body of legislative action, judicial opinion and academic commentary that explain, interpret and critique the 1961 and 1981 Acts and the Federal Administrative Procedure Act. In the past two decades state legislatures, dissatisfied with agency rulemaking and adjudication, have enacted statutes that modify administrative adjudication and rulemaking procedure... What has been learned from the experience in those states can be used to improve this Act." RMSAPA, 2.

127 For example, in Florida, "Rulemaking is not a matter of agency discretion. Each agency statement defined as a rule by s. 120.52 shall be adopted by the rulemaking procedure provided by this section as soon as feasible and practicable." Fla. Stat. § 120.54(1)(a) (2009).

128 *Sierra Club v. Thomas*, 828 F.2d 783 (D.C. Cir. 1987).

129 PUBLIC LAW 104–142—MAY 13, 1996 110 STAT. 1329.

130 40CFR273 (July 1, 2018).

131 "State Universal Waste Programs in the United States," *US EPA* (accessed July 30, 2020) https://www.epa.gov/hw/state-universal-waste-programs-united-states.

132 Beck, George A. and Mehmet Konar-Steenberg, eds. *Minnesota Administrative Procedure*, 3rd edition (Mitchell Hamline School of Law, 2014), ebook.

133 Luxton, Jane C. "Agency Efforts to Circumvent Rulemaking Requirements Proliferating," *Pepper Hamilton, LLP* (September 25, 2012) https://www.jdsupra.com/legalnews/agency-efforts-to-circumvent-rulemaking-91572/.

134   Kerwin, Cornelius M. *Rulemaking: How Government Agencies Write Law and Make Policy*, 3rd edition (CQ Press: Thousand Oaks, California, 2003), 107.

135   For example, in California, "NOTICE OF PROPOSED RULEMAKING ACTION," *California State Mining and Geology Board* (November 1, 2019) https://www.conservation.ca.gov/smgb/Documents/NOPA-OTC.pdf.

136   For example, "Florida Sample FOIA Request," *National Freedom of Information Coalition* (accessed January 23, 2021) https://www.nfoic.org/florida-sample-foia-request.

137   "Lobbyists: Definitions and Prohibited Activities," *Council of State Governments* (2005) http://www.csg.org/knowledgecenter/docs/BOS2005-LobbyistInfoTables.pdf.

138   For example in Kentucky, "An Executive Agency Lobbyist is any person who is engaged for compensation to influence executive agency decisions or to conduct executive agency lobbying activity regarding a *substantial issue* as one of his or her *main purposes*. This also includes associations, coalitions, or public interest entities formed for the purpose of promoting or otherwise influencing executive agency decisions." "Executive Branch Lobbying," *Executive Branch Ethics Commission* (Accessed July 2, 2020) https://ethics.ky.gov/lobbying/Pages/default.aspx.

139   For example in Louisiana, "To preserve and maintain the integrity of executive branch action and state government, the legislature also declares it is necessary that the identity of persons who attempt to influence actions of the executive branch and certain expenditures by those persons be publicly disclosed." "Executive Branch Lobbying," La. Stat. Ann. § 49:71-78.1 (2019) http://ethics.la.gov/Pub/Laws/Title49ExecutiveLobbying.pdf, 1.

140   For example in Maine, "Anyone may petition an agency to adopt or change a rule. When a petition is submitted by 150 or more registered voters of the State, the agency must begin rulemaking proceedings within 60 days." "Guide To Rulemaking," *Maine*

APA-Office, Secretary of State (accessed July 28, 2020) https://www.maine.gov/sos/cec/rules/guide.html.

141 "The use of the word 'wit' ... here refers to knowledge, wisdom, intelligence and humor, as it was used for wisdom and intelligence during the Shakespearean era. Hence, this phrase has won proverbial approval, which means that knowledge and intelligence need be expressed in as few words as possible." "Brevity is the Soul of Wit," *Literary Devices* (accessed June 30, 2020) https://literarydevices.net/brevity-is-the-soul-of-wit/.

142 "(c) Unless a hearing is required by law of this state other than this [act], an agency is not required to hold a hearing on a proposed rule but may do so. A hearing must be open to the public, recorded, and held at least [10] days before the end of the public comment period." SECTION 306. PUBLIC PARTICIPATION, RMSAPA.

143 "Under the APA, a rulemaking agency has the option whether to hold a public hearing on a proposed rulemaking action. If an agency does not schedule a public hearing, any interested person can submit a written request for a hearing to be held. The written request for a hearing must be submitted at least 15 days prior to the close of the written public comment period. If timely requested, the agency must hold a public hearing. (Government Code section 11346.8.) If a public hearing is held, the hearing must be scheduled for a date at least 45 days after the notice of proposed action was published. At the public hearing, both written and oral comments must be accepted." "About the Regular Rulemaking Process," *California Office of Administrative Law* (2020) https://oal.ca.gov/rulemaking_participation/.

144 This is a useful example of a definition of this term. "An ex parte communication is a communication to a board member from any person about a pending water board matter that occurs in the absence of other parties to the matter and without notice and opportunity for all parties to participate in the communication. People often refer to these communications as 'one-sided,'

'off-the-record,' or private communications between a board member and any person concerning a matter that is pending or impending before the applicable water board." Lauffer, Michael A.M. "Memorandum Transmittal of Ex Parte Communications Questions and Answers Document" and attachment "Ex Parte Questions and Answers," State Water Resources Control Board and California Regional Water Quality Control Boards (April 25, 2013) https://www.waterboards.ca.gov/laws_regulations/docs/exparte.pdf.

145 "Home Box Office, Inc. v. Federal Commc'ns Comm'n, 567 F.2d 9, 57 (D.C. Cir. 1977); see also Sierra Club v. Costle, 657 F.2d 298, 400-01 (D.C. Cir. 1981)." "'Ex Parte' Communications in Informal Rulemaking," *Administrative Conference of the United States* (June 25, 2014) https://www.acus.gov/recommendation/ex-parte-communications-informal-rulemaking#_ftn3.

146 "It bears emphasizing that such communications 'are completely appropriate so long as they do not frustrate judicial review or raise serious questions of fairness'." "'Ex Parte' Communications in Informal Rulemaking." Id.

147 Santaniello, Neil. "POWER LINE RULES SET BY PANEL LIMITS ESTABLISHED FOR MAGNETIC FIELDS," *Florida Sun Sentinel* (April 16, 1988) https://www.sun-sentinel.com/news/fl-xpm-1988-04-16-8801240088-story.html.

148 "Why do these conversations take place? In short, information collection is costly to the bureaucrat, and ex parte communications mitigate these costs." Susan Yackee, "The Hidden Politics of Regulation: Interest Group Influence on Agency Rule Development," 8. (link expired) Dr. Yackee has written much on this topic. See, "Susan Webb Yackee's research while affiliated with University of Wisconsin–Madison and other places," *ResearchGate* https://www.researchgate.net/scientific-contributions/Susan-Webb-Yackee-25624881.

149 A rule implementation plan is a master schedule for adopting proposed regulations. For each rule, section by section, it lays

out necessary activities, dates, and geographical regions to create an enforcement mechanism. In some states, the rule implementation plan is a formal published document. For example, see the "PQAC New Rules Live Implementation Plan," (Washington State) *Pharmacy Quality Assurance Commission* (accessed October 23, 2020) https://www.doh.wa.gov/Portals/1/Documents/2300/2020/PQAC-NewRulesLiveImplementationPlan.pdf. In another state, you have to ask for it and it may be an informal document known only to those in rule development, enforcement, or perhaps the Office of General Counsel. Do not be shocked if, upon asking for it, you get a blank stare from someone not involved in its development. But someone in the agency has the rollout plan itemized so contact the agency's internal rule development committee, Office of General Counsel, or the section within the agency charged with enforcement. Knowing it will help you prepare for compliance and estimate costs that may be incurred by your principal.

150 Kerwin, Cornelius M. *Rulemaking, 3rd edition*, Id., 36.

151 Kerwin, Id.

152 Kerwin, Id.

153 "When the legislative and executive powers are united in the same person or body... there can be no liberty, because apprehensions may arise lest THE SAME monarch or senate should ENACT tyrannical laws to EXECUTE them in a tyrannical manner." James Madison, Federalist 47 (Emphases in Madison's original).

154 "Voltaire > Quotes > Quotable Quote," *Good Reads* (accessed December 31, 2020) https://www.goodreads.com/quotes/88924-i-was-never-ruined-but-twice-once-when-i-lost.

155 For example, bill drafting services, legislative counsel, bill room, sergeant at arms, other chamber support services.

156 For example, Speaker's and President's or President Pro Tem-

pore's offices, committee and subcommittee chairs, members of committees of jurisdiction, majority, minority, and specialty caucus leadership, caucus staff, and other key chamber leaders.

157 Ranked in order of importance in enacting a bill are: special interests, legislative staff, executive agency staff, lawmakers themselves, governor's office, lawmakers' supporters, lawmakers' voters, and lawmakers' constituents. For example, Guyer, Robert L. *Insiders Talk: Winning with Lobbyists, Professional Edition* (Engineering THE LAW, Inc., 2018).

158 "2021 Governors and Legislatures," *MultiState Associates* (accessed January 26, 2021) https://www.multistate.us/resources/2021-governors-and-legislatures.

159 "Full and Part-Time Legislatures," *National Conference of State Legislatures* (June 14, 2017) https://www.ncsl.org/research/about-state-legislatures/full-and-part-time-legislatures.aspx.

160 For example, Florida has 31 executive agencies estimated by extrapolating the number of State Personnel System - Agency Human Resource Offices. "State Personnel System - Agency Human Resource Offices," *Department of Management Services - State of Florida* (accessed December 14, 2020) https://www.dms.myflorida.com/workforce_operations/human_resource_management/state_personnel_system_agency_human_resource_offices.

161 For example, consider in Oregon, which is a mid-sized, regulation-heavy state, the number of regulatory bodies. "State Agencies A-Z," *Oregon Blue Book* https://sos.oregon.gov/blue-book/Pages/state/list.aspx. (Accessed February 24, 2021) Note: Oregon is ranked 27th in population size but it has the sixth greatest number of regulations per Kaia Hubbard.

162 Hubbard, Kaia. "The 10 Most and Least Heavily Regulated States," *Regulatory Transparency Project* (November 3, 2020) https://regproject.org/news/the-10-most-and-least-heavily-regulated-states.

163 Champ, Norm. "Building Effective Relationships with Regulators," *Harvard Law School Forum on Corporate Governance* (September 1, 2015) https://corpgov.law.harvard.edu/2015/10/22/building-effective-relationships-with-regulators/.

164 Id.

165 For example in Florida, "CHALLENGES TO PROPOSED AGENCY RULES PURSUANT TO SECTION 120.56(2).— If the appellate court or administrative law judge declares a proposed rule or portion of a proposed rule invalid pursuant to s. 120.56(2), a judgment or order shall be rendered against the agency for reasonable costs and reasonable attorney's fees, unless the agency demonstrates that its actions were substantially justified or special circumstances exist which would make the award unjust." Fla. Stat. §120.595(2) (2015) https://www.flsenate.gov/laws/statutes/2015/120.595.

166 "Those involved in decision making in a government agency, including decision making that is done during the course of rulemaking, strive for a result that can be embraced by the agency's external clients and constituents, whether they are beneficiaries or regulated entities." Kerwin, 3rd edition, 107.

167 "Due to their non-flammability, chemical stability, high boiling point and electrical insulating properties, PCBs were used in hundreds of industrial and commercial applications including: Electrical, heat transfer and hydraulic equipment, plasticizers in paints, plastics and rubber products, pigments, dyes and carbonless copy paper." "Learn about Polychlorinated Biphenyls (PCBs)," *USEPA* (accessed July 31, 2020) https://www.epa.gov/pcbs/learn-about-polychlorinated-biphenyls-pcbs.

168 The kinds of rules an agency adopts are decided broadly by its *authorizing* statute(s) and specifically directed by topic-specific *enabling* statutes. The *authorizing* statute creates the agency and prescribes each agency's broad authority and duties. Many statutes confer wide-ranging powers to some state agencies regarding matters that directly affect the general public. The *enabling*

statute is a legislative mandate to a specific authorized agency that it carry out the stated legislative objectives of the enabling legislation. The legislature directs and funds the agency to undertake precise and detailed regulatory actions or programs. To that end, the legislature delegates to the agency its legislative authority to set policy and promulgate rules consonant with statutory implementation. It is in the rule adoption process that each page of broad statutory law leads to ten pages of detailed administrative law.

169   For example in Montana, "Rulemaking under MAPA involves four steps. (a) Contact with the primary sponsor. When an agency begins to work on the substantive content and the wording of a proposal notice for a rule that initially implements legislation, the agency shall contact the legislator who was the primary sponsor of the legislation. See 2-4-302, MCA." Mont. Admin. R. 1.3.07(4)(a) (accessed December 22, 2020) http://www.mtrules.org/gateway/RuleNo.asp?RN=1%2E3%2E307.

170   The differences between USEPA Methods 5 and 17 for measuring compliance with USEPA fossil fuel generator emission standards were the basis for the Florida Electric Power Coordinating Group's technical meeting with the Florida Department of Environmental Regulation and consulting services of Walt Smith mentioned in Chapter 2. Method 17 became the preferred emissions measurement method for fossil fuel steam generating plants in demonstrating compliance with the USEPA particulate emissions standard. The standard limited weight of particulate matter per volume of combustion gas emitted. Preference for Method 17 over Method 5 came about because Method 17 avoided the added particulate load that came from condensation of SO_2 (Sulphur dioxide) gas into solid sulphates. SO_2 is a gas released from the combustion of fossil fuels. SO_2 gas condenses into sulphate particulates as the boiler gases cool as they move along the channel used by power plants to exhaust combustion gases into the air. The added weight from condensed sulphate particulates as measured by Method 5 resulted in noncompliance with particulate air emissions standards, whereas Method

17 measured particulates in the hotter part of the channel before S02 condensed into particulates. Using Method 5 resulted in non-compliance with USEPA standards while using Method 17 demonstrated compliance, both measuring the same steam of combustion gases just at different temperatures along the exhaust route.

171   ISO = International Standards Organization. ASTM = American Society for Testing or Materials. "A standards organization, standards body, standards developing organization (SDO), or standards setting organization (SSO) is an organization whose primary activities are developing, coordinating, promulgating, revising, amending, reissuing, interpreting, or otherwise producing technical standards that are intended to address the needs of a group of affected adopters." "Standards Organization," *Wikipedia* (June 24, 2020) https://en.wikipedia.org/wiki/Standards_organization.

172   "Drinking Water & Groundwater Quality Standards/Advisory Levels," *Wisconsin Department of Natural Resources* (accessed January 1, 2021) https://dnr.wisconsin.gov/topic/DrinkingWater/HealthAdvisoryLevels.html.

173   "Rule Title: Other Contaminants Without a Standard." *Florida Department of Environmental Protection* (November 19, 1987) https://www.flrules.org/gateway/ruleno.asp?id=62-550.330&-Section=0.

174   For example, "Idaho Office of the Administrative Rules Coordinator," *Division of Financial Management* (accessed January 4, 2021) https://adminrules.idaho.gov/bulletin/index.html.

175   For example, "Proposed Regulations under Review," *California Office of Administrative Law* (OAL) (accessed (January 4, 2021) https://oal.ca.gov/proposed-regulations/.

176   For example, "Wyoming Administrative Rules," *Wyoming Secretary of State* (accessed January 4, 2021) https://rules.wyo.gov/.

177   "When an agency adopts a final rule, the agency shall issue a concise explanatory statement that contains: (1) the agency's reasons for adopting the rule, including the agency's reasons for not accepting substantial arguments made in testimony and comments;" SECTION 313. CONCISE EXPLANATORY STATEMENT. RMSAPA.

178   "Under the Administrative Procedures Act ('APA'), we uphold a final agency action unless it is 'arbitrary, capricious, an abuse of discretion or otherwise not in accordance with law.' 5 U.S.C. § 706(2). [Footnote omitted.] The standard is 'highly deferential, presuming the agency action to be valid and affirming the agency action if a reasonable basis exists for its decision.' *Bahr v. EPA*, 836 F.3d 1218, 1229 (9th Cir. 2016) (citation and internal quotation marks omitted). *Yazzie v. US Environmental Protection Agency*, (9th Cir. 2017)." Gauthier, Gary. "The Arbitrary and Capricious Standard Under the APA," *Landmark Publications* (May 23, 2017) http://www.landmark-publications. com/2017/05/the-arbitrary-and-capricious-standard.html. Blog post.

179   Id.

180   SECTION 404. EVIDENCE IN CONTESTED CASE. RMSAPA.

181   "As of May 2012, the Bureau of Labor Statistics found that, on average, workers employed by federal, state and local governments made more than those employed by the private sector. Private sector employees in all industries reported an average salary of $44,600 per year. During the same period, government workers reported an average annual salary of $51,840 -- $7,240 per year more than private-sector employees." Tambien, Erica. "The Average Salary of Government Employees," *Career Tend* (July 05, 2017*)* https://careertrend.com/facts-7470700-average-salary-government-employees.html.

182   "In addition to higher average salaries, public sector employees tend to have more access to employee benefits. For example, the

235

Bureau of Labor Statistics reports that 89 percent of local and state government workers had access to retirement benefits as of March 2013, compared to 64 percent of workers in private industry." Id.

183   *Effective Negotiating*, Karrass (accessed January 25, 2021) https://www.karrass.com/en.

184   "Peak Oil Superfund Site Tampa, Florida and Bay Drums De Minimis Administrative Order on Consent, Docket No. 95-8-C," *USEPA* (Last updated January 14, 2015) https://www.epa.gov/foia/peak-oil-superfund-site-tampa-florida-and-bay-drums-de-minimis-administrative-order-consent.

185   The constitutional problems with *delegation of legislative authority*, which took a century of constitutional litigation to develop, were discussed in Chapter 1 but, for us practitioners, these problems are not ours but belong to academics.

186   Erickson, Brenda and Kae Warnock. "Separation of Powers—Delegation of Legislative Power," *National Conference of State Legislatures* (accessed June 9, 2020) https://www.ncsl.org/research/about-state-legislatures/delegation-of-legislative-power.

187   Administrative analogs for the familiar legislative terms *bill, enroll, enact,* and *law* are *proposed rule, concurrence, adopt,* and *rule*, respectively.

188   "Enrollment, also called certification, occurs when the Speaker and Clerk of the House of Representatives and the President and Secretary of the Senate by their signatures certify that each chamber passed the bill being presented to the Governor." See Guyer, Robert L. *Insiders Talk Glossary of Legislative Concepts and Representative Terms* (Engineering THE LAW, Inc., 2019).

189   For a useful process primer, see, "The Administrative Rules Promulgation Process: A Primer," *South Dakota Legislature, Legislative Research Council* (August 2018) https://mylrc.sdlegisla-

ture.gov/api/Documents/72131.pdf.

190   "(30) 'Rule' means the whole or a part of an agency statement of general applicability that implements, interprets, or prescribes law or policy or the organization, procedure, or practice requirements of an agency and has the force of law." SECTION 102. DEFINITIONS. RMSAPA.

191   For example in Washington state, "'Rule' means any agency-order, directive, or regulation of general applicability (a) the violation of which subjects a person to a penalty or administrative sanction; (b) which establishes, alters, or revokes any procedure, practice, or requirement relating to agency hearings; (c) which establishes, alters, or revokes any qualification or requirement relating to the enjoyment of benefits or privileges conferred by law; (d) which establishes, alters, or revokes any qualifications or standards for the issuance, suspension, or revocation of licenses to pursue any commercial activity, trade, or profession; or (e) which establishes, alters, or revokes any mandatory standards for any product or material which must be met before distribution or sale. The term includes the amendment or repeal of a prior rule, but does not include (i) statements concerning only the internal management of an agency and not affecting private rights or procedures available to the public, (ii) declaratory rulings issued pursuant to RCW 34.05.240, (iii) traffic restrictions for motor vehicles, bicyclists, and pedestrians established by the secretary of transportation or his or her designee where notice of such restrictions is given by official traffic control devices, or (iv) rules of institutions of higher education involving standards of admission, academic advancement, academic credit, graduation and the granting of degrees, employment relationships, or fiscal processes." Wash. Rev. Code § 34.05.010 (16) (Effective January 1, 2020.)

192   "The essential part of this definition [of rule] is the requirement of general applicability of the statement... Applicability of a rule may be general, even though at the time of the adoption of the rule there is only one person or firm affected: persons or firms in

the future who are in the same situation will also be bound by the standard established by such a rule." RMSAPA. Comment Section 102. Definitions. (30) "Rule." 17.

193 For example, "Generally speaking, the U.S. Department of Agriculture (USDA) and FDA (Food and Drug Administration) are responsible for the core consumer protections in this complex web of regulations, largely leaving states and local governments to administer federal rules by conducting inspections and enforcing standards." Bellos, Nicholas. "How State and Federal Food Regulations Can—and Should—Work Together," *The Regulatory Review* (Nov 2, 2018) https://www.theregreview.org/2018/11/02/bellos-how-state-federal-food-regulations-work-together/.

194 Esworthy, Robert. "Federal Pollution Control Laws: How Are They Enforced?" *Congressional Research Service* (October 7, 2014) https://fas.org/sgp/crs/misc/RL34384.pdf, 11.

195 A broad overview or rulemaking may be found at "Rulemaking / Writing Agency Regulations," *Justia* (April 2018) https://www.justia.com/administrative-law/rulemaking-writing-agency-regulations/.

196 For example in Iowa, "A rule-making proceeding is pending from the time it is commenced, by publication in the Iowa Administrative Bulletin of a Notice of Intended Action pursuant to Iowa Code section 17A.4(1)'a,' to the time it is terminated, by publication of a Notice of Termination in the Iowa Administrative Bulletin or the rule becoming effective." Iowa Code 591—4.3(3) (17A).

197 "If an agency finds that an imminent peril to the public health, safety, or welfare or the loss of federal funding for an agency program requires the immediate adoption of an emergency rule and publishes in a record its reasons for that finding, the agency, without prior notice or hearing or on any abbreviated notice and hearing that it finds practicable, may adopt an emergency rule without complying with Sections 304 through 307." SECTION

309. EMERGENCY RULE. RMSAPA.

198   For example in Wisconsin, "Purpose. If preservation of the public peace, health, safety, or welfare necessitates placing a rule into effect prior to the time it could be effective if the agency were to comply with the notice, hearing, legislative review, and publication requirements, of the statutes, the agency may adopt that rule as an emergency rule." Wis. Stat. § 227.24(1).

199   Governors may declare states of emergency that agencies carry-out by publishing implementation orders. Many states empower their legislatures to nullify a Governor's order. "Legislative Oversight of Emergency Executive Powers," *National Conference of State Legislatures* (Jul 16, 2020) https://www.ncsl.org/research/about-state-legislatures/legislative-oversight-of-executive-orders.aspx.

200   Tenn. Code Ann. § 4-5-209. Public necessity rules. (accessed July 22, 2020).

201   "A rule may incorporate by reference all or any part of a code, standard, or rule that has been adopted by an agency of the United States, this state, or another state, or by a nationally recognized organization or association, if... [criteria]." SECTION 314. INCORPORATION BY REFERENCE. RMSAPA.

202   For example in Montana, "(1) An agency may adopt by reference any model code, federal agency rule, rule of any agency of this state, or other similar publication if: (a) the publication of the model code, rule, or other publication would be unduly cumbersome, expensive, or otherwise inexpedient; and (b) it is reasonable for the agency to adopt the model code, rule, or other publication for the state of Montana." Omissions from ARM or register. Mont. Code Ann. § 2-4-307.

203   "(b) Not later than [two years] after a notice of proposed rulemaking is published, the agency shall adopt the rule or terminate the rulemaking by publication of a notice of termination in the [administrative bulletin]. [The agency may extend the time for

adopting the rule once for an additional [two years] by publishing a statement of good cause for the extension but must provide for additional public participation as provided in Section 306 before adopting the rule.]" SECTION 307. TIME LIMIT ON ADOPTION OF RULE. RMSAPA.

204   For example in New York, "… a notice of proposed rulemaking shall expire and be ineffective for the purposes of this section, unless the proposed rule is adopted by the agency and filed with the Secretary of State in the manner prescribed by law, within three hundred sixty-five days…" NY State APA § 202-E (2016). https://codes.findlaw.com/ny/state-administrative-procedure-act/sap-sect-202.html.

205   For example in Minnesota, "An agency shall publish a notice of intent to adopt rules or a notice of hearing within 18 months of the effective date of the law authorizing or requiring rules to be adopted, amended, or repealed." Minn. Stat. § 14-25.

206   For example in Texas, "A proposed rule is withdrawn six months after the date of publication of notice of the proposed rule in the Texas Register if a state agency has failed by that time to adopt, adopt as amended, or withdraw the proposed rule." Tex. Gov't Code § 2001.027. WITHDRAWAL OF PROPOSED RULE.

207   "(b) An agency may engage in negotiated rulemaking by appointing a committee to comment or make recommendations on the subject matter of a proposed rulemaking under active consideration within the agency. In making appointments to the committee, the agency shall make reasonable efforts to establish a balance in representation among members of the public known to have an interest in the subject matter of the proposed rulemaking." ADVANCE NOTICE OF PROPOSED RULEMAKING; NEGOTIATED RULEMAKING. SECTION 303. RMSAPA.

208   "(d) This section does not prohibit an agency from obtaining information and opinions from members of the public on the subject of a proposed rule by any other method or procedure." Id.

209   A workgroup might consist of sub-office topic specific manag-
        ers, Office of General Counsel, policy specialists, subject matter
        experts, drafting experts, economists, interagency personnel,
        and others.

210   "Any person may petition an agency to adopt a rule. An agency
        shall prescribe by rule the form of the petition and the procedure
        for its submission, consideration, and disposition. Not later than
        [60] days after submission of a petition, the agency shall: (1)
        deny the petition in a record and state its reasons for the denial;
        or (2) initiate rulemaking." SECTION 318. PETITION FOR
        ADOPTION OF RULE. RMSAPA.

211   Id.

212   "Agency decisions that decline to adopt a rule are judicially
        reviewable for abuse of discretion (See Massachusetts v. EPA
        127 S. Ct. 1438 (2007) *(sic)* (EPA decision to reject rulemaking
        petition and therefore not to regulate greenhouse gases associ-
        ated with global warming was judicially reviewable and decision
        was arbitrary and capricious.))." SECTION 318. PETITION
        FOR ADOPTION OF RULE. RMSAPA. Comment.

213   "If an agency receives a petition requesting rulemaking, the APA
        requires the agency within 60 days to either deny the petition in
        writing, stating the reasons for denial, or initiate a rulemaking
        proceeding. There is no right under the APA for a person to seek
        judicial review from an agency's denial of a petition for rulemak-
        ing or based on an agency's failure to adopt a rule. Similarly, the
        court has held that the APA does not create a right to judicial
        review of an agency's failure to grant a public hearing pursu-
        ant to APA § 2001.029 when the agency denies a petition for
        rulemaking." "2020 Administrative Law Handbook," (Texas)
        Administrative Law Division, https://www.texasattorneygen-
        eral.gov/sites/default/files/files/divisions/general-oag/admin-
        law_hb.pdf, 53.

214   To illustrate: Office of Administrative Law (OAL), California;
        Administrative Rules Coordinator, Iowa; Michigan Office of

Administrative Hearings and Rules (MOAHR); State Budget Office to Office of Management and Budget (SBA/OMB) Indiana; Governor's Office, Minnesota; State Budget Office and Governor's Office, North Carolina; Governor's Office, Wisconsin.

215 "Forty-one states have some type of authority to review administrative rules, although not all of them have the power to veto rules. In the states that have veto authority, the action may be required through enactment of a statute (13 states) or passage of a resolution (15 states). State courts have heard challenges to a legislative veto of administrative rules in at least 11 states, with all but two ruling that the power—or the process being used—was unconstitutional. Court decisions in Idaho and Missouri illustrate the differing perspectives." Erickson, Brenda and Kae Warnock, "Separation of Powers--Legislative Oversight," *National Conference of State Legislatures* (accessed July 17, 2020) https://www.ncsl.org/research/about-state-legislatures/separation-of-powers-legislative-oversight.aspx.

216 For example in Oregon, "If an agency appoints an advisory committee for consideration of a rule under subsection (1) of this section, the agency shall seek the committee's recommendations on whether the rule will have a fiscal impact, what the extent of that impact will be and whether the rule will have a significant adverse impact on small businesses." Or. Rev. Stat. § 183.333(3). Policy Statement. (accessed July 17, 2020) Also see, Oregon's "Rulemaking Flow Chart," https://www.oregon.gov/wcb/Documents/wcbrule/rule-flowcharta.pdf.

217 For example in Pinal County, Arizona, "Stakeholder Definition: A person or group having an interest in the rulemaking process. In order to exercise your right to comment, you must first know what rules are being developed, when the stakeholders are meeting, when the proposed rule comment period begins, and many other details of the rulemaking process." "What is the Rulemaking Process?" *Pinal County Government* (accessed August 3, 2020) https://www.pinalcountyaz.gov/AirQuality/

Pages/Rulemaking.aspx.

218   SECTION 303. RMSAPA. Id.

219   For example in Florida, "An agency must hold public workshops, including workshops in various regions of the state or the agency's service area, for purposes of rule development if requested in writing by any affected person, unless the agency head explains in writing why a workshop is unnecessary." Fla. Stat. § 120.54(2) (c) (2019).

220   "An agency shall prepare a regulatory analysis for a proposed rule that has an estimated economic impact of more than $[]. The analysis must be completed before notice of the proposed rulemaking is published." REGULATORY ANALYSIS. SECTION 305. RMSAPA.

221   "Guide to Public Participation in the Regulatory Process," *Office of Administrative Law* (accessed November 18, 2020) https://www.oal.ca.gov/wp-content/uploads/sites/166/2017/05/How-2-Participate-102016.pdf, 15.

222   For example in Arizona, "Close of the Record. The close of the record for a proposed rule occurs on the date the agency chooses as the last date it will accept public comments. An agency shall not complete a rulemaking until the record is closed." Ariz. Admin. Code § R1-1-505. (March 23, 2004).

223   "Legislative Note: State laws vary on the length of public comment periods and on whether a rulemaking hearing is required. The bracketed number of days in subsections (a) and (d) should be interpreted to require that, if a rulemaking hearing is held, it will be held before the end of the public comment period. In that case, the minimum time period would be 50 days rather than 30 days." PUBLIC PARTICIPATION. SECTION 306. RMSAPA.

224   For example in Minnesota, "[T]he agency shall give notice of its intention to adopt a rule without public hearing. The notice

must be given by publication in the State Register and by United States mail or electronic mail to persons who have registered their names with the agency under section 14.14, subdivision 1a... The notice must include a statement advising the public that if 25 or more persons submit a written request for a public hearing within the 30-day comment period, a public hearing will be held..." Minn. Stat. § 14.22. Subd. 1. (2019).

225 Tharp, Stacey M. "Legislative Powers of Rules Review in the States and Congressional Powers of Rules," *Virginia Administrative Law Advisory Committee* (undated, accessed July 17, 2020) http://codecommission.dls.virginia.gov/documents/alac/studies/2001/legrev1.pdf.

226 Levinson, Harold. *Legislative and Executive Veto of Rule of Administrative Agencies: Models and Alternatives*, 24 Wm. & Mary L. Rev. 79 (1982), https://scholarship.law.wm.edu/wmlr/vol24/ iss1/3.

227 For example in Louisiana, "The Governor, by executive order, may suspend or veto any rule or regulation or body of rules or regulations adopted by a state department, agency, board or commission, except as provided in R.S. 49:967, within thirty days of their adoption. Upon the execution of such an order, the Governor shall transmit copies thereof to the speaker of the House of Representatives and president of the Senate." La. Stat. Ann § 49:970. Gubernatorial suspension or veto of rules and regulations. https://biotech.law.lsu.edu/cases/la/adlaw/apa/LAAPA27.htm.

228 For example in Tennessee, "No rule shall become effective until approved by the Attorney General and reporter pursuant to the provisions of § 4-5-211 and filed in the office of the Secretary of State pursuant to the provisions of § 4-5-206. Further, no rule, unless filed as an emergency rule pursuant to the provisions of § 4-5-208 or filed as a public necessity rule pursuant to the provisions of § 4-5-209, shall become effective until the expiration of the seventy-five-day period immediately following the filing

of the original of such rule in the office of the secretary of state." Tenn. Code Ann. § 4-5-207. Effective dates of rules.

229 Disclosure: Bob for many years has assisted the American Association of Nurse Anesthetists, State Government Affairs office in training state associations, member-advocates, and association staff in state level advocacy.

230 "Anesthesiology Assistants Work States," *American Academy of Anesthesiologist Assistants* (June 2019) https://www.anesthetist. org.

231 Fla. Stat. § 458.3475 (2020).

232 For example in Texas, "All state agencies must review and consider for re-adoption all rules not later than the fourth anniversary date of their effective date and every four years thereafter. The review 'must include an assessment of whether the reasons for initially adopting the rule continue to exist.' As part of rule review, an agency will determine whether a new rule is needed or if an existing rule is no longer necessary and should be repealed." "Administrative Law Handbook 2020," *Administrative Law Division, Office of the Attorney General of Texas* (2020) https://www.texasattorneygeneral.gov/sites/default/files/files/divisions/general-oag/adminlaw_hb.pdf, 52.

233 PETITION FOR ADOPTION OF RULE. SECTION 318. RMSAPA.

234 For example, "In re: Florida Pool & Spa Association, Inc. d/b/a, the Florida Swimming Pool Association and John Nance Garner, Sr., Petition to Initiate Rulemaking." http://www.floridapoolpro.com/wp-content/uploads/2017/01/bottom-FSPA.John-Garner.Petition-to-Initiate-Rulemaking-to-CILB.pdf.

235 "If an agency finds that an imminent peril to the public health, safety, or welfare or the loss of federal funding for an agency program requires the immediate adoption of an emergency rule and publishes in a record its reasons for that finding, the agency,

without prior notice or hearing or on any abbreviated notice and hearing that it finds practicable, may adopt an emergency rule without complying with Sections 304 through 307." EMERGENCY RULE. SECTION 309. RMSAPA.

236   For example in Wisconsin, "We conclude that Emergency Order 28 is a rule under the controlling precedent of this court, [cite] and therefore is subject to statutory emergency rulemaking procedures established by the Legislature. Emergency Order 28 is a general order of general application within the meaning of Wis. Stat. § 227.01(13), which defines "Rule." Accordingly, the rulemaking procedures of Wis. Stat. § 227.24 were required to be followed during the promulgation of Order 28. Because they were not, Emergency Order 28 is unenforceable.6." *Wisconsin Legislature v. Andrea Palm* (Wisconsin Department of Health Services), 2020 WI 42.

237   "Nonetheless, by the early 1990s many agencies eschewed rulemaking and chose to apply 'incipient' policy, a means of implementing delegated legislative authority that was permitted by the courts but was frustrating to regulated persons and entities." Blanton, Donna. "State Agency Rulemaking Procedures and Rule Challenges," *Florida Bar Journal*, vol. 75, no. 1, 2001, 34.

238   "Sue and Settle: Regulating Behind Closed Doors," *U.S. Chamber of Commerce* (March 6, 2018) https://www.uschamber.com/report/sue-and-settle-regulating-behind-closed-doors.

239   Hayes, Kelli. "Sue and Settle: Forcing Government Regulation Through Litigation," 40 U Dayton L. Rev. 1 (2015), 106. https://Udayton.Edu/Law/_Resources/Documents/Law_Review/Vol40_No1/Sue_And_Settle.pdf.

240   Barron, Lisa. "12 States Sue EPA Over Settlements with Green Groups," *Newsmax* (July 17, 2013) https://www.newsmax.com/US/epa-settlements-green-groups/2013/07/17/id/515601/.

241   "A lesser-known provision in the [Federal] APA is a petition

mechanism through which any interested party can request an agency to issue, amend, or repeal a rule (Section 553(e)). Such petitions are sometimes referred to as 553(e) petitions, petitions for rulemaking, petitions for reconsideration, administrative petitions, or citizens' petitions. The APA petition mechanism is a potentially efficient (and arguably underused) means for an individual or stakeholder to call on an agency to take a particular action." "Petitions for Rulemaking: An Overview," *Congressional Research Service* (January 23, 2020) https://fas.org/sgp/crs/misc/R46190.pdf.

242   "Any interested person may petition an agency for a declaration of the applicability of any rule or prior order issued by the agency." SECTION 203. DECLARATIONS BY AGENCY. RMSAPA. (2005 Draft).

243   "Any person may petition an agency to adopt a rule. An agency shall prescribe by rule the form of the petition and the procedure for its submission, consideration, and disposition. Not later than [60] days after submission of a petition, the agency shall: (1) deny the petition in a record and state its reasons for the denial; or (2) initiate rulemaking. Agency decisions that decline to adopt a rule are judicially reviewable for abuse of discretion." SECTION 318. PETITION FOR ADOPTION OF RULE. RMSAPA.

244   For example in Oregon, "Any interested citizen can request that the Marine Board adopt, amend, or repeal a boating regulation through a petition. Complete the fillable PDF from the link below and submit to osmb.rulemaking@oregon.gov. Incomplete petitions may be returned by the agency director." "Petition and Rulemaking Process," *Oregon State Marine Board* (accessed January 9, 2020) https://www.oregon.gov/osmb/info/Pages/PetitionRulemakingProcess.aspx.

245   "Regulation development is an iterative process with many opportunities for stakeholders and the public to engage with CARB [California Air Resource Board] staff to help inform

potential requirements and provide comments prior to Board consideration of the proposed rule." "Commercial Harbor Craft Rulemaking - Opportunities for Public Participation in Rulemaking Process," *California Air Resource Board* (April 7, 2020) https://ww2.arb.ca.gov.

246 "Boards and Commissions," *Office of the Minnesota Secretary of State* (accessed November 10, 2020) https://commissionsandap-pointments.sos.state.mn.us/Agency.

247 "Appointing Authority," *Office of the Minnesota Secretary of State* (accessed February 26, 2021) https://commissionsandappoint-ments.sos.state.mn.us/AppointingAuthority.

248 "Members," *Office of the Minnesota Secretary of State* (accessed February 26, 2021) https://commissionsandappointments.sos.state.mn.us/Member.

249 For example, "The Florida Environmental Regulation Commission (ERC) is a non-salaried, seven-member board selected by the governor that represents agriculture, the development industry, local government, the environmental community, residents, and members of the scientific and technical community." "Environmental Regulation Commission," *Florida Department of Environmental Protection* (accessed November 10, 2020) https://floridadep.gov/ogc/ogc/content/environmental-regulation-commission.

250 For example, for a sense of how boards and commissions are populated in Florida see, "State Boards and Commissions," *Florida Department of State, Division of Library and Information Services* (accessed November 10, 2020) https://dos.myflorida.com/library-archives/research/florida-information/government/state-government-bodies/state-boards-and-commissions/.

251 For example, "The person conducting the hearing may: (a) Limit oral presentations if the hearing would be unduly lengthened by repetitious testimony." 227.18(2)(a), Wisconsin Statutes; "The presiding officer may place time limitations on individual oral

presentations when necessary to ensure the orderly and expeditious conduct of the oral proceeding." X.5(3)d.(1), Iowa Statutes; "The agency representative appointed under Section 306(e) to preside over a public hearing under Section 306(c) has the authority to manage the hearing and to set reasonable limits on public participation at the public hearing." 306. PUBLIC PARTICIPATION. RMSAPA. Comment on 306(e).

252   "Agencies feel obliged to make the basic decisions before the comment period begins, because they would not have enough time for full deliberation thereafter. This pattern tends to defeat the purpose of having a comment period." Levin, Ronald M. "Rulemaking Under the 2010 Model State Administrative Procedure Act," 20 Widener Law J. (2011) Washington University in St. Louis Legal Studies Research Paper No. 11-08-05, Available at SSRN: https://ssrn.com/abstract=1919256.

253   For example in California, "Once an agency determines that the adoption, amendment or repeal of regulations is necessary, the agency performs legal and factual research needed to develop and support the documents required to conduct a formal APA rulemaking proceeding. While much of this research is done internally by the agency, some agencies involve the public during this stage through workshops or other informal proceedings where the agency may invite interested persons to provide input or information. The APA provides that an agency must engage in pre-notice public discussions regarding complex proposals or large proposals. However, a decision whether to engage in such discussions is not subject to review by OAL or the courts." "Guide to Public Participation in the Regulatory Process," Id., 10.

254   Hoover, Kent. "Tennessee claims state agency recommendations are exempt from open records law," *Muckrock* (September 13, 2019) https://www.muckrock.com/news/archives/2019/sep/13/tennessee-claims-state-agency-recommendations-are-/.

255   For example, "(2)(a) Afford all interested persons reasonable

opportunity to submit data, views, comments, or arguments, orally or in writing. In case of substantive rules, opportunity for oral presentation or argument must be granted if requested within twenty days after publication of the rule as provided in this Subsection, by twenty-five persons, by a governmental subdivision or agency, by an association having not less than twenty-five members, or by a committee of either house of the legislature to which the proposed rule change has been referred under the provisions of R.S. 49:968." La. Stat. Ann. § 49:1:953(A)(2)(a).

256   "Scope of review. (a) General rule. -- A party who proceeded before a Commonwealth agency under the terms of a particular statute shall not be precluded from questioning the validity of the statute in the appeal, but such party may not raise upon appeal any other question not raised before the agency (notwithstanding the fact that the agency may not be competent to resolve such question) unless allowed by the court upon due cause shown." 2 Pa. Cons. Stat. § 703(a).

257   "According to the *Daily Environment Report*, however, it became apparent that the petitioners' 'significant contribution' argument may not have been raised during the rule's public comment period. This posed a 'significant problem,' the news organization quoted Judge Griffith as saying, because petitioners may only litigate issues they brought to the agency's attention in comments." "Federal Court Panel Hears Cross-State Rule Arguments," *Power* (April 8, 2012) https://www.powermag.com/federal-court-panel-hears-cross-state-rule-arguments/.

258   "The requirement of an official agency rulemaking record in subsection (a) should facilitate a more structured and rational agency and public consideration of proposed rules. It will also aid the process of judicial review of the validity of rules." SECTION 302. RULEMAKING RECORD. RMSAPA. Commentary.

259   For example in Tennessee, "Except to the extent that this chap-

ter or another statute provides otherwise, the agency record shall constitute the exclusive basis for agency action in adjudicative proceedings under this chapter, and for judicial review thereof." Tenn. Code Ann. § 4-5-319(d).

260   For example in Idaho, "Except as otherwise required by a provision of law, the agency rulemaking record need not constitute the exclusive basis for agency action on that rule or for judicial review thereof." Idaho Code Ann. § 5225(3). (accessed July 22, 2020) Other state APAs have similar or identical wording.

261   For example in Louisiana, "The Governor, by executive order, may suspend or veto any rule or regulation or body of rules or regulations adopted by a state department, agency, board or commission, except as provided in R.S. 49:967, within thirty days of their adoption." La. Stat. Ann. §49:970 (accessed January 11, 2021)

262   For example in Minnesota, "The Governor may veto all or a severable portion of a rule of an agency as defined in section 14.02, subdivisions 2 and 4, by submitting notice of the veto to the State Register within 14 days of receiving a copy of the rule from the secretary of state. . ." Minn. Stat. § 14.05 Subd. 6. (accessed January 11, 2021).

263   "Forty-one states have some type of authority to review administrative rules, although not all of them have the power to veto rules. In the states that have veto authority, the action may be required through enactment of a statute (13 states) or passage of a resolution (15 states). State courts have heard challenges to a legislative veto of administrative rules in at least 11 states, with all but two ruling that the power—or the process being used— was unconstitutional." Erickson and Warnock, "Separation of Powers--Legislative Oversight," Id.

264   For example in Louisiana, Legislative veto, amendment, or suspension of rules, regulations, and fees, "In addition to the procedures provided in R.S. 49:968 for review of the exercise of the rulemaking authority delegated by the legislature to state agen-

cies, as defined by this Chapter, the legislature, by Concurrent Resolution, may suspend, amend, or repeal any rule or regulation or body of rules or regulations, or any fee or any increase, decrease, or repeal of any fee, adopted by a state department, agency, board, or commission." La. Stat. Ann. § 49:969.

265 Haskins, Debbie. "Legislative Oversight of State Agency Rule-making," *Colorado LegiSource* (September 4, 2014) https://legisource.net/2014/09/04/legislative-oversight-of-state-agency-rule-making/.

266 Micheli, Chris. "Legislative oversight of rulemaking bodies," *Cap impact* (February 1, 2018) https://www.capimpactca.com/2018/02/legislative-oversight-rulemaking-bodies/.

267 Micheli, Chris. "An Additional Role for the Legislature in Agency Rulemaking," *Fox & Hounds* (December 14th, 2016) https://www.foxandhoundsdaily.com/2016/12/additional-role-legislators-agency-rulemaking/.

268 "A litigant should exhaust any prescribed administrative remedies available before seeking judicial review. Where relief is available from an administrative agency, the plaintiff is ordinarily required to pursue that avenue of redress before proceeding to the courts. Until that recourse is exhausted, the suit is premature and must be dismissed." "Exhaustion of Administrative Remedies," *USLegal* (accessed July 22, 2020) https://administrativelaw.uslegal.com/judicial-review-of-administrative-decisions/exhaustion-of-administrative-remedies/.

269 Whellan, Michael J. "Exhaustion of Administrative Remedies," *18th Annual Land Development Seminar* (October 29, 2010) https://www.baustin. exhaustion_of_administrative_remedies. pdf.

270 Samson, Anthony and Chris Micheli. "Regulations at the heart of governance," *Capitol Weekly* (June 13, 2017) https://capitolweekly.net/regulations-governance-repeal-amend-lawmakers-petition/.

271   For example in Florida, "(a) "Any person substantially affected by a rule or a proposed rule may seek an administrative determination of the invalidity of the rule on the ground that the rule is an invalid exercise of delegated legislative authority." Fla. Stat. § 120.56(1)(a) (2019).

272   ARTICLE 4. ADJUDICATION IN CONTESTED CASE. RMSAPA.

273   Webendorfer, J. Wesley. "Challenging a State Agency Regulation," *Wisconsin Lawyer* (November 1, 2017) https://www.wisbar.org/NewsPublications/WisconsinLawyer/Pages/Article.aspx?ArticleID=25970.

274   For example in Texas, "(a) The validity or applicability of a rule, including an emergency rule adopted under Section 2001.034 , may be determined in an action for declaratory judgment if it is alleged that the rule or its threatened application interferes with or impairs, or threatens to interfere with or impair, a legal right or privilege of the plaintiff." Tex. Gov. Code § 2001.038(a).

275   For example in Oregon, "The validity of any rule may be determined upon a petition by any person to the Court of Appeals in the manner provided for review of orders in contested cases..." Or. Rev. Stat. § 183.400(1).

276   "(7) 'Contested case' means an adjudication in which an opportunity for an evidentiary hearing is required by the federal constitution, a federal statute, or the constitution or a statute of this state." SECTION 102. DEFINITIONS. RMSAPA.

277   SECTION 506. EXHAUSTION OF ADMINISTRATIVE REMEDIES. RMSAPA.

278   "After the meeting, which lasted less than 15 minutes, Republican Rep. Tom Demmer, of Dixon, said lawmakers had been hearing significant opposition to the order from the public. 'I know every member of this committee has received thousands of emails and phone calls from people who were concerned about

this rule… So, I think there were a number of angles and all those added up to the rule not being sustainable.'" Hancock, Peter. "Governor reverses rule calling for misdemeanors against defiant businesses," *Illinois Business Journal* (May 20, 2020) https://www.ibjonline.com/2020/05/20/Governor-reverses-rule-calling-for-misdemeanors-against-defiant-businesses/.

279   "The Mercury-Containing and Rechargeable Battery Management Act - Public Law 104-142," *USEPA* (accessed December 8, 2020) https://www.epa.gov/rcra/mercury-containing-and-rechargeable-battery-management-act-public-law-104-142.

280   "Statistics and Historical Comparison," *GovTrack* (accessed January 27, 2021) https://www.govtrack.us/congress/bills/statistics.

281   For example, "The Court will not substitute its judgment for that of the Board as to the weight of the evidence on questions of fact. Stated differently, the findings of the agency will be upheld even though a reasonable mind might have reached a contrary result." *Lisa J. Betcher v. Department of Labor and Training Board of Review and The Kitchen Countertop Center of New England, LLC.* A.A. No. 11-80 (September 17, 2012) https://www.courts.ri.gov/Courts/districtcourt/Appeals/decisions/11-80.pdf.

282   See also, "Review of Agency Decisions," *United States Court of Appeals for the Ninth Circuit* (accessed December 9, 2020) http://cdn.ca9.uscourts.gov/datastore/uploads/guides/stand_of_review/IV_Review_AD.html.

283   Chisenhall, Garnett. "Practice Tips for Private Attorneys New to Administrative Law," *Florida Bar Journal*, vol. 86, no. 8, 2012, 61. https://www.floridabar.org/the-florida-bar-journal/practice-tips-for-private-attorneys-new-to-administrative-law/.

284   These percentages are for illustration as our general estimates. These are not statistically researched numbers. See also, "The administrative state's dominance over the notion that the Constitution vests lawmaking power solely in the elected Congress is all but complete." Crews, Clyde Wayne, Jr. "The 2021 'Uncon-

stitutionality Index' 19 Federal Rules and Regulations for Every Law Congress Passes," *Forbes* (February 2, 2021) https://www. forbes.com/sites/waynecrews/2021/02/02/the-2021-uncon-stitutionality-index-19-federal-rules-and-regulations-for-ev-ery-law-congress-passes/?sh=72db178e5522.

285 "Different Standards of Proof," *HG.org Legal Resources* (accessed July 23, 200) https://www.hg.org/legal-articles/different-stan-dards-of-proof-6363.

286 Id.

287 Id.

288 "Administrative Law - Definitions," *Oregon Land Use Board of Appeals* (December 14, 2018) https://www.oregon.gov/LUBA/docs/headnotes/1.6.2.pdf.

289 "Generally, courts infer that agencies make rules according to the prescribed procedures. [iv] Courts also assume that the agency regulations created are valid and within the bounds of an enabling act. The party challenging the validity of an agency rule must produce evidence to show that it is an unreasonable rule beyond doubt. The challenger is supposed to prove that an administrative agency did not follow the rulemaking proce-dures, the rules created are illegal, arbitrary and unreasonable, the rules created lack support of evidence, and the rulemaking authority acted in an unconstitutional manner exceeding its statutory authority. [v] However, courts when considering the validity of an agency rule should give the benefit of presumption that the created rule abides by all procedures." "Proceedings to Determine Validity of Rules," *USLegal* (accessed July 23, 2020) https://administrativelaw.uslegal.com/administrative-agen-cy-rulemaking/proceedings-to-determine-validity-of-rules/.

290 Conference Speaker, "Take Back the Conversation," March 6, 2016. Oldsmar, Florida.

291 "Animal Welfare Act and Animal Welfare Regulations," *USDA*

Animal Care (May 2019) https://www.aphis.usda.gov/animal_ welfare/downloads/bluebook-ac-awa.pdf.

292   Laboratory Animal Welfare Act of 1966, P.L. 89-544. 80 Stat. 350. https://bit.ly/3kpMchf.

293   Per the conference speaker attorney, USDA piles on so many charges that some will stick such that they win on appeal almost 100% of the time. He noted in his client's case the top of the training stand was just tall enough such that the minimum distance between it and the top of the training enclosure was not met resulting in a sure loss. Inspection of USDA's Office of the Judicial Office, Summary of Decisions at https://www.dm.usda. gov/ojo/index.htm suggests that legal counsel may be correct that the licensees almost never win on appeal.

294   "The inspector must complete an official Inspection Report as soon as possible at the end of the inspection. . . . Remember that Inspection Reports with a Direct NCI must be completed and delivered to the licensee/registrant immediately after the inspection. The Inspection Report should follow the format of the Inspection Report template in the Animal Care Information System (ACIS)." *USDA Animal Welfare Inspection Guide*, United States Department of Agriculture (March 11, 2020) https://www.aphis.usda.gov/animal_welfare/downloads/Animal-Care-Inspection-Guide.pdf, 3-21.

295   "MTA spokesman Shams Tarek blames 'collective bargaining agreements' and 'third-party arbitrators' who decide the cases for making it 'significantly more difficult' to fire transit employees." Post Editorial Board, "Endanger the public, keep your job: Why these workers are so hard to fire," *New York Post* (June 10, 2019) https://nypost.com/2019/06/10/endanger-the-public-keep-you-job-why-these-workers-are-so-hard-to-fire/.

296   "As a result, states where public employees were more likely to be in unions had higher rates of overall union representation. In New York, the nation's most unionized state, 70% of public sector employees were union members, the highest percent-

age in the nation. By contrast, in North Carolina, the nation's least unionized state, slightly less than 10% were union members." Calio, Vince. et al. "5 States with the Absolute Toughest Unions," Time (May 30, 2014) https://time.com/135975/unions. Note: Despite *Janus v. AFSCME* (2018) non-union government workers are forced to make "fair share" payments to public employee unions. A state employee in a heavily unionized state interviewed for this book reported regular uninvited office visits by union representatives who keep recruitment efforts to just within the bounds of legal.

297 "A CBS News investigation looks at how hard it is for the U.S. government to discipline or fire employees who behave badly. With examples ranging from extravagant to explicit, civil service rules meant to protect public workers from political pressure may be backfiring, and costing you big, reports CBS News correspondent Don Dahler." "Red tape keeps some bad gov't workers from being fired," *CBS NEWS* (March 2, 2015) https://www.cbsnews.com/news/civil-servant-protection-system-could-keep-problematic-government-employees-from-being-fired/.

298 Carter, Terry. "The Maricopa Courthouse War," *ABA Journal* (April 1, 2010) https://www.abajournal.com/magazine/article/the_maricopa_courthouse_war/.

299 Manuel, H. Alexander, Id.

300 Teachout, Zephyr. "The Anti-Corruption Principle." Id.

301 "The most common method of scale control is to maintain the cooling water chemistry such that the solubility of mineral scale is not exceeded. Traditionally, sulfuric acid is used to adjust the carbonate and bicarbonate alkalinity to maintain the pH of the cooling water in the 6.5 to 7.5 range." Harfst, William (Bill). "Scale and Fouling Control in Cooling Tower Systems," *Water Technology Report* (January 2, 2018).

302   Goodnow, F, *Comparative Administrative Law: An Analysis of the Administrative Systems, National and Local, of the United States, England France and Germany* (1893).

303   Freund, E., "Cases on Administrative Law", *West Publishing Company* (1911).

304   See, Harriman, E.A, "The Development of Administrative Law in the United States," 25 Yale L.J. (1916). In *Prentis v. Atlantic Coast Line Co.*, 211 U. S. 210 (1908), the Supreme Court explained: "So far as the Federal Constitution is concerned, a state may, by constitutional provision, unite legislative and judicial powers in the same body. A judicial inquiry investigates, declares and enforces liabilities as they stand on present or past facts and under existing laws, while legislation looks to the future and changes conditions, making new rules to be thereafter applied."

305   A convicted person or prisoner cannot file an appeal on the grounds that "I am innocent." *Herrera v. Collins*, 506 U.S. 390 (1993). Instead, he or she must prove that the lack of evidence, biased judge or jury, or unfair process led to the conviction. We all enjoy a due process right to the presumption of innocence, and to be convicted on a proof standard requiring reasonable doubt. See, *Cochran v. United States*, 157 U.S. 286, 299 (1895). But, "innocence" or regulatory wrongdoing is a factual issue, and whether it is a criminal law or administrative law case, courts cannot disregard the facts if they were established in accordance with due process of law and the applicable legal standard, "reasonable doubt" for crimes, "substantial evidence in the record" for regulatory wrongdoing.

306   Article I, Section 8 of the Constitution is considered the primary source of federalist principles, and the limitations on the scope of federal power. The 10th Amendment to the Constitution is more explicit: "The powers not delegated to the United States by the Constitution, nor prohibited by it to the States, are reserved to the States respectively, or to the people." Article IV, Section 2

of the U.S. Constitution states: "The United States shall guarantee to every State in this Union a Republican Form of Government ***."

307   The Supremacy Clause is stated in Article VI, para. 2 of the Constitution: "This Constitution, and the laws of the United States which shall be made in pursuance thereof; and all treaties made, or which shall be made, under the authority of the United States, shall be the supreme law of the land; and the judges in every state shall be bound thereby, anything in the Constitution or laws of any State to the contrary notwithstanding." Based on this supremacy of federal statutes, the Supreme Court has stated "we have long recognized that state laws that conflict with federal law are without effect." See, *Maryland v. Louisiana*, 451 U. S. 725, 746 (1981).

308   The Full Faith and Credit Clause is contained in Article IV, Section 1 of the Constitution: "Full Faith and Credit shall be given in each State to the public Acts, Records, and judicial Proceedings of every other State. And the Congress may by general Laws prescribe the Manner in which such Acts, Records and Proceedings shall be proved, and the Effect thereof."

309   Many statutes enacted by state legislatures and Congress assign duties to multiple agencies creating overlapping regulatory jurisdiction. To avoid conflicts with each other, as well as to efficiently use resources, these agencies may enter into jurisdictional "agreements" or "memoranda of understanding" regarding which agency will take the lead on which issues. Additionally, you should ascertain whether the agency adjudicating your case serves as the official "state agency" for administering combined federal and state statutes. For example, the federal Equal Employment Opportunity Commission (EEOC) has designated the comparable state office or "human rights" office as the EEOC's "state agency" for processing federal discrimination claims in addition to those filed under applicable state law.

310   "Persuasive authority refers to cases, statutes, regulations, or sec-

ondary sources that the court may follow but does not have to follow. Thus, the holding from a court in another jurisdiction or a lower court in the same jurisdiction is persuasive authority." *When and How to Use Secondary Sources and Persuasive Authority to Research and Write Legal Documents*, The Writing Center at Georgetown University Law Center (2004).

311   The Uniform Law Commission was created in 1892 and "provides states with non-partisan, well-conceived and well-drafted legislation that brings clarity and stability to critical areas of state statutory law." See, Uniform Law Commission, https:// www.uniformlaws.org/aboutulc/overview. A list of these uniform laws may be viewed at https://my.uniformlaws.org/acts/catalog/current.

312   Here are a few examples of overlapping or parallel regulations:

(1) A nuclear power plant is regulated by the Nuclear Regulatory Commission, the Department of Energy, the Environmental Protection Agency, and state environmental regulators.

(2) Regulation of a retail food product may be under the jurisdiction of the United States Department of Agriculture, the Food and Drug Administration, the Consumer Product Safety Commission, and state regulators.

(3) Airline operations may be regulated by the Federal Aviation Administration, the Department of Transportation, the Department of Homeland Security, and a state airport authority.

(4) A farming operation you might think is regulated only by the state Department of Agriculture, but may also be subject to regulations and adjudications of the state's Department of Environmental Quality regarding water purity, the state's Department of Transportation regarding movement of livestock and crops, and the state's Fish and Wildlife Department as to the effects of farm pesticides.

313   See, *S.E.C. v. Chenery Corp.*, 332 U.S. 194, 196, 67 S. Ct. 1575,

91 L. Ed. 1995 (1947): "That is, we cannot substitute our judgment of what would be a more adequate or proper ground for a decision if the agency's decision did not rest on those grounds. To do so would propel the court into the domain which Congress has set aside exclusively for the administrative agency." See also, *NLRB v. Pittsburgh S. S. Co.*, 340 U.S. 498, 503 (1951): "This is not the place to reverse a Court of Appeals because were we in its place we would find the record tilting one way rather than the other."

314   All fifty states have enacted right-to-farm laws that seek to protect qualifying farmers and ranchers from nuisance lawsuits filed by individuals who move into a rural area where normal farming operations exist, and who later use nuisance actions to attempt to stop those ongoing operations. While the overall statutory schemes might be similar, each state has noticeably different content in the specific details of the laws. See, "States' Right-To-Farm Statutes," *National Agricultural Law Center*, https://nationalaglawcenter.org/state-compilations/right-to-farm.

315   *Marbury v. Madison*, 5 U.S. (1 Cranch) 137, 155 (1803).

316   Section 2 of Article II of the US Constitution, provides that "the president shall nominate, and, by and with the advice and consent of the senate, shall appoint ambassadors, other public ministers and consuls, and all other officers of the United States, whose appointments are not otherwise provided for." Section 3 provides that "he shall commission all the officers of the United States."

317   The case is so famous in constitutional history because the Court also held that the Supreme Court was not the proper venue for the case, and that Congress could not tell the Supreme Court what cases to hear or not hear, because that is strictly governed by the constitution.

318   Here is a 1977 dramatization of the Marbury v. Madison story (a government funded 30-minute movie), at https://www.c-span.org/video/?310956-1/marbury-vs-madison. Skip to minute

11 and watch Thomas Jefferson spit vitriol, hatred of the other party, and lawlessness in hiding or destroying 43 judicial and other commissions issued by his predecessor John Adams. It is the depiction of modern-day politics as well. If you watch the whole movie (it is fabulous), the rendition of the overtly political court system seems just like our court over 200 years later.

INDEX

CPSIA information can be obtained
at www.ICGtesting.com
Printed in the USA
BVHW081227200421
605390BV00005B/34